CANADA'S ECONOMIC ACTION PLAN
YEAR 2

BUDGET 2010

Leading the Way on Jobs and Growth

Tabled in the House of Commons
by the Honourable James M. Flaherty, P.C., M.P.
Minister of Finance

March 4, 2010

D1511452

CANADA'S ECONOMIC
ACTION
PLAN

All requests for permission to reproduce this document
or any part thereof shall be addressed to
Public Works and Government Services Canada.

Available through your local bookseller or by mail from
Publishing and Depository Services
Public Works and Government Services Canada
Ottawa, Ontario KIA OS5

Telephone: 613-941-5995
Orders only: 1-800-635-7943 (Canada and U.S.A.)
Fax: 613-954-5779 or 1-800-565-7757 (Canada and U.S.A.)
Internet: http://publications.gc.ca

Cat. No.: F1-23/3-2010E
ISBN: 978-0-660-19957-3

This document is also available on the Internet at www.fin.gc.ca

Cette publication est aussi disponible en français.

Table of Contents

Canadians in all regions have already benefited from the implementation of Canada's Economic Action Plan in year 1:

- Commitments are in place for almost 16,000 projects across the country. Over 12,000 of these projects have begun or have been completed.

- One objective of the Economic Action Plan was to maintain or create 220,000 jobs. The Action Plan is on track. It has contributed to the creation of over 135,000 jobs recorded in Canada since July 2009.

At the same time, the Action Plan will advance the objectives set out in our long-term economic plan, *Advantage Canada*.

New Investments in Jobs and Economic Growth

In addition to delivering Year 2 of Canada's Economic Action Plan, Budget 2010 introduces a limited number of new and targeted actions to protect Canadians from the global recession and create the jobs and economy of tomorrow.

Jobs Protection and Youth Employment Measures

Budget 2010 invests in measures that will directly protect jobs. This includes extensions to work-sharing and investments in training and skills development for youth.

Creating Economic Growth and Jobs Through Innovation

Budget 2010 builds on earlier investments with over $600 million over three years to help develop and attract talented people, to strengthen our capacity for world-leading research and development, and to improve the commercialization of research.

Encouraging Investment and Trade to Create Jobs and Growth

Budget 2010 takes action to improve the environment for investment, enhance competition and reduce barriers for businesses. This includes making Canada a tariff-free zone for manufacturers, by eliminating all remaining tariffs on productivity-improving machinery and equipment and goods imported for further manufacturing in Canada. This initiative, when fully implemented, will provide $300 million in annual duty savings to Canadian business.

Proposed improvements to the international tax system to attract new investment, cuts to red tape for businesses and increased competition for telecommunications will also foster investment and create jobs for Canadians.

Canada will emerge from the recession with a highly competitive tax system

- This year, Canada will have the lowest overall tax rate on new business investment in the G7.

- By 2012, Canada will have the lowest statutory corporate income tax rate in the G7.

- The Government introduced the Tax-Free Savings Account, the most important new vehicle for savings since the introduction of the Registered Retirement Savings Plan.

- The Government introduced the Working Income Tax Benefit, lowering the "welfare wall," making work more attractive for low-income Canadians.

- Canada's federal tax-to-GDP (gross domestic product) ratio is at its lowest level since 1961.

A highly competitive tax system will support the creation of jobs in Canada.

Green Jobs and Growth

Budget 2010 builds on Canada's position as an energy superpower with measures to encourage investments in energy projects and clean energy generation. The budget also includes measures to preserve Canada's natural heritage through environmental protection in the North and further protection of the Great Lakes.

Modernizing Canada's Infrastructure

Budget 2010 strengthens the Government's commitment to rebuild Canada's aging infrastructure by making priority investments in projects designed to ensure that Canadians have access to safe and effective transportation. This includes support for the operations of Atlantic ferry services, investments in federal bridges and new funding for aviation security.

Strengthening the Financial Sector

Canada's financial sector has been widely acknowledged as being one of the strongest in the world. Budget 2010 will further strengthen the sector by moving forward with the majority of provinces and territories toward a Canadian securities regulator, extending access to financing for Canadian businesses, and enhancing disclosure and financial institutions' business practices to better protect consumers.

Supporting Families and Communities and Standing Up for Those Who Helped Build Canada

Budget 2010 also introduces measures to support single parents and persons with disabilities, makes investments to assist Aboriginal Canadians and their communities, and provides support for participation in sport. Budget 2010 also recognizes those who helped build our country, with measures for military families, investments to recognize the efforts of veterans, and additional support for seniors.

Honouring Canada's International Commitments

Canada is a global leader and continuously demonstrates this by honouring its international commitments. The importance of accountability for promises will be a defining feature of Canada's G8 and G20 Summit year. Budget 2010 fulfills Canada's commitment to double international assistance by increasing the International Assistance Envelope by $364 million, bringing it to $5 billion in ongoing annual support.

The Three-Point Plan to Return to Budget Balance

The actions taken by the Government over the last two years are working. Stimulus measures are maintaining and creating jobs and securing the economic recovery. As the economy improves, the Government will refocus its attention on its long-term economic plan. The cornerstone of this plan is a return to balanced budgets.

Budget 2010 outlines a three-point plan for returning to budget balance once the economy has recovered.

- First, the Government will follow through with the exit strategy built into the Economic Action Plan. Temporary measures in the Action Plan will be wound down as planned.

- Second, the Government will restrain spending through targeted measures. Towards achieving this objective, Budget 2010 proposes $17.6 billion in savings over five years.

- Third, the Government will undertake a comprehensive review of government administrative functions and overhead costs in order to identify opportunities for additional savings and improve service delivery.

The Government will not raise taxes and will not cut major transfers to persons and other levels of government.

As a result of the expiration of the Economic Action Plan and the measures in this budget, the deficit is projected to decline by almost half over the next two years to $27.6 billion in 2011–12, and by two-thirds to $17.5 billion in 2012–13. In 2014–15, the deficit is projected to be $1.8 billion.

Canada's fiscal health is the envy of the world. The Government is fully committed to sustaining our fiscal advantage.

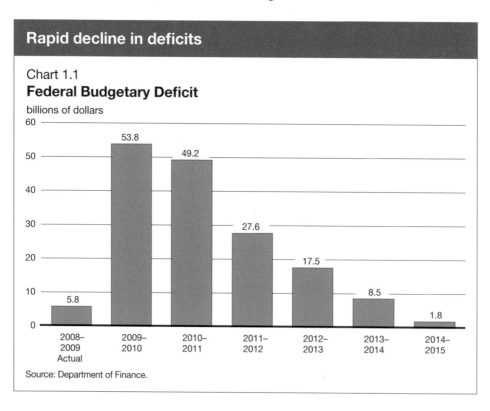

Rapid decline in deficits

Chart 1.1
Federal Budgetary Deficit

billions of dollars

Source: Department of Finance.

Chapter

Recent Economic
Developments
and Prospects

Highlights

✓ The global economy has begun to stabilize after undergoing a deep and synchronized recession, which stemmed from the worst global financial crisis since the 1930s.

✓ With support from the extraordinary measures in Canada's Economic Action Plan, the Canadian economy has started to recover.

✓ Canada has weathered the global recession better than all other major industrialized countries, reflecting several important financial, economic and fiscal strengths.

✓ Canadian labour markets have fared much better than in the U.S., where job losses to date have been proportionately more than three times as large as in Canada.

✓ Domestic demand in Canada has also rebounded more strongly than in all other Group of Seven (G7) countries since the beginning of 2009.

✓ While unemployment remains a concern, the rise in the unemployment rate has been smaller than was initially forecast by private sector forecasters.

✓ The Department of Finance conducted a survey of private sector forecasters in December 2009. In early February, private sector forecasters met with the Minister of Finance to discuss the economic forecast from the survey as well as the risks associated with that forecast.

✓ The average private sector economic forecast from the December 2009 survey forms the basis of the Government's fiscal planning.

✓ The use of private sector forecasts introduces an element of independence into the Government's economic and fiscal forecast.

This chapter incorporates data available up to and including March 1, 2010, unless otherwise indicated. All rates are reported at annual rates unless otherwise noted.

✓ Over the short term, the average private sector economic forecast has improved somewhat since the September 2009 Update of Economic and Fiscal Projections. Private sector forecasters expect the Canadian economic recovery to build momentum through 2010.

✓ Private sector forecasters have not materially changed their medium-term outlook since the September Update. Over the medium term, the level of uncertainty surrounding the outlook has declined since the Update but remains high.

✓ The average private sector forecast from the December survey provides a prudent basis for fiscal planning.

Introduction

The global economy has begun to stabilize after undergoing a deep and synchronized recession, which stemmed from the worst global financial crisis since the 1930s. Since then, global financial markets have improved and confidence is returning, leading to a tentative resumption of global economic growth.

Reflecting these positive developments, together with the impact of Canada's Economic Action Plan and significant monetary policy stimulus, economic activity in Canada has also strengthened. The near-term outlook has improved since the Government's September 2009 Update of Economic and Fiscal Projections. Both gross domestic product (GDP) and employment have increased, and private sector economists continue to believe that the recovery will gain momentum through 2010. However, the economic recovery is expected to be modest, and uncertainty surrounding the economic outlook remains elevated.

This chapter reviews the major global and Canadian economic developments since the September 2009 Update, describes the private sector economic forecast that forms the basis for the fiscal projections, and discusses the risks and uncertainties surrounding this economic outlook.

Financial Market Developments

The global financial crisis of late 2008 and early 2009 resulted in a pronounced tightening in credit conditions worldwide, which had significant impacts on global economic activity. Global financial conditions have improved considerably since early 2009 due to the extraordinary policy measures introduced by governments and central banks to support the financial system worldwide. Wholesale borrowing costs of banks have declined, and spreads between corporate and government bond rates have narrowed considerably (Chart 2.1). World equity markets have also rebounded strongly over the past year, with most major benchmark indices rising between 50 per cent and 65 per cent since March 2009.

While global financial conditions have improved markedly over the past year, they have yet to fully normalize. In some markets, credit conditions remain relatively tight in terms of both the availability and price of credit, particularly at longer maturities.

In Canada, financial conditions were less affected by the global financial crisis than in most other countries. Wholesale bank borrowing costs rose much less in Canada and improved faster than in other countries, while corporate bond rate spreads remain below those of the U.S. and Europe. As a result, credit growth in Canada has remained solid, mainly due to continued strong household credit growth. Business credit growth is showing some signs of stabilization after decelerating in late 2008 and most of 2009 due to the impact of the recession on both the demand for and supply of credit. A continued recovery in bond and equity market financing shows that businesses have greater access to capital.

Financial market conditions have improved significantly since early 2009

Chart 2.1

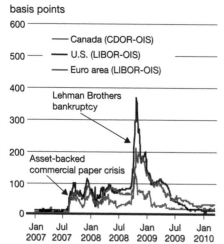

Short-Term Financing Spreads

basis points

- Canada (CDOR-OIS)
- U.S. (LIBOR-OIS)
- Euro area (LIBOR-OIS)

Lehman Brothers bankruptcy

Asset-backed commercial paper crisis

Notes: These spreads are a measure of banks' funding costs relative to a risk-free rate and are a gauge of financial market stress and banks' financing pressures. The rate on the overnight-indexed swap (OIS) is used as a proxy for expected overnight rates. LIBOR is the London Interbank Offered Rate. CDOR is the Canadian Dealer Offered Rate. Daily data up to and including February 19, 2010.
Source: Bloomberg.

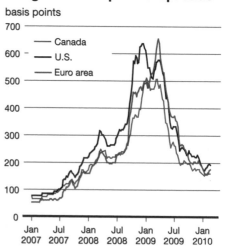

Long-Term Corporate Spreads

basis points

- Canada
- U.S.
- Euro area

Notes: The spreads are the difference between corporate and government bond yields with a maturity between 7 and 10 years. Weekly data up to and including February 19, 2010.
Source: Merrill Lynch.

The U.S. dollar has depreciated by about 10 per cent on a trade-weighted basis since March 2009 against a broad group of currencies. This, together with higher commodity prices, has contributed to an appreciation of about 20 cents in the Canadian dollar relative to the U.S. dollar since the beginning of March 2009, peaking at US97.5 cents on January 14, 2010 (Chart 2.2). The Canadian dollar has accounted for a large share of the broad depreciation of the U.S. dollar.

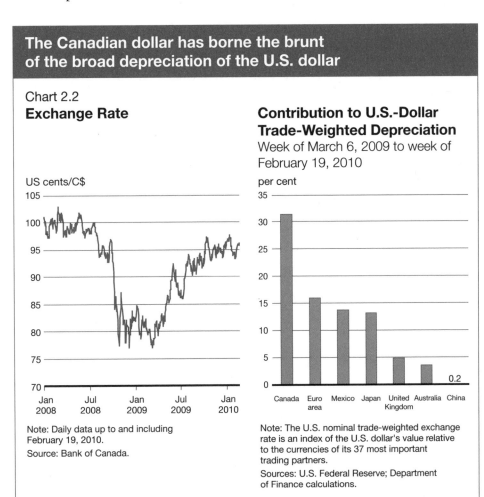

The Canadian dollar has borne the brunt of the broad depreciation of the U.S. dollar

Chart 2.2

Exchange Rate

US cents/C$

Note: Daily data up to and including February 19, 2010.

Source: Bank of Canada.

Contribution to U.S.-Dollar Trade-Weighted Depreciation
Week of March 6, 2009 to week of February 19, 2010

per cent

Note: The U.S. nominal trade-weighted exchange rate is an index of the U.S. dollar's value relative to the currencies of its 37 most important trading partners.

Sources: U.S. Federal Reserve; Department of Finance calculations.

Global Economic Developments and Outlook

The global economy began to expand in the second half of 2009, supported by extraordinary policy stimulus. The policy-induced recovery, in turn, has led to a recovery in global trade and an end to the inventory liquidation cycle. Nonetheless, the recovery in most advanced economies is expected to be weak by historical standards.

The recovery remains fragile in advanced economies. Most of the advanced economies emerged from recession in the third quarter of 2009, although the recovery in some countries appears to have stalled in the fourth quarter, primarily within the euro area. Most major industrialized economies are experiencing weaker domestic demand growth than overall GDP growth. In these countries, the economic recovery is led by export growth and an end to the cycle of inventory liquidation. Canada is unique in that the economic recovery is being led by strong domestic demand growth.

After having previously contracted for five consecutive quarters, real GDP in the euro area recorded a second consecutive modest increase in the fourth quarter of 2009 (0.4 per cent). However, growth in a number of member countries, including Germany and Italy, was flat or negative in the fourth quarter. Real GDP grew 1.1 per cent in the United Kingdom in the fourth quarter of 2009 after having contracted for six quarters. After a year-long recession, real GDP in Japan has expanded in two of the last three quarters, including a 4.6-per-cent increase in the fourth quarter.

The economic recovery is strongest in emerging and developing countries, led by Asian economies, particularly China, where massive fiscal stimulus has buoyed domestic demand. This in turn has supported a recovery in global trade. Despite the severe global downturn and the disruption of trade, the Chinese economy grew 8.7 per cent in 2009, including a 10.7-per-cent year-over-year increase in the fourth quarter of 2009, the fastest pace in two years.

Looking forward, the forces currently driving the recovery in advanced economies are expected to gradually weaken, as positive contributions to growth from inventories diminish and as the impact of fiscal stimulus fades toward the end of 2010 and early 2011. A sustained recovery will require increased support from private sector spending. The International Monetary Fund (IMF) expects global economic activity to grow by 3.9 per cent in 2010 and 4.3 per cent in 2011, led by developing Asian countries and China (Chart 2.3).

The expected rebound is relatively modest compared to previous recoveries, especially given the sharp drop in output last year. Based on the IMF outlook, the output lost during the recession is not expected to be recouped over the medium term. The IMF outlook suggests that the level of global GDP will be about 7.5 per cent lower in 2014 than it would have been if pre-recession trends had continued. This loss reflects the view that the level of activity prior to the crisis was unsustainably high, as it was based on excessive risk taking, an unsustainably low cost of financing, and rising leverage.

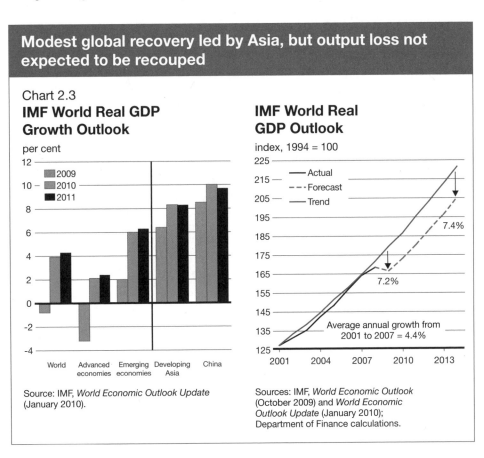

Modest global recovery led by Asia, but output loss not expected to be recouped

Chart 2.3

IMF World Real GDP Growth Outlook

per cent

Source: IMF, *World Economic Outlook Update* (January 2010).

IMF World Real GDP Outlook

index, 1994 = 100

Average annual growth from 2001 to 2007 = 4.4%

7.2%

7.4%

Sources: IMF, *World Economic Outlook* (October 2009) and *World Economic Outlook Update* (January 2010); Department of Finance calculations.

United States

Economic growth in the United States has resumed. This follows a peak-to-trough decline in real GDP of 3.8 per cent, which has resulted in a record loss of 8.4 million jobs (or 6.1 per cent of U.S. jobs) and left the unemployment rate at 9.7 per cent, near a 26-year high (Chart 2.4). Real GDP rose 2.2 per cent in the third quarter of 2009 and accelerated to a six-year high of 5.9 per cent in the fourth quarter. Final domestic demand in the U.S. remains weak, growing by only 1.6 per cent in the fourth quarter and accounting for less than a third of overall growth in the quarter.

The depreciation of the U.S. dollar since March 2009 and the continued improvement in global growth have supported the U.S. trade sector. In the fourth quarter of 2009, these developments were accompanied by a substantial rebound in inventory investment from very low levels, resulting in significantly stronger U.S. growth than was anticipated by private sector forecasters in the Department of Finance December 2009 survey.

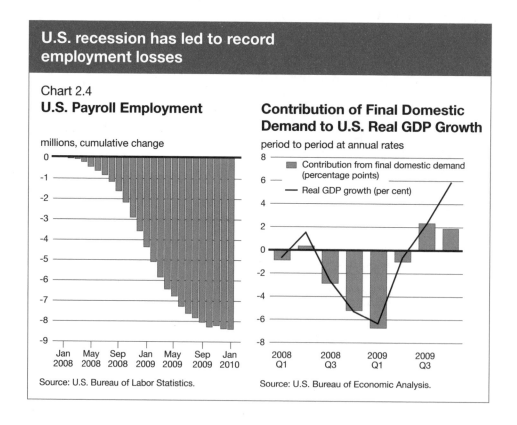

U.S. recession has led to record employment losses

Chart 2.4

U.S. Payroll Employment

millions, cumulative change

Contribution of Final Domestic Demand to U.S. Real GDP Growth

period to period at annual rates

Contribution from final domestic demand (percentage points)

Real GDP growth (per cent)

Source: U.S. Bureau of Labor Statistics.

Source: U.S. Bureau of Economic Analysis.

However, the unexpectedly strong growth in the fourth quarter has not significantly altered the quarterly private sector outlook for 2010, since fourth-quarter growth mainly reflected a large temporary contribution from inventories. In December, private sector forecasters expected real GDP growth to average about 3 per cent through 2010, reflecting still-modest private domestic demand growth, the gradual withdrawal of fiscal stimulus toward the end of the year, and the winding down of the temporary boost provided by the end of the inventory liquidation cycle (Chart 2.5).

There remains considerable uncertainty surrounding the U.S. outlook due to high U.S. unemployment and ongoing deleveraging, as well as large U.S. deficits and rising public debt.

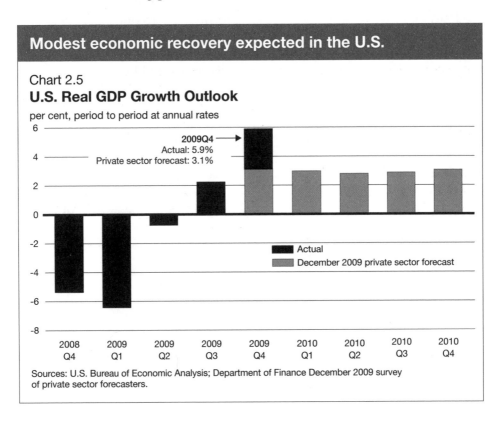

Modest economic recovery expected in the U.S.

Chart 2.5
U.S. Real GDP Growth Outlook

per cent, period to period at annual rates

Sources: U.S. Bureau of Economic Analysis; Department of Finance December 2009 survey of private sector forecasters.

Canadian Recent Economic Developments

The global recession did not start within Canadian borders. Nevertheless, the Canadian economy has been significantly affected by the global economic recession. However, reflecting several important financial, economic and fiscal strengths, Canada has been able to weather the crisis better than all other major industrialized countries. Indeed, Canada was the last G7 country to enter recession. These strengths, together with the extraordinary measures provided by Canada's Economic Action Plan, helped Canada emerge from recession in mid-2009.

The economic recovery in Canada strengthened over the second half of 2009, with real GDP increasing 0.9 per cent in the third quarter and 5.0 per cent in the fourth quarter. The resumption of positive economic growth followed three quarters of negative growth in Canada, beginning in the fourth quarter of 2008. Over the course of the recession, the level of real GDP declined by 3.6 per cent—similar to the decline in output that occurred during the recession of the early 1990s. However, the decline in Canadian real GDP was virtually the smallest of all G7 countries (Chart 2.6).

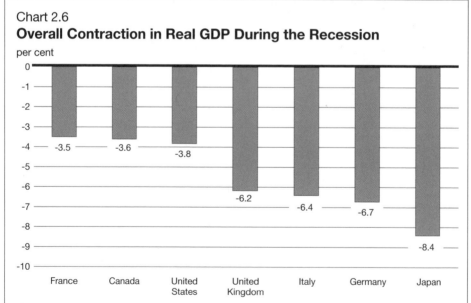

Canada has fared better than virtually all other G7 countries during the global recession

Chart 2.6
Overall Contraction in Real GDP During the Recession

Note: The overall contraction in GDP is measured by the peak-to-trough decline in real GDP in each country: 2008Q2-2009Q3 for United Kingdom; 2008Q2-2009Q2 for Italy; 2008Q2-2009Q1 for France, Germany and Japan; 2008Q3-2009Q2 for United States; 2008Q4-2009Q2 for Canada.

Sources: Statistics Canada; U.S. Bureau of Economic Analysis; Japan Cabinet Office; U.K. Office for National Statistics; Deutsche Bundesbank; Institut national de la statistique et des études économiques; Istituto nazionale di statistica.

Several factors account for Canada's ability to weather the global recession better than most other industrialized countries. First, Canada's banks and other financial institutions were better capitalized and less leveraged than their international peers. In the corporate sector, debt-to-equity ratios were very low going into the recession and have increased far less than in other countries since the start of the financial crisis.

In the household sector, net worth relative to personal disposable income declined significantly less than in many other countries. This reflects the fact that Canada entered the global recession without the type of major housing market imbalances that were present in many other advanced economies at the time, and as a result, Canadian house prices declined far less than elsewhere.

More recently, there are broad signs of recovery in the Canadian housing market, with resale housing activity and prices returning back to pre-recession levels. Canada's housing market remains healthy and stable. As recently confirmed by the IMF, our housing market is supported by sound economic factors such as low interest rates, rising incomes and a growing population. Moreover, mortgage arrears—overdue mortgage payments—have remained low both during and after the recession. The Government has taken proactive steps to maintain the long-term stability of Canada's housing market. The rules for government-backed insured mortgages have been adjusted to help Canadians prepare for higher interest rates, to ensure home ownership is an effective way to save, and to limit speculation.

Canada's strong fiscal situation has been another key source of strength. With the lowest debt-to-GDP ratio in the G7, the Government has been able to undertake unprecedented actions to support the economy without jeopardizing Canada's long-term fiscal position and causing uncertainty about future tax increases (Chart 2.7). Unlike other jurisdictions which will be forced to consider tax increases, Canada will be able to keep taxes low and to continue with planned tax cuts.

Canada entered the recession with the strongest fiscal position in the G7

Chart 2.7
Total Government Net Debt in 2007

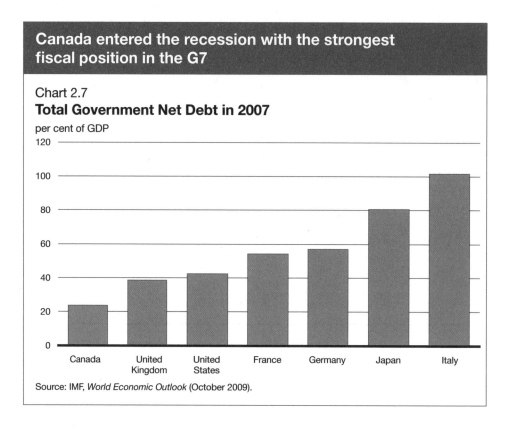

Source: IMF, *World Economic Outlook* (October 2009).

These strengths, together with low interest rates and the substantial support provided by Canada's Economic Action Plan, have supported a recovery of domestic demand in Canada. Since the start of 2009, final domestic demand in Canada has grown significantly faster than in any other G7 country (Chart 2.8). The higher level of domestic economic activity led the resumption of Canadian GDP growth in the second half of 2009. Strong domestic demand growth in Canada was partly offset by a weak export performance over much of 2009, reflecting weak demand from our major trading partners, particularly the United States, and the impact of the appreciation of the Canadian dollar.

Final domestic demand in Canada grew significantly faster than in any other G7 country over 2009

Chart 2.8
Real Final Domestic Demand Growth from 2009Q1 to 2009Q4

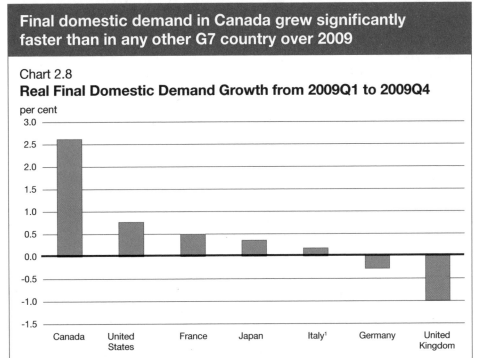

[1] Data for 2009Q4 for Italy is based on Moody's Economy.com Global Outlook published on February 23, 2010.
Sources: Statistics Canada; U.S. Bureau of Economic Analysis; Japan Cabinet Office; U.K. Office for National Statistics; Deutsche Bundesbank; Institut national de la statistique et des études économiques; Istituto nazionale di statistica; Department of Finance calculations.

27

The recovery of domestic demand in Canada has been broad-based and provides strong evidence that the Economic Action Plan is working. Growth in real consumer spending on goods and services averaged more than 3.5 per cent over the second half of 2009. Residential investment has also rebounded strongly, supported by the Home Renovation Tax Credit, increasing 9.5 per cent in the third quarter and 29.7 per cent in the fourth quarter, following double-digit declines at the onset of the recession. These developments have been accompanied by a swift recovery of consumer and business confidence to historical norms (Chart 2.9).

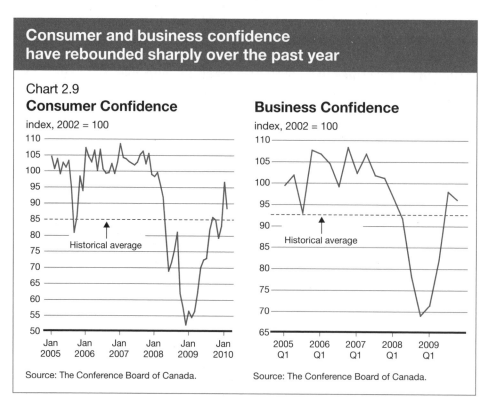

Consumer and business confidence have rebounded sharply over the past year

Chart 2.9

Consumer Confidence

index, 2002 = 100

Business Confidence

index, 2002 = 100

Source: The Conference Board of Canada.

Source: The Conference Board of Canada.

The Economic Action Plan has also substantially increased funding for infrastructure. Government investment in infrastructure increased by 25.1 per cent in the third quarter—the largest increase in nearly a decade— and 16.3 per cent in the fourth quarter, contributing significantly to the broader recovery of domestic demand. A more detailed analysis of the impact of the Economic Action Plan on the Canadian economy is presented in Annex 1.

The price of Canadian-produced goods and services has also rebounded from the lows of early 2009, increasing by 3.4 per cent in the third quarter and 4.5 per cent in the fourth quarter. These increases have largely reflected a recovery of Canada's terms of trade, as world prices for Canadian commodities have rebounded after declining sharply during the global recession. These price gains, combined with an increase in the volume of output in the last two quarters, led to a rebound in nominal GDP growth. After three consecutive quarters of decline, nominal GDP increased by 4.3 per cent in the third quarter and 9.8 per cent in the fourth quarter.

Reflecting the improved economic performance of the Canadian economy over the second half of 2009, labour market conditions have improved markedly since early 2009. In particular, over 135,000 jobs have been created in Canada since July 2009. As a result, the unemployment rate has declined modestly from the peak of 8.7 per cent reached in mid-2009. However, at 8.3 per cent in January 2010, the unemployment rate remains of concern.

The Economic Action Plan is on track to meet its objective of maintaining or creating 220,000 jobs

One objective of the Economic Action Plan was to maintain or create 220,000 jobs by the end of 2010. The Action Plan is on track. In the first year of implementation, an estimated 130,000 jobs have been created or maintained as a result of the Economic Action Plan. In addition, over 160,000 Canadians are benefiting from the work-sharing program (see Annex 1). Overall, this has contributed to the net creation of over 135,000 jobs recorded in Canada since July 2009.

Canada's labour market performance has been significantly stronger than in the United States (Chart 2.10). Since the start of the U.S. recession in January 2008, employment in the U.S. has declined by 8.4 million jobs, or 6.1 per cent. In contrast, since the start of the Canadian recession in October 2008, employment has declined by 1.6 per cent. This means that job losses in the U.S. have been proportionately more than three times as large as in Canada. The unemployment rate in the U.S. has exceeded that in Canada for almost one and a half years, and over the last five months the difference has averaged 1.6 percentage points. The last time the Canada-U.S. unemployment rate gap was so large was in the mid-1970s. Canada's relatively better labour market performance compared to that of the U.S. reflects Canada's later entry into recession as well as the relatively early stabilization of Canadian domestic demand in 2009.

The Canadian labour market has been significantly stronger than in the U.S.

Chart 2.10

Unemployment Rate

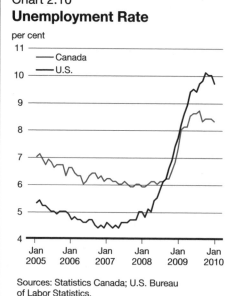

Sources: Statistics Canada; U.S. Bureau of Labor Statistics.

Total Employment

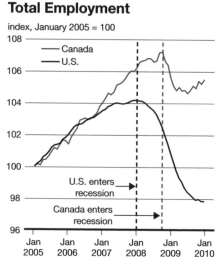

Sources: Statistics Canada; U.S. Bureau of Labor Statistics.

Commodity Prices

Commodity prices have rebounded solidly from the sharp declines observed in late 2008 and early 2009. In particular, crude oil prices have nearly doubled since February 2009, while base metal prices are up over 70 per cent over the same period, reflecting the improvement in global economic and financial conditions and the global outlook (Chart 2.11). Forestry prices have also increased since February 2009, in line with signs of stabilization in the U.S. housing market. Moderate gains were seen in natural gas prices over the period, despite a temporary decline in mid-2009 reflecting strong production and weak U.S. industrial demand.

As a result, prices for many commodities are now close to levels observed at the time of the October 2007 Economic Statement. Crude oil futures contracts suggest prices will continue to increase modestly in coming months, averaging US$81 per barrel in 2010, up from an average of US$62 per barrel in 2009. Futures contracts also suggest natural gas prices will average US$5.39 per MMBtu in 2010 compared to US$3.95 in 2009.

There remains considerable uncertainty surrounding the outlook for commodity prices over the near term, reflecting high inventory levels for most commodities and risks surrounding the pace and timing of the global economic recovery. However, most experts expect commodity prices to continue to increase as the global economic recovery continues to gain strength.

Prices for key Canadian commodities have rebounded since early 2009

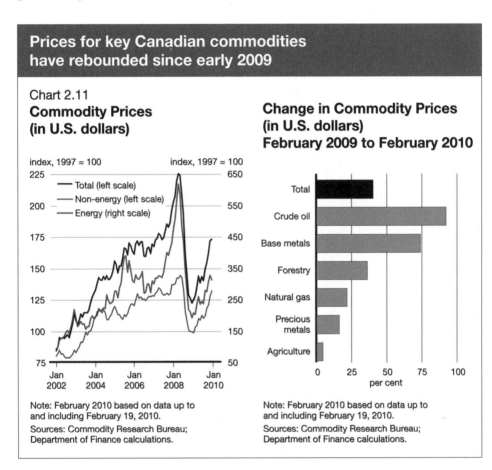

Chart 2.11
Commodity Prices (in U.S. dollars)

Change in Commodity Prices (in U.S. dollars) February 2009 to February 2010

Note: February 2010 based on data up to and including February 19, 2010.
Sources: Commodity Research Bureau; Department of Finance calculations.

Note: February 2010 based on data up to and including February 19, 2010.
Sources: Commodity Research Bureau; Department of Finance calculations.

Canadian Economic Outlook—
Private Sector Forecasts

The Department of Finance regularly surveys private sector economic forecasters on their views on the outlook for the Canadian economy. The economic forecasts reported in this budget, and which form the basis of the Department's fiscal forecasts, are based on a survey that closed on December 18, 2009 and includes the views of 15 private sector economic forecasters.

The December 2009 survey of private sector forecasters included Bank of America Merrill Lynch, BMO Capital Markets, Caisse de dépôt et placement du Québec, CIBC World Markets, The Conference Board of Canada, Desjardins, Deutsche Bank of Canada, Laurentian Bank Securities, Global Insight, National Bank Financial, Royal Bank of Canada, Scotiabank, TD Bank Financial Group, UBS Warburg, and the University of Toronto (Policy and Economic Analysis Program).

The use of private sector forecasts introduces an element of independence into the Government's economic and fiscal forecast.

Private sector economists continue to believe that the recovery will gain momentum through 2010. The short-term private sector economic forecast is now stronger than at the time of the September 2009 Update of Economic and Fiscal Projections. Forecasts for both GDP and employment have been revised up.

Over the medium term, the December average private sector outlook calls for a moderate economic recovery and a gradual improvement in labour market conditions. This is expected to be accompanied by an increase in interest rates and a stabilization of consumer price inflation near the mid-point of the Bank of Canada's inflation target band (Table 2.1).

The private sector forecast for the unemployment rate in 2010 has been revised down again. In May 2009, private sector economists were forecasting an unemployment rate of 9.2 per cent for 2010. The forecast was revised down to 9.0 per cent in the September Update and then to 8.5 per cent in the December survey.

Table 2.1
Average Private Sector Forecast

	2009	2010	2011	2012	2013	2014	2009–2014
	(per cent, unless otherwise indicated)						
Real GDP growth							
January 2009 private sector forecast	-0.8	2.4	3.4	3.1	2.9	2.6	2.3
September 2009 Update	-2.3	2.3	3.2	3.3	3.0	2.7	2.0
March 2010 budget	-2.5	2.6	3.2	3.0	2.8	2.6	2.0
GDP inflation							
January 2009 private sector forecast	-0.4	1.7	2.2	2.3	2.1	2.1	1.7
September 2009 Update	-2.3	1.8	2.0	2.3	2.2	2.2	1.4
March 2010 budget	-2.1	2.2	2.1	2.2	2.1	2.0	1.4
Nominal GDP growth							
January 2009 private sector forecast	-1.2	4.2	5.7	5.5	5.0	4.7	4.0
Budget 2009 planning	-2.7	4.3	6.4	6.1	5.3	5.0	4.1
September 2009 Update	-4.6	4.1	5.3	5.6	5.3	5.0	3.5
March 2010 budget	-4.6	4.9	5.4	5.3	4.9	4.7	3.4
Nominal GDP level (billions of dollars)							
January 2009 private sector forecast	1,590	1,657	1,751	1,847	1,940	2,031	–
Budget 2009 planning	1,560	1,627	1,731	1,837	1,935	2,031	–
September 2009 Update	1,527	1,590	1,674	1,768	1,862	1,955	–
March 2010 budget	1,527	1,601	1,688	1,778	1,865	1,953	–
3-month treasury bill rate							
January 2009 private sector forecast	0.8	1.7	3.2	4.0	4.3	4.4	3.1
September 2009 Update	0.4	0.8	2.5	3.9	4.2	4.3	2.7
March 2010 budget	0.3	0.7	2.4	3.8	4.3	4.4	2.6
10-year government bond rate							
January 2009 private sector forecast	2.8	3.4	4.5	5.0	5.2	5.2	4.3
September 2009 Update	3.3	3.8	4.4	4.9	5.1	5.2	4.5
March 2010 budget	3.3	3.7	4.3	4.9	5.2	5.3	4.5
Exchange rate (US cents/C$)							
January 2009 private sector forecast	81.1	85.4	91.5	94.5	95.6	95.9	90.7
September 2009 Update	86.7	91.9	95.2	96.1	97.1	96.5	93.9
March 2010 budget	87.9	95.5	98.3	97.7	99.3	98.5	96.2

Table 2.1 *(cont'd)*
Average Private Sector Forecast

	2009	2010	2011	2012	2013	2014	2009–2014
	(per cent, unless otherwise indicated)						
Unemployment rate							
January 2009 private sector forecast	7.5	7.7	6.9	6.4	6.2	6.1	6.8
September 2009 Update	8.5	9.0	8.5	7.8	7.1	6.8	7.9
March 2010 budget	8.3	8.5	7.9	7.4	6.9	6.6	7.6
Consumer Price Index inflation							
January 2009 private sector forecast	0.7	1.9	2.1	2.1	2.0	2.0	1.8
September 2009 Update	0.5	1.8	2.0	2.1	2.1	2.1	1.8
March 2010 budget	0.3	1.7	2.2	2.1	2.1	2.1	1.7
U.S. real GDP growth							
January 2009 private sector forecast	-1.8	2.1	3.5	3.2	3.0	2.7	2.1
September 2009 Update	-2.6	2.0	3.2	3.8	3.5	3.2	2.2
March 2010 budget	-2.5	2.7	3.0	3.4	3.1	2.9	2.1

Note: March 2010 budget figures for 2009 are from the December 2009 survey of private sector forecasters and have not been adjusted to include data released since December 18, 2009.

Sources: Budget 2009; September 2009 Update of Economic and Fiscal Projections; Department of Finance January 2009, August 2009 and December 2009 surveys of private sector forecasters.

As the global economy continues to stabilize following the deepest recession since the 1930s, the uncertainty surrounding the medium-term outlook has diminished significantly since the September Update. The difference between the average of the three highest and three lowest forecasts for the level of nominal GDP in 2013 is $54 billion, down from the record $98-billion difference at the time of the September Update. However, the gap still remains high by historical standards, reflecting the still-fragile global economic recovery and the inherent difficulty in providing a medium-term forecast (Chart 2.12).

The uncertainty surrounding the medium-term outlook has diminished but remains high

Chart 2.12
Private Sector Forecast Distribution of Nominal GDP Level in 2013

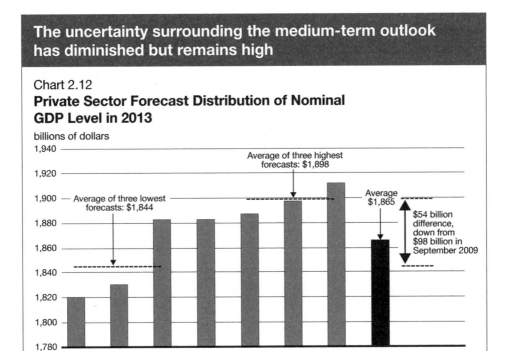

Source: Department of Finance December 2009 survey of private sector forecasters.

Risks to the Private Sector Forecast

On February 2, 2010, the Minister of Finance met with private sector economists to discuss the economic forecast from the December 2009 survey as well as the risks associated with those projections.

The forecasters were of the view that the short-term growth outlook was likely to be stronger than suggested by the December survey given a number of positive economic developments since the survey closed on December 18th. However, the private sector forecasters also expressed concerns about the risks to economic growth over the medium term. In particular, they noted that a sustained recovery in the global economy, particularly in the United States, and in financial markets may take some more time to fully materialize. At the same time, many forecasters noted that medium-term risks to the outlook were to some extent incorporated in the average private sector forecast.

35

Since the meeting with the private sector forecasters, their views on upside risks to the short-term growth outlook have largely materialized. At the time of the December 2009 private sector survey, forecasters expected real GDP growth of 3.4 per cent and nominal GDP growth of 5.6 per cent in the fourth quarter of 2009 (Chart 2.13). Both real and nominal GDP growth in the fourth quarter, released by Statistics Canada on March 1, 2010, were stronger than expected. Private sector forecasters' expectations for real GDP growth were more than 1.5 percentage points lower than actual real GDP growth of 5.0 per cent, while expectations for nominal GDP growth were more than 4 percentage points lower than actual nominal GDP growth of 9.8 per cent, reflecting higher real GDP growth as well as significant increases in commodity prices. If sustained, this would represent a $14-billion increase in nominal income in each year of the forecast.

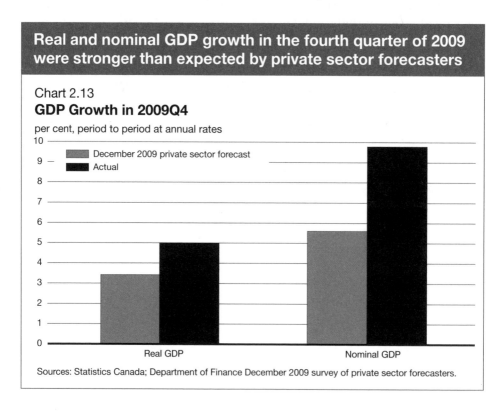

Real and nominal GDP growth in the fourth quarter of 2009 were stronger than expected by private sector forecasters

Chart 2.13
GDP Growth in 2009Q4

per cent, period to period at annual rates

Sources: Statistics Canada; Department of Finance December 2009 survey of private sector forecasters.

Over the medium term, private sector forecasters, on average, expect the level of real GDP in Canada between 2009 and 2014 to be about $95 billion lower each year compared to what they were expecting at the time of the October 2007 Economic Statement, just before the beginning of the U.S. recession.

The medium-term average private sector forecast for GDP inflation is nearly identical to the forecast for Consumer Price Index (CPI) inflation. GDP inflation, which is the broadest measure of price changes for goods and services produced in Canada, tends to be broadly in line with CPI inflation when the terms of trade is stable. The terms of trade, which is the ratio of export prices to import prices, is influenced by movements in the exchange rate and commodity prices. The close similarity of GDP and CPI inflation in the average private sector forecast is consistent with broadly unchanged terms of trade and commodity prices over the next five years.

Fiscal Planning

The average private sector economic forecast from the December 2009 survey forms the basis of the Government's fiscal planning. The Department of Finance considers that this economic forecast is a prudent basis for fiscal planning. The fiscal outlook is presented in Chapter 4.

Chapter

3

New Investments in Jobs and Economic Growth

Introduction

Budget 2010 takes actions in three broad areas, all of which contribute to the overarching objective of sustaining Canada's economic advantage.

First, the Government will follow through on its commitments to Canadians and its G7 and G20 partners to complete the implementation of Canada's Economic Action Plan. These investments will maintain and create jobs now.

Second, Budget 2010 invests in a limited number of targeted initiatives that build jobs and growth for the economy of tomorrow by improving skills, innovation, and our competitiveness.

Third, Budget 2010 charts a course to bring Canada's finances back to balance over the medium term and well before any other G7 country.

This chapter reviews the $19 billion in new federal stimulus measures that will take effect in 2010–11 under Canada's Economic Action Plan, as well as new actions Budget 2010 is proposing to build jobs and growth for the future. Chapter 4 reviews actions to reduce the deficit and return to balanced budgets. Chapter 5 provides a detailed report on the status of implementation of Canada's Economic Action Plan.

3.1

Delivering Year 2
of Canada's Economic
Action Plan

$19 Billion in New Stimulus in 2010-11

Highlights

Budget 2010 will deliver Year 2 of Canada's Economic Action Plan, with $19 billion in new federal stimulus in 2010–11, by:

✓ Providing $3.2 billion in personal income tax relief to support growth and job creation.

✓ Delivering $1.6 billion to strengthen benefits for the unemployed.

✓ Providing $1 billion to enhance training opportunities for all Canadian workers.

✓ Freezing the Employment Insurance premium rate at $1.73 per $100 of insurable earnings to the end of 2010—the lowest rate since 1982—in order to leave more money in the hands of employers and employees.

✓ Providing $7.7 billion in new stimulus to modernize infrastructure, support home ownership, and improve social housing across Canada.

✓ Investing almost $1.9 billion in post-secondary education infrastructure, research, technology innovation and environmental protection.

✓ Providing $2.2 billion in stimulus spending to support adjustment and secure job opportunities in regions, communities and industries that have been most affected by the economic downturn.

✓ Introducing new measures to strengthen Canada's financial sector, allowing businesses to continue growing and creating jobs.

C anada's Economic Action Plan is a two-year $62-billion plan to protect and create jobs in response to the deepest global recession since the Second World War. Chapter 5 describes the full Action Plan and reports on the Government's progress in its implementation. This section briefly reviews the main elements of the Action Plan that will be in effect for 2010–11.

In the first year of the Action Plan (2009–10), a significant amount of stimulus has been provided to support the economy and Canadians. The Government is ready to begin delivering Year 2 of the Economic Action Plan. The Action Plan will continue to maintain and create jobs, and help Canadian workers and families manage through still difficult economic conditions. Year 2 delivers $19 billion in new federal stimulus spending, with an additional $6 billion in stimulus from provinces, territories, municipalities and other partners. Even before the start of the fiscal year, 92 per cent of Year 2 funding is committed and ready to be delivered. This includes:

- $3.2 billion in personal income tax relief.
- More than $4 billion in actions to create and protect jobs and help the unemployed.
- $7.7 billion to modernize infrastructure and improve housing across Canada.
- $1.9 billion to create the economy of tomorrow.
- $2.2 billion to support industries and communities.

Actions under the Economic Action Plan that come into effect in 2010–11 are described below.

Reducing the Tax Burden for Canadians

Tax reductions in the Economic Action Plan are an essential part of the Government's effort to stimulate the economy and to create and maintain jobs. The Economic Action Plan will deliver $3.2 billion in personal income tax relief in 2010–11. This includes allowing Canadians to earn more income before paying federal income tax and before being subject to higher tax rates. It includes the enhanced Working Income Tax Benefit, which reduces the welfare wall by making work pay better for many low-income Canadians. Eligible beneficiaries will begin to receive enhanced benefits upon filing their 2009 tax returns. Tax measures for 2010–11 also include higher child benefits for parents and lower taxes for low- and middle-income seniors.

Tax measures in 2010–11 will continue to support the housing market. First-time home ownership is being encouraged through the First-Time Home Buyers' Tax Credit and additional access to Registered Retirement Savings Plan savings to purchase or build a home.

Millions of Canadian families took advantage of the Home Renovation Tax Credit before its expiry on January 31, 2010, and will be able to claim the credit when they file their 2009 income tax returns.

Tax relief will also continue to benefit Canadian businesses in the coming year. The measures included in Canada's Economic Action Plan, as well as actions taken by this Government since 2006, are positioning Canadian businesses to emerge stronger and better equipped to compete globally as the economy recovers.

The Government is lowering the federal general corporate income tax rate from 22.12 per cent (including the corporate surtax) in 2007 to 15 per cent in 2012. Canada's business tax advantage is being strengthened as the Government of Canada, provinces and territories progress toward the goal of a 25-per-cent combined federal-provincial corporate income tax rate. These broad-based corporate income tax reductions foster investment and help build a strong foundation for job creation and higher rates of productivity growth. As a result of these actions, Canada will have the lowest corporate income tax rate in the G7 in 2012.

Canada will have the lowest corporate income tax rate in the G7 in 2012

Chart 3.1.1
Corporate Income Tax Rates in 2012[1]

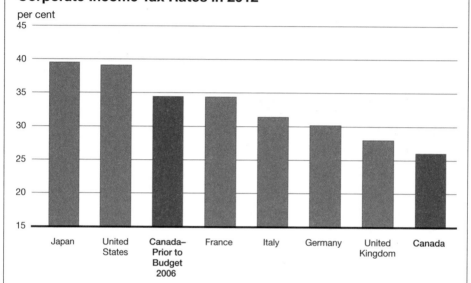

per cent

[1] Includes national and sub-national corporate income tax rates.
Sources: Organisation for Economic Co-operation and Development; Department of Finance.

These lower tax rates help us and companies like us keep more capital at work and achieve our priority in reinvesting in the business for future growth in our company.

— Tim Hortons Chief Financial Officer Cynthia Devine
"Canada Regains Tims Bragging Rights,"
Edmonton Journal, September 23, 2009

Tax Achievements Since 2006

The Government has reduced taxes on individuals, families and businesses by an estimated $220 billion over 2008–09 and the following five fiscal years. The Government's tax reduction efforts began in 2006—well before the introduction of Canada's Economic Action Plan.

Individuals and families at all income levels are benefiting from tax relief, with proportionately greater savings for those with lower incomes. For example:

- All Canadians—even those who do not earn enough to pay personal income tax—are benefiting from the 2-percentage-point reduction in the Goods and Services Tax (GST) rate. Maintaining the GST credit level while reducing the GST rate by 2 percentage points translates into more than $1.1 billion in GST Credit benefits annually for low- and modest-income Canadians.

- All taxpayers are benefiting from personal income tax relief, which includes reducing the lowest personal income tax rate to 15 per cent from 16 per cent and increasing the basic amount that Canadians can earn without paying federal income tax.

- The Working Income Tax Benefit (WITB) introduced in Budget 2007 and enhanced in the Economic Action Plan will provide $1.1 billion annually in benefits for low-income working Canadians. The WITB, in combination with other tax relief introduced by this Government, has substantially improved work incentives and the financial circumstances of many low-income Canadians.

- The Tax-Free Savings Account (TFSA) is improving incentives to save through a flexible, registered general-purpose account that allows Canadians to earn tax-free investment income while saving for their individual needs such as for a car, a home or retirement. The TFSA is the single most important personal savings vehicle since the introduction of the Registered Retirement Savings Plan (RRSP).

The Government has also introduced measures targeted to help families, students, seniors and pensioners, workers, persons with disabilities and communities. Examples of such measures include:

- A Child Tax Credit in recognition of the expenses associated with raising children.

- Exempting from tax primary, secondary and post-secondary scholarship, bursary and fellowship income in support of academic studies.

- The introduction of pension income splitting, the doubling of the Pension Income Credit and two $1,000 increases to the Age Credit amount, which provide substantial tax savings to seniors and pensioners.

- The Canada Employment Credit, which recognizes work-related expenditures such as home computers, uniforms and supplies.

Tax Achievements Since 2006 *(cont'd)*

- The Registered Disability Savings Plan (RDSP), which helps ensure the financial security and well-being of children with severe disabilities.
- The Children's Fitness Tax Credit, which promotes physical fitness among children.
- A tax credit for public transit passes.

This Government's previous tax achievements also include actions to make Canada's business tax system more competitive, which is essential to encouraging new investment, growth and job creation in Canada. Examples include:

- Substantial, broad-based tax reductions that will reduce the federal general corporate income tax rate from 22.12 per cent (including the corporate surtax) in 2007 to 15 per cent in 2012.
- An increase in the amount of small business income eligible for the reduced federal income tax rate to $500,000 effective January 2009, following an earlier increase to $400,000 from $300,000—as well as a reduction of the federal income tax rate applying to qualifying small business income to 11 per cent effective January 2008.
- The alignment of capital cost allowance (CCA) rates for a number of assets, including non-residential buildings, computers, railway locomotives, carbon dioxide pipelines, natural gas distribution pipelines, and liquefied natural gas facilities, to better reflect their useful life—this both reduces the tax burden on investment and ensures neutral tax treatment of different capital assets, encouraging investment to flow to its most productive uses.
- The elimination in 2006 of the federal capital tax, a particularly damaging tax for business investment. In 2007, a temporary financial incentive was introduced to encourage provinces to eliminate their general capital taxes and to eliminate or replace their capital taxes on financial institutions with a minimum tax. All provincial general capital taxes will be eliminated by 2012.
- An enhancement of the financial support for small and medium-sized research and development performers, which was announced in 2008. The expenditure limit for the enhanced refundable Scientific Research and Experimental Development Investment Tax Credit was increased to $3 million and extended to medium-sized companies by phasing out access to this benefit over increased taxable capital and income ranges.

Actions to Create and Protect Jobs and Help the Unemployed

While the unemployment rate has stabilized and there are signs that the economy is improving, too many Canadians are still unemployed. In 2010–11, Canada's Economic Action Plan will provide more than $4 billion in additional benefits, training opportunities and Employment Insurance (EI) premium relief to help unemployed Canadians through this difficult period, and help ensure that they are equipped to re-enter the workforce and prosper in the future.

The Government is providing $1.6 billion in 2010–11 to strengthen benefits for the unemployed. This support includes providing up to an extra five weeks of EI regular benefits for all EI-eligible claimants, providing greater access to EI regular benefits for long-tenured workers, and extending the duration and the scope of the work-sharing program.

The Government is providing almost $1.0 billion in 2010–11 to enhance training opportunities for all Canadian workers. This includes additional support to the provinces and territories to expand training and skills development. It also includes helping youth to gain work experience and necessary skills and offering more opportunities to Aboriginal Canadians.

The Government is maintaining the freeze of the EI premium rate at $1.73 per $100 of insurable earnings to the end of 2010—the lowest rate since 1982 (Chart 3.1.2). In Budget 2009, this action was estimated to leave more than $1.6 billion in the hands of employers and employees in 2010–11.

When the temporary freeze of EI premiums is lifted in 2011, premium rates will be set by an independent arms's length Crown corporation, the Canada Employment Insurance Financing Board (CEIFB). Under the EI financing regime announced in Budget 2008, the CEIFB will set EI premium rates in order to balance the EI program over time, subject to a 15-cent limit on annual changes. Consistent with the Government's commitment in Budget 2009, the CEIFB will not be mandated to recover any EI deficits resulting from the benefit and training enhancements announced in Budget 2009.

Freeze in EI premium rate leaves money in the hands of employers and employees in 2010–11

Chart 3.1.2
Employment Insurance Premium Rates

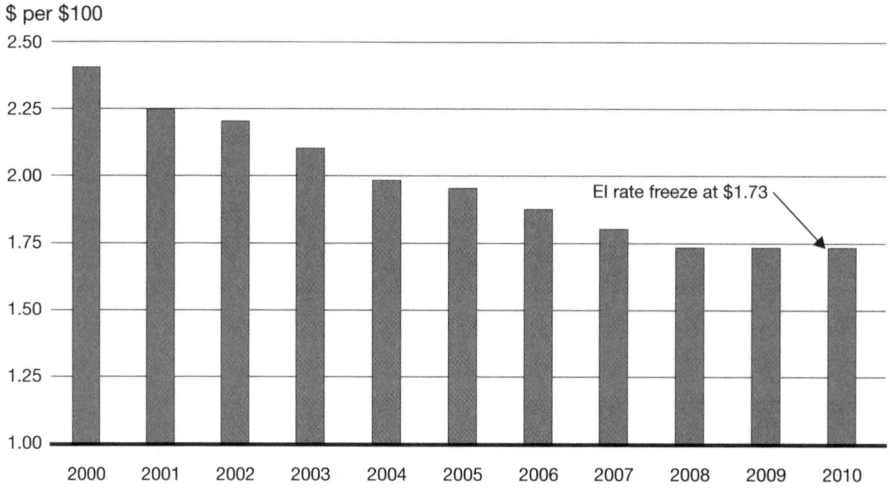

$ per $100

EI rate freeze at $1.73

Actions to Create and Protect Jobs

Canada's Economic Action Plan is a $62-billion stimulus plan aimed at creating and maintaining 220,000 jobs by the end of 2010. The Action Plan is on track to meet its objective, with 130,000 jobs created or maintained to date.

Canada's Economic Action Plan also targets $7.0 billion over two years in direct support to those workers most affected by the recession, providing them with additional benefits and expanded access to training and skills development.

Strengthening Benefits—$2.7 Billion

- Up to an extra five weeks of Employment Insurance benefits—$1.15 billion
- Enhanced work-sharing—$200 million
- Extended benefits for long-tenured workers—$1.3 billion
- Wage earner protection—$50 million

Enhancing Availability of Training—$1.9 Billion

- Enhanced Employment Insurance training programs—$1 billion
- Strategic Training and Transition Fund—$500 million
- Youth employment—$55 million
- Targeted Initiative for Older Workers—$40 million
- Apprenticeship Completion Grant—$80 million
- Foreign credential recognition—$50 million
- Aboriginal Skills and Employment Partnerships—$80 million
- Aboriginal Skills and Training Strategic Investment Fund—$75 million
- Aboriginal Human Resources Development Strategy—$25 million

Employment Insurance Premium Rates—$2.4 Billion

- Freezing Employment Insurance premium rates at $1.73 per $100 of insurable earnings for 2010

Building Infrastructure to Create Jobs

During 2010–11, communities, businesses and individuals from across Canada will continue to see the benefits of infrastructure investments under Canada's Economic Action Plan. The Action Plan will provide $7.7 billion in stimulus in 2010–11 to modernize infrastructure, support home ownership, stimulate the housing sector and improve social housing across Canada. This builds on the $8.3 billion in infrastructure and housing stimulus delivered in 2009–10.

In 2010–11, the Economic Action Plan will invest more than $4 billion in provincial, territorial and municipal infrastructure, $285 million in First Nations community infrastructure and $780 million in priority federal projects. These investments will create jobs and ensure that Canada emerges from the economic downturn with a more modern and greener infrastructure.

In addition, the Economic Action Plan will provide over $2 billion in 2010–11 to renew Canada's social housing stock. This funding provides significant support for provinces, territories and municipalities to renovate their social housing, including housing for low-income seniors and persons with disabilities. The Action Plan also invests in First Nations and northern housing.

Infrastructure investments will continue to create jobs over the coming year

In 2009–10 and 2010–11, the Government will deliver the following infrastructure programs as part of the Economic Action Plan:

Immediate Action to Build Infrastructure—$8.2 Billion

- Infrastructure Stimulus Fund—$4.0 billion

- Accelerating payments under the Provincial/Territorial Base Funding Initiative—$441 million

- Bonus for Community Projects under the Building Canada Fund—$500 million

- Green Infrastructure Fund—$400 million

- Recreational Infrastructure Canada—$500 million

- First Nations infrastructure—$515 million

- Federal infrastructure projects—$1.8 billion

Stimulating Housing Construction—$7.8 Billion

- Support for home ownership and the housing sector—$3.8 billion

- Investments in social housing for Canadians—$4.1 billion

These Action Plan initiatives and their progress are described in Chapter 5.

Creating the Economy of Tomorrow

In designing Canada's Economic Action Plan, the Government incorporated measures to help create the economy of tomorrow. In 2010–11, the Action Plan will invest almost $1.9 billion in post-secondary education, infrastructure, research, technology innovation, and environmental protection. This builds on 2009–10 investments of over $2.1 billion to support these strategic investments.

In 2010–11, the Government will provide $1 billion to support deferred maintenance, repair and construction at Canada's colleges and universities. This investment will help keep Canadian research and educational facilities at the forefront of scientific advancement and will help to ensure that high-paid jobs are maintained and created in Canada.

Funding to create the economy of tomorrow will also extend access to broadband Internet in remote communities, develop carbon capture and storage technology, and fund other strategic investments in science, technology and research.

Supporting Industries and Communities

Canada's Economic Action Plan is providing $2.2 billion in stimulus spending in 2010–11 to support adjustment and secure job opportunities in regions, communities and industries that have been hard hit by the economic downturn.

In 2010–11, the Government will provide $1.3 billion in support to affected sectors, including forestry, agriculture, small business, tourism, shipbuilding and culture. These investments will help to maintain and create jobs across the country.

Building on tariff measures implemented in the Economic Action Plan, in this budget the Government is eliminating all remaining tariffs on manufacturing inputs and machinery and equipment. This historic step will position Canada as the first among its G20 partners to establish itself as a tariff-free zone for manufacturers. Full details regarding tariff reductions can be found in Chapter 3.3.

In addition, over $900 million will be invested in communities that have been particularly hard hit by the economic downturn. This includes $500 million through the Community Adjustment Fund, which is designed to help communities with fewer than 250,000 people deal with industrial restructuring by investing in new economic opportunities.

Strengthening Canada's Financial Sector

The Extraordinary Financing Framework (EFF) introduced as part of Canada's Economic Action Plan helped to ensure that credit continued to be available in Canada throughout the financial crisis, allowing businesses to continue to grow and create jobs. Financing conditions in Canada have improved markedly since the EFF was introduced. Accordingly, certain initiatives under the EFF, including the Insured Mortgage Purchase Program and the Canadian Secured Credit Facility, will end as planned as of March 31, 2010. Others, such as the Business Credit Availability Program, will remain in place to support the growth in business credit that will be needed during the economic recovery.

Budget 2010 builds on the strengths of Canada's financial sector, further bolstering Canada's advantage in global capital markets. New measures will support Canada's strong and competitive financial sector, help businesses access the financing they need to support the recovery, and protect Canadian financial consumers.

Table 3.1.1

Year 2 of Canada's Economic Action Plan—$19 Billion in New Stimulus in 2010–11

	Year 1	Year 2	
	2009–10 Stimulus	2010–11 Stimulus	Total Action Plan
	(millions of dollars—cash basis)		
Reducing the Tax Burden for Canadians			
Personal income tax relief for all taxpayers	1,885	1,950	3,835
Increases to the National Child Benefit supplement and the Canada Child Tax Benefit	230	310	540
Enhancing the Working Income Tax Benefit	580	580	1,160
Targeted relief for seniors	325	340	665
Total—Reducing the Tax Burden for Canadians	**3,020**	**3,180**	**6,200**
Actions to Create and Protect Jobs and Help the Unemployed			
Strengthening benefits for Canadian workers	1,115	1,550	2,665
Enhancing the availability of training	919	986	1,905
Maintaining low EI premium rates	818	1,631	2,449
Total—Actions to Create and Protect Jobs and Help the Unemployed	**2,852**	**4,167**	**7,019**
Building Infrastructure to Create Jobs			
Investments in provincial, territorial and municipal infrastructure	1,710	4,156	5,866
Investments in First Nations infrastructure	230	285	515
Investments in federal infrastructure projects	1,007	780	1,786
Support for home ownership and the housing sector	3,340	425	3,765
Investments in social housing for Canadians	2,025	2,050	4,075
Total—Building Infrastructure to Create Jobs	**8,312**	**7,696**	**16,007**

Table 3.1.1 *(cont'd)*

Year 2 of Canada's Economic Action Plan—$19 Billion in New Stimulus in 2010–11

	Year 1	Year 2	
	2009–10 Stimulus	2010–11 Stimulus	Total Action Plan
	(millions of dollars—cash basis)		
Creating the Economy of Tomorrow			
Action to invest in post-secondary education and research	1,089	1,155	2,244
Investing in science and technology	1,049	725	1,774
Total—Creating the Economy of Tomorrow	**2,139**	**1,880**	**4,018**
Supporting Industries and Communities			
Support for industries	1,171	1,296	2,467
Support for communities	879	935	1,813
International partnerships to support the auto sector	9,718	0	9,718
Total—Supporting Industries and Communities	**11,768**	**2,231**	**13,998**
Economic Action Plan stimulus	**28,090**	**19,152**	**47,242**
Assumed provincial and territorial actions	8,441	5,978	14,419
Total Economic Action Plan stimulus (with leverage)	**36,531**	**25,131**	**61,661**

Note: Totals may not add due to rounding.

3.2

Sustaining Canada's Economic Advantage

The measures in Canada's Economic Action Plan are designed to protect Canadians from the immediate challenges posed by the global recession. These actions will also improve Canada's long-term economic growth and prosperity. By ensuring that Canada emerges from the recession with a more modern infrastructure, a more skilled and flexible labour force, lower taxes and a more competitive economy, the measures in the Action Plan will also contribute to sustaining and building on Canada's economic advantages.

In 2006, the Government set out its long-term plan for the economy in *Advantage Canada*. *Advantage Canada* is about building a strong foundation for Canada's economic future by focusing on the main drivers of productivity: human capital, physical capital, and sound regulatory, tax and fiscal frameworks. To that end, the plan is centered on building five key strategic advantages for Canada:

A **Tax Advantage**—reducing the tax burden on Canadians and Canadian businesses.

A **Knowledge Advantage**—fostering skills, training and education.

An **Infrastructure Advantage**—building a modern, world-class infrastructure.

An **Entrepreneurial Advantage**—making product and financial markets more efficient.

A **Fiscal Advantage**—strengthening Canada's fiscal position for current and future generations.

Since 2006, the Government has made significant progress in implementing all elements of *Advantage Canada*.

- The Government has made major progress in developing a Canadian tax advantage: it has reduced taxes in every way that it collects revenues, and is ensuring that Canadian families, students, workers, seniors and businesses large and small continue to keep more of their hard-earned money.

- Building on progress in creating a Tax Advantage, Canada's Economic Action Plan has introduced over $20 billion in new tax relief in 2008–09 and over the following five fiscal years. This will bring total tax relief for individuals, families and businesses from measures introduced since 2006 to an estimated $220 billion over this period.

Canada will emerge from the recession with one of the world's most competitive tax systems

- This year, Canada will have an overall tax rate on new business investment that is the lowest in the Group of Seven (G7) and below the average of the Organisation for Economic Co-operation and Development (OECD). Canada's business tax advantage is supporting investment, job creation and growth in all sectors of the economy, improving productivity and providing Canadians with more and better jobs.

- By 2012, Canada will have the lowest statutory corporate income tax rate in the G7. With a federal rate of 15 per cent in 2012, and provinces and territories converging towards the goal of a 10-per-cent rate, a 25-per-cent combined federal-provincial corporate income tax rate makes Canada a country of choice for investment.

- The Government introduced the Tax-Free Savings Account—the most important new vehicle for savings since the introduction of the Registered Retirement Savings Plan—which has improved the incentives for all Canadians to save.

- The Government introduced the Working Income Tax Benefit, lowering the "welfare wall", making work more attractive for low-income Canadians.

- Canada's federal tax-to-GDP (gross domestic product) ratio is at its lowest level since 1961.

- To ensure Canada has the best-educated, most-skilled and most flexible workforce in the world, the Government has made significant new investments in education, training, a modernized Canada Student Loans Program, the new Vanier Canada Graduate Scholarships, and innovation, science and technology. Canada's immigration system has also been streamlined to better respond to the needs of the labour market.

- Historic federal infrastructure investments are enhancing Canada's future by increasing productivity and competitiveness, cleaning up the environment and strengthening communities as vibrant centres of commerce, learning and recreation.

- To build a more competitive business environment, the Government has signed bilateral free trade agreements, implemented unilateral tariff reductions and strengthened Canada's financial system.

- All of these achievements are sustainable. In contrast to the situation in other major industrialized countries, Canada's fiscal position is strong. Canada entered the recession with a total government net debt-to-GDP ratio of 23.5 per cent. Looking ahead, Canada's net debt burden is projected to increase by just 5.9 percentage points between 2007 and 2014. This compares to an expected increase of between 24 and 63 percentage points for other G7 nations (Chart 3.2.1).

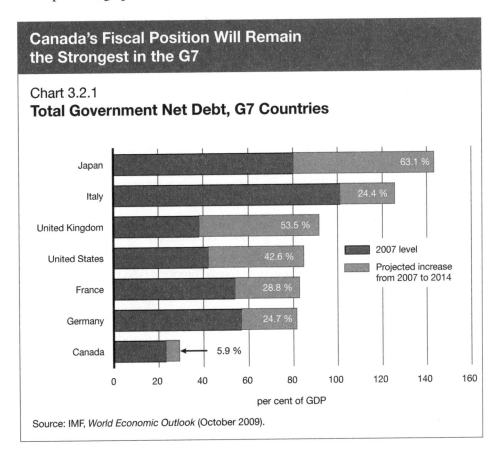

Canada's Fiscal Position Will Remain the Strongest in the G7

Chart 3.2.1
Total Government Net Debt, G7 Countries

Source: IMF, *World Economic Outlook* (October 2009).

The Government is committed to maintaining this strong Fiscal Advantage and returning to balanced budgets over the medium term. The Government's plan to return to balance is detailed in Chapter 4. Budget 2010 also introduces a number of targeted actions, at limited fiscal cost, that will provide additional support to the economy by protecting and creating jobs, furthering the objectives of *Advantage Canada*, and addressing other priorities. These actions are outlined in the next section.

Building on a Strong Economic Foundation

3.3

Highlights

Jobs Protection and Youth Employment Measures

Budget 2010 builds on the Economic Action Plan with targeted actions to protect Canadian workers from the effects of the global economic recession by:

✓ Temporarily extending the maximum length of work-sharing agreements to protect jobs.

✓ Supporting the next generation of business leaders with $10 million in new funding for the Canadian Youth Business Foundation.

✓ Providing $60 million in 2010–11 to assist more young Canadians while the labour market recovers.

✓ Investing $20 million in support of Pathways to Education Canada's work to support disadvantaged youth.

✓ Committing $30 million to support better elementary and secondary education outcomes for First Nations students.

Creating Economic Growth and Jobs Through Innovation

Budget 2010 makes targeted changes to improve Canada's productivity growth through innovation by:

✓ Providing $45 million over five years to establish a post-doctoral fellowship program to help attract the research leaders of tomorrow to Canada.

✓ Delivering $222 million in funding over five years to strengthen the world-leading research taking place at TRIUMF, Canada's premier national laboratory for nuclear and particle physics research.

✓ Increasing the combined annual budgets of Canada's research granting councils by an additional $32 million per year, plus an additional $8 million per year to the Indirect Costs of Research Program.

✓ Providing Genome Canada with an additional $75 million for genomics research.

✓ Doubling the budget of the College and Community Innovation Program with an additional $15 million per year.

✓ Providing $135 million over two years to the National Research Council Canada's regional innovation clusters program.

✓ Providing $48 million over two years for research, development and application of medical isotopes.

✓ Providing a total of $497 million over five years to develop the RADARSAT Constellation Mission.

✓ Launching a new Small and Medium-sized Enterprise Innovation Commercialization Program with $40 million over two years.

✓ Renewing and making ongoing $49 million in annual funding for the regional development agencies to support innovation across Canada.

Encouraging Investment and Trade to Create Jobs and Growth

Budget 2010 takes further action to improve conditions for investment, enhance competition, and reduce barriers for businesses by:

✓ Making Canada a tariff-free zone for industrial manufacturers by eliminating all remaining tariffs on machinery and equipment and goods imported for further manufacturing. When fully implemented, this will provide $300 million in annual duty savings for Canadian business to support investment and growth and create jobs.

✓ Improving Canada's system of international taxation to facilitate investment, cut red tape, and streamline the compliance process associated with the taxation of cross-border activity.

✓ Establishing a new Red Tape Reduction Commission.

✓ Providing $7.2 million over two years to improve canadian fish and seafood industry access to the international marketplace.

✓ Delivering $75 million over three years to support investments by Canadian cattle processing plants to help improve their operations to ensure cattle producers have access to competitive cattle processing operations in Canada.

Green Jobs and Growth

Budget 2010 includes measures to promote energy investments, help develop and deploy clean energy technologies, and protect and enrich Canada's unique environmental heritage by:

✓ Establishing the Next Generation Renewable Power Initiative, with $100 million over the next four years to support the development, commercialization and implementation of advanced clean energy technologies in the forestry sector.

✓ Modernizing the regulatory system for project reviews, and supporting consultation with Aboriginal peoples on major resource projects.

✓ Expanding eligibility for accelerated capital cost allowance for investment in clean energy generation assets.

Modernizing Canada's Infrastructure

Budget 2010 strengthens the Government's already significant investments in Canada's infrastructure by:

✓ Providing $175 million over two years to renew Marine Atlantic's fleet and shore facilities and improve its services.

✓ Providing $28 million to ensure Atlantic ferry services continue to operate in a safe and reliable condition.

✓ Providing $51 million over two years to The Jacques Cartier and Champlain Bridges Incorporated to maintain the safety of Montréal's bridges.

Strengthening the Financial Sector

Budget 2010 introduces measures that will support Canada's strong and competitive financial sector by:

✓ Moving forward with the majority of provinces and territories to establish a Canadian securities regulator within the next three years.

✓ Extending access to financing through continuation of the Business Credit Availability Program (BCAP) and the creation of the Vehicle and Equipment Financing Partnership under BCAP.

✓ Moving ahead with a Code of Conduct for the Credit and Debit Card Industry in Canada and proposing legislation to provide the Minister of Finance with the authority to regulate the market conduct of the credit and debit card networks, if required.

✓ Introducing a legislative framework to enable credit unions to incorporate and continue federally, which will promote the continued growth and competitiveness of the sector and enhance financial stability.

✓ Enhancing the financial consumer protection framework through new measures to improve the business practices and disclosure regime for federally regulated financial institutions.

The Government is taking targeted actions to create and maintain jobs and encourage economic growth. Budget 2010 builds on Canada's Economic Action Plan with initiatives to protect jobs, harness innovation to further improve Canada's economic advantage, support increased business investment and access to the international marketplace, create a more sustainable environment, modernize transportation infrastructure, and strengthen the financial system.

Jobs Protection and Youth Employment Measures

Canada's Economic Action Plan takes decisive action to support the economy and Canadians during the deepest global economic recession since the Second World War. In the first year of the Plan (2009–10), significant stimulus has been provided to protect and create jobs. Year 2 of the Action Plan delivers $19 billion in new federal stimulus spending, including $4 billion to create and protect jobs through additional Employment Insurance (EI) benefits by maintaining low EI premium rates and improving access to training and skills development. The Economic Action Plan has contributed to the stabilization of labour market conditions. Nevertheless, many Canadians are struggling to find jobs. In recognition of this, Budget 2010 includes additional measures to support those workers.

Work-Sharing

Work-sharing avoids layoffs by offering Employment Insurance income benefits to qualifying workers willing to work a reduced work week while their employer recovers. The Economic Action Plan extended work-sharing agreements by 14 weeks, to a maximum of 52 weeks, and increased access to work-sharing agreements by providing greater flexibility in the qualifying criteria and streamlining processes for employers. More than 160,000 workers are currently participating in nearly 6,000 work-sharing agreements.

Budget 2010 extends this measure. Existing or recently terminated work-sharing agreements will be extended by an additional 26 weeks, to a maximum of 78 weeks. Greater flexibility in the qualifying criteria for new work-sharing agreements will also continue to be provided. Both of these enhancements will be in place until March 31, 2011.

This measure, estimated to cost $106 million over two years, means even more workers will keep their jobs, while employers will also be able to retain skilled employees with years of experience. This extended enhancement to work-sharing will continue to reduce the financial impact of the downturn on workers and their communities.

Building Skills for Youth

Young workers have been significantly affected by the recession. Budget 2010 invests $108 million over three years to assist young people looking to gain skills and experience. This includes additional support for the education of First Nations children and youth.

Youth Internships

Recent post-secondary graduates are facing an uncertain job market. The Youth Employment Strategy is the Government's key labour market program to help young people. To help more new graduates obtain valuable work experience in their field, Budget 2010 provides a one-year $30-million increase in funding for the Career Focus component of the Youth Employment Strategy. This measure will provide additional support to Canadian employers and organizations willing to offer valuable career-related work experience to college and university graduates, including more internships in green sectors of the economy. This will allow more young Canadians to get that vital first job in their field of study.

Supporting Young Entrepreneurs

The Canadian Youth Business Foundation is a national organization that helps young Canadians become successful entrepreneurs by providing mentorship, learning resources and start-up financing where commercial lending is unavailable. Through its presence in communities across Canada, the Foundation supports the next generation of business leaders in developing the skills and experience necessary to thrive in today's competitive economy. Budget 2010 provides $10 million in 2009–10 to the Canadian Youth Business Foundation to support its work with Canada's young entrepreneurs.

Youth at Risk

The Skills Link component of the Youth Employment Strategy was developed to assist youth in a range of circumstances, including persons with disabilities, single parents, Aboriginal Canadians, recent immigrants, those living in rural and remote areas, and those who have not completed high school. Skills Link provides funding to organizations to help these young Canadians develop the broad range of skills, knowledge and work experience they need to participate and succeed in the job market.

Budget 2010 provides a one-year $30-million increase in funding for Skills Link to assist more young Canadians while the labour market recovers. This initiative will provide more opportunities for young Canadians to successfully join the labour market.

Pathways to Education Canada

A gap continues to exist between the post-secondary participation rates of youth from lower-income backgrounds and youth from higher-income backgrounds. Research shows that many of the barriers are not financial, and that some youth need other supports to reach their goals. Pathways to Education Canada is a unique program of early interventions and support for high school students. It has an established record of reducing high school drop-out rates and increasing post-secondary enrolment of students from inner city high schools. This community-based, volunteer-supported program provides tutoring, mentoring, counselling and financial support to disadvantaged youth and their families.

Budget 2010 provides $20 million for Pathways to Education Canada to partner with the private sector, other governments and non-governmental organizations and work with communities in support of disadvantaged youth. This funding will enable Pathways to extend its reach to more young Canadians who are facing barriers to their pursuit of post-secondary education.

Supporting Better Education Outcomes for First Nations

The Government is committed to working with First Nations and provinces to ensure that First Nations children receive the education they require for success.

Budget 2010 provides $30 million over two years to support an implementation-ready tripartite K-12 education agreement. This agreement will ensure First Nations students benefit from comparable education and achieve comparable results whether the classroom is located on or off reserve.

The Government will work with First Nations groups and other willing partners to develop options, including new legislation, to improve the governance framework and clarify accountability for First Nations elementary and secondary education.

In addition, the Government will engage in a new approach to providing support to First Nations and Inuit post-secondary students to ensure that students receive the support they need to attend post-secondary education. The new approach will be effective and accountable, and will be coordinated with other federal student support programs.

Helping youth acquire skills and participate in the labour market

Strong Record of Support for Youth

The Government recognizes the importance of high quality education and skills training for young Canadians. A number of programs are already in place to help youth get an education, acquire skills and get a job:

- $342 million per year for the Youth Employment Strategy to give young Canadians needed support as they pursue an education and careers.

- $2.2 billion per year to help students deal with the costs of education through grants, scholarships and loan programs.

- $100 million per year for the Apprenticeship Incentive Grant and $40 million per year for the Apprenticeship Completion Grant to encourage more young Canadians to pursue apprenticeships.

- $80 million per year for a tax credit to a maximum of $2,000 per apprentice per year through the Apprenticeship Job Creation Tax Credit to encourage employers to hire apprentices.

- $20 million per year for two years under the Economic Action Plan to enhance student employment opportunities under the Canada Summer Jobs Program and the Federal Student Work Experience Program.

Budget 2010 provides a further $108 million over three years to support young people looking to gain skills and experience.

Creating Economic Growth and Jobs Through Innovation

As the global economy emerges from the recent downturn, nations that prosper will be those that can most effectively utilize their resources and create a unique competitive advantage. Securing sustained economic growth and a rising standard of living for Canadians will require that businesses and individuals have the tools, the drive and the creativity to lead this global race.

For Canada, the key challenge will be to improve the rate at which our productivity is growing. Faster productivity growth will allow us to produce more with fewer resources, increasing our wealth and helping us deal with challenges such as an aging population and a stronger currency. Being more productive does not mean working more for less pay. It means becoming better at what we do, so that we can attract more investment, create more jobs, and have the resources to support the public services we want.

There is no single factor that drives productivity growth. For this reason, the Government has pursued a broad approach, as set out in its long-term economic plan, *Advantage Canada,* to put in place strategic advantages that will allow our country to prosper. Significant progress has been achieved to date in implementing *Advantage Canada.* This progress includes historic tax reductions that are helping to provide Canada with the lowest overall tax rate on new business investment in the G7 this year. It also includes the strengthening of Canada's investment and competition policies, and significant investments in critical infrastructure across the country.

Budget 2010 builds on earlier investments by providing new resources to help develop and attract talented people, strengthen our capacity for world-leading research, improve commercialization, accelerate private sector investment, enhance the ability of Canadian firms to participate in global markets, and create a more competitive business environment. This budget will also make Canada a tariff-free manufacturing zone by positioning Canada as the first of the G20 countries to allow industrial manufacturers to operate without the burden of tariffs and diversify their linkages to new markets.

Strengthening Canada's Tax Advantage

The tax reductions in the Economic Action Plan reinforce the Government's ambitious agenda of tax relief aimed at creating a tax system that improves standards of living, and fuels job creation and investment in Canada. Over the medium term, the Government will continue to strengthen Canada's Tax Advantage.

Canada's business tax advantage is being strengthened as the Government of Canada, provinces and territories progress toward the goal of a 25-per-cent combined federal-provincial corporate income tax rate.

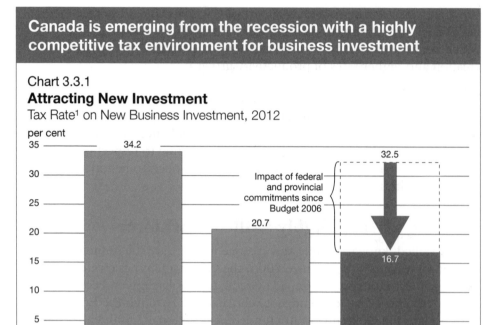

Canada is emerging from the recession with a highly competitive tax environment for business investment

Chart 3.3.1
Attracting New Investment
Tax Rate[1] on New Business Investment, 2012

[1] The Marginal Effective Tax Rate (METR) includes measures announced as of February 1, 2010. It excludes resource and financial sectors and tax provisions related to research and development.
[2] Excludes Canada.
Source: Department of Finance.

The federal general corporate income tax rate was reduced to 18 per cent on January 1, 2010. It will be further reduced to 16.5 per cent on January 1, 2011 and to 15 per cent on January 1, 2012. With Ontario, British Columbia, New Brunswick and Manitoba having announced their own rate reductions, and Alberta already at 10 per cent, the provinces and territories are converging towards a 10-per-cent corporate income tax rate. The benefits of continued provincial and territorial corporate income tax rate convergence include:

- A strengthening of Canada's business tax advantage, resulting in the business investment necessary to create new and better jobs and increase living standards for Canadians.

- A better allocation of investment in Canada, thereby promoting higher rates of productivity and economic growth.

- A reduced incentive for unproductive interprovincial tax planning, thereby protecting the tax bases of the provinces and territories and simplifying tax compliance for corporations.

Provinces and territories are a vital part of Canada's Tax Advantage. They have taken important actions to improve Canada's tax competitiveness, which are helping build a solid foundation for economic growth, job creation and higher rates of productivity growth.

The Government of Canada has a number of tax agreements with provinces and territories that result in greater efficiency and simplicity of the tax system. Work is always ongoing to improve and enhance the application and administration of these agreements. We will continue to respect provincial decisions in their areas of jurisdiction and remain open to negotiating in good faith with them.

Creating a More Highly Skilled Workforce

Highly skilled, knowledgeable and creative workers are the foundation of an innovative economy. Since 2006, the Government has created 500 new prestigious Vanier Canada Graduate Scholarships and created 1,000 permanent Canada Graduate Scholarships. Through the Economic Action Plan, the Government has funded an additional 2,500 scholarships in response to the global economic downturn, introduced the Canada Excellence Research Chairs initiative, and created additional Industrial Research and Development internships. These initiatives help attract leading researchers to Canada, enhance the incentives for young Canadians to pursue advanced education, and encourage businesses to create high quality jobs for recent graduates.

Post-doctoral research is a valuable way for recent doctoral graduates to gain additional experience prior to embarking on a faculty or applied research career. Building on the significant investments made since 2006, Budget 2010 provides $45 million over five years to the granting councils to establish a new and prestigious post-doctoral fellowships program to attract top-level talent to Canada.

The proposed new post-doctoral fellowship program will be designed to be internationally competitive. These fellowships will be valued at $70,000 each per year for two years. The first fellowships will be awarded in 2010–11. At maturity, the new program will fund 140 fellowships annually.

World-Leading Research Infrastructure

In recent budgets, the Government has made significant new investments to modernize and upgrade infrastructure at Canadian post-secondary institutions. The Economic Action Plan introduced the $2-billion Knowledge Infrastructure Program to accelerate repairs, maintenance and construction at universities, colleges and research hospitals.

Building on these investments, Budget 2010 provides significant new funding for cutting-edge research facilities to help create the jobs of the future.

Canadian High Arctic Research Station

Science and technology play an important role in reinforcing Canada's sovereignty in the Arctic by helping to achieve economic, environmental and strategic objectives in the North. Canada's Economic Action Plan laid the groundwork for delivering on the Government's commitment to build a world-class Canadian High Arctic Research Station by providing $2 million over two years for a feasibility study for the proposed facility. Budget 2010 is taking a further step by providing $18 million over five years to Indian and Northern Affairs Canada to commence the pre-construction design phase for the station.

TRIUMF

The TRIUMF facility in British Columbia is Canada's premier national laboratory for nuclear and particle physics research and is home to the world's largest cyclotron. In addition to fundamental research in subatomic physics, TRIUMF has gained an international reputation as a leader in advanced medical imaging, nuclear medicine, and research in the environmental and material sciences. TRIUMF collaborates with industry partners to commercialize its scientific breakthroughs, including its successful relationship with MDS Nordion in the production of radioisotopes and radiation-related technologies used to diagnose, prevent and treat disease.

Budget 2010 provides $126 million over five years to strengthen the
world-leading research taking place at TRIUMF. In combination with
$96 million to be provided from existing resources of the National Research
Council Canada, federal support for TRIUMF's core operations will total
$222 million over the next five years.

Supporting Advanced Research

The Government has made significant investments to strengthen our
post-secondary research environment in recent budgets, including the
additional $4.9 billion provided through Canada's Economic Action Plan
to support post-secondary infrastructure and advanced research, and create
new scholarships and internships for promising students. Budget 2010
builds on these important investments by providing additional resources
for advanced research at Canada's post-secondary institutions.

The Research Granting Councils

The three federal granting councils—the Natural Sciences and Engineering
Research Council of Canada (NSERC), the Canadian Institutes of Health
Research (CIHR), and the Social Sciences and Humanities Research Council
of Canada (SSHRC)—are the primary institutions through which the federal
government supports research at Canada's universities, colleges and research
hospitals. They fund breakthrough research projects, support the training
of graduate students and help accelerate the translation of knowledge into
practical applications. These investments contribute to the creation of high-
paid jobs in Canada.

Budget 2010 increases the annual budgets of the three granting councils
by an additional $32 million per year, starting in 2010–11. This new
funding will enable the councils to sustain their overall support for research
and lead to increased commercialization in Canada. The new resources for
the councils will be allocated as follows:

- $16 million per year to the CIHR to support outstanding health-related
  research and development.

- $13 million per year to NSERC, including $8 million per year to
  strengthen its support for advanced research, and $5 million per year to
  foster closer research collaborations between academic institutions and the
  private sector through NSERC's Strategy for Partnerships and Innovation.

- $3 million per year to SSHRC to support world-leading research
  in the social sciences and humanities.

Budget 2010 also provides an additional $8 million per year to the Indirect Costs of Research Program. This enhanced funding will help institutions support the additional research activities enabled by the new resources provided to the federal granting councils through Budget 2010.

Genome Canada

Genome Canada is a not-for-profit corporation dedicated to establishing Canada as a research leader in genomics, an area of science that has seen some of the most dramatic advances in the past two decades. Genomics research has the potential to improve lives through better health, a cleaner environment and more sustainable use of natural resources. Genome Canada has been successful in establishing world-calibre genomics science capacity in Canada by funding first-class research, establishing cutting-edge innovation centres and helping train the next generation of researchers. To date, the Government has provided $840 million to Genome Canada, which along with funding from other partners will result in over $1.7 billion in genomics research in Canada.

Budget 2010 provides Genome Canada with an additional $75 million in 2009–10 to launch a new targeted research competition focused on forestry and the environment and sustain funding for the regional genomics innovation centres.

Rick Hansen Foundation

The Rick Hansen Foundation is a not-for-profit organization dedicated to accelerating the discovery of a cure for spinal cord injury and improving the quality of life of people with spinal cord injuries. This year, the Foundation is celebrating the 25th anniversary of Rick Hansen's Man in Motion World Tour, which saw him visit more than 30 countries and raise over $26 million for spinal cord research. To mark the occasion, the Foundation will launch the new Rick Hansen Institute, building on existing federal support to create an international centre of excellence in spinal cord care and research.

Budget 2010 provides $9 million over two years to support the Rick Hansen Foundation, including the 25th anniversary of the Man in Motion Tour and the new Rick Hansen Institute. This funding will contribute to advancing knowledge and research that will improve the lives of people suffering from spinal cord injuries in Canada and abroad.

Knowledge Transfer and Commercialization

Canada is a world leader in post-secondary research, but to fully realize value from our investments in this area, we must improve the translation of research discoveries into new goods, services and technologies.

The Government has recognized the need to better link researchers and businesses, and has introduced a number of initiatives that promote collaborative research partnerships and knowledge transfer to businesses. Budget 2010 provides additional resources to support commercialization and enable innovative companies to benefit from federal investments in research, leading to the creation of additional high-value jobs and an increased standard of living for Canadians.

Supporting College Innovation

Colleges make important contributions to advancing Canada's innovation capacity by working with businesses and playing a key role in translating knowledge into practical applications that open new markets and create high-value jobs. The applied research and training capacity at colleges and polytechnics is a tremendous resource for building a more knowledge-driven economy. Our 150 colleges and polytechnics, with locations in over 1,000 communities, are uniquely placed to work with businesses and industries to address real-life market needs and opportunities.

The College and Community Innovation Program (CCIP) successfully enables applied research collaborations between colleges and local firms focused on specific company needs. Through Budget 2010, the Government is doubling the budget of the CCIP by providing an additional $15 million per year starting in 2010–11. The new resources will support additional collaborative projects in colleges across the country, strengthen the competitiveness of small and medium-sized businesses through innovation, and enable additional young Canadians to prepare for the jobs of tomorrow.

National Research Council Canada Regional Innovation Clusters

The National Research Council Canada's (NRC) regional innovation clusters program aims to foster knowledge-based partnerships among business, academia and other levels of government, helping regions and communities build a competitive advantage through research and innovation in targeted areas. Program funding supports 11 technology clusters across all 10 provinces. These cluster initiatives support the development of dynamic Canadian firms, generate jobs and transform local economies.

Budget 2010 provides $135 million over the next two years to build on the success to date of the cluster initiatives in developing networks of innovative businesses, NRC scientists and communities, promoting regional economic growth through innovation, and levering Canada's investment in research into economic and social benefits for all Canadians.

Diversifying the Supply of Medical Isotopes

Provinces and Canadian health researchers are exploring new avenues for the production and use of medical isotopes. The Government of Canada is taking action to help support these efforts. Budget 2010 provides $35 million over two years to Natural Resources Canada to support research and development of new technologies for the production of isotopes.

An additional $10 million over two years will be provided to the Canadian Institutes of Health Research for a clinical trials network to help move research on isotopes and imaging technologies into clinical practice, and $3 million over two years will be provided to Health Canada to work with stakeholders to optimize the use of medical isotopes in the health system.

Canadian Space Agency

Canada's space industry is a sophisticated research and innovation leader, successfully turning its investment in knowledge into a global advantage in several niche areas, including robotics and satellite communications. Through the Canadian Space Agency, the Government of Canada has played a crucial role in the development of the Canadian space sector and the creation of high-paid jobs, by investing in new industry-developed space technologies and applications.

Canada's RADARSAT-1 and RADARSAT-2 satellites provide a wide range of enhanced capabilities, including more advanced maritime surveillance, support for operations of Canadian Forces at home and abroad, weather and climate change assessment, disaster management and ecosystem monitoring.

To ensure that Canada maintains its strong position in this important field, Budget 2010 provides the Canadian Space Agency with $397 million over five years to work with the Canadian space industry to develop the RADARSAT Constellation Mission, the next generation of advanced radar remote sensing satellites. Together with $100 million from existing resources of the Canadian Space Agency, $497 million will be invested over five years in advanced research, technology development and construction associated with the Constellation Mission. The bulk of this spending will occur after 2011–12.

Promoting Innovation by Small and Medium-Sized Businesses

Small and medium-sized businesses are an important component of our economy, estimated to account for about 98 per cent of all businesses in Canada and employing more than 5 million people, roughly half of the private sector workforce. Becoming more innovative will allow Canadian small and medium-sized businesses to grow faster and create additional high-value jobs. Yet in many cases, smaller Canadian companies that develop new and innovative products and technologies struggle to find buyers due to the higher risk associated with untested products. The federal government can play an important role in helping smaller businesses introduce innovations into the marketplace by providing an opportunity for companies to demonstrate the successful application of new concepts on a commercial scale.

Recognizing this, the Government will support innovation in Canada's small business sector by launching a new Small and Medium-sized Enterprise Innovation Commercialization Program, a two-year pilot initiative through which federal departments and agencies will adopt and demonstrate the use of innovative prototype products and technologies developed by small and medium-sized businesses. Budget 2010 provides $40 million over two years to support up to 20 demonstration projects. To help small and medium-sized businesses take advantage of this initiative, the Government will organize regional trade shows so that companies can showcase their innovative concepts to federal departments. Further details regarding this initiative will be announced later in the spring of 2010.

International Science and Technology Partnerships

Budget 2010 will provide $8 million over two years to extend the International Science and Technology Partnerships Program (ISTPP). The ISTPP was launched to promote collaborative research and development activities with international partners such as India, China and Brazil. As a "seed fund," the ISTPP helps to foster strategic international partnerships that accelerate the commercialization of research and development, leading to new market opportunities for Canadian businesses, particularly small and medium-sized enterprises.

Advancing the Digital Economy

Canadian businesses lag their international competitors in the development and adoption of innovative information and communications technologies (ICT). The ICT sector creates high-skilled, high-paying jobs in Canada, and the adoption of information and communications technologies helps to raise business productivity. A strong digital economy will contribute to a more prosperous and competitive Canada.

The Government will develop a Digital Economy Strategy that will enable the ICT sector to create new products and services, accelerate the adoption of digital technologies, and contribute to improved cyber security practices by industry and consumers.

Supporting Regional Innovation

Regional economic development agencies play an important role by promoting innovation and the commercialization of research in communities throughout Canada. The agencies work with innovative businesses, post-secondary research institutes and not-for-profit organizations to increase opportunities for knowledge-based industries and apply innovative solutions to regional needs. To strengthen the important activities of the regional development agencies in promoting growth through innovation across Canada, Budget 2010 is providing new resources to the agencies.

Atlantic Canada Opportunities Agency

The Atlantic Canada Opportunities Agency (ACOA) has made significant progress in supporting knowledge and entrepreneurial initiatives and facilitating the development of emerging technology clusters in Atlantic Canada. By enhancing the region's innovative capacity, ACOA has strengthened the economic base of Atlantic communities and has helped to create better business opportunities.

Budget 2010 will provide ACOA with $19 million per year, ongoing starting in 2010–11. This funding will allow the agency to extend the Atlantic Innovation Fund, a competitively allocated initiative that helps regional businesses, universities and research institutions to develop and commercialize new technologies, builds research capacity and encourages the creation of research and development partnerships. The funding will also support ACOA's Innovative Communities Fund, which will help Atlantic communities adapt to new economic realities and opportunities. Through these programs and additional funding raised from other private and public sources, ACOA will help to create jobs, strengthen community infrastructure and accelerate business growth in Atlantic Canada.

Canada Economic Development for Quebec Regions

Canada Economic Development for Quebec Regions (CEDQ) is supporting the long-term economic development of the regions of Quebec, with special attention to helping vulnerable communities to diversify their economies and become more knowledge-based.

Budget 2010 will provide CEDQ with $14.6 million per year, ongoing starting in 2010–11, to increase the vitality of communities and help small and medium-sized businesses and communities to enhance their competitiveness. This funding will play a key role in ensuring that communities in all areas of Quebec can fully participate in the economy of tomorrow and benefit from a higher quality of life.

Western Economic Diversification Canada

Western Economic Diversification Canada (WD) is successfully promoting economic growth and diversification throughout Manitoba, Saskatchewan, Alberta and British Columbia. WD is focusing on supporting projects that strategically position western businesses to grow, innovate, compete and create jobs in the knowledge-based economy.

Budget 2010 will provide WD with $14.7 million per year, ongoing starting in 2010–11, for activities to support commercialization, enhance global competitiveness and drive economic growth and development in communities. WD will undertake initiatives to promote research and development capabilities and help communities and businesses in Western Canada take advantage of domestic and international opportunities. WD will also work to foster federal-provincial-municipal economic development partnerships in urban, rural and northern communities.

Improving Support for Innovation

The Government is taking steps to improve its support for innovation and ensure that investments are effective and yield the best possible results for Canadians.

The Government of Canada provides substantial support for research and development (R&D) in the education, private and not-for-profit sectors, estimated at more than $7 billion in 2009. This includes about $4 billion in direct federal support for R&D undertaken by post-secondary researchers, the private sector, not-for-profit organizations and other research performers. Canada's investment in higher-education R&D as a proportion of the economy is the highest among G7 countries (see Chart 3.3.2).

In addition, Canada's Scientific Research and Experimental Development Tax Incentive Program is the single largest federal program supporting business R&D in Canada, providing over $3 billion in tax assistance in 2009.

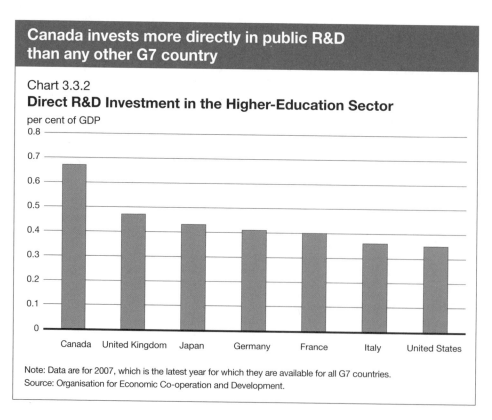

Canada invests more directly in public R&D than any other G7 country

Chart 3.3.2
Direct R&D Investment in the Higher-Education Sector
per cent of GDP

Note: Data are for 2007, which is the latest year for which they are available for all G7 countries.
Source: Organisation for Economic Co-operation and Development.

Despite the high level of federal support, we continue to lag behind other advanced economies with respect to overall innovation performance, private sector investment in R&D, and the commercialization of research.

To ensure that federal funding is yielding maximum benefits for Canadians, the Government, in close consultation with business leaders from all sectors and our provincial partners, will conduct a comprehensive review of all federal support for R&D to improve its contribution to innovation and to economic opportunities for business. This review will inform future decisions regarding federal support for R&D. The Government is currently developing the terms of reference for the review.

Encouraging Investment and Trade to Create Jobs and Growth

Investment by businesses in modern machinery and equipment improves an economy's productivity. It makes businesses more competitive in international markets, allowing them to expand and create jobs here in Canada. Governments can help create the conditions that encourage businesses to make these investments by reducing taxes and tariffs and streamlining regulation as well as burdensome and slow approval processes.

The Government has improved the business environment since 2006. Budget 2010 takes further action to improve conditions for investment, enhance competition and reduce barriers for businesses.

Making Canada a Tariff-Free Zone for Industrial Manufacturers

In recognition of the importance of open markets for global economic recovery, Canada and its G20 partners have committed to resist trade protectionism and complete the World Trade Organization Doha Round to further liberalize markets worldwide. Canada, as a nation whose prosperity is greatly dependent on trade, clearly understands the importance of open markets.

For this reason, and in view of its responsibilities as host and co-host of the G8 and G20 Leaders Summits in 2010, the Government is taking steps to demonstrate its commitment to free trade and provide new trade advantages to Canadian business. It is doing this through a strategy that includes unilateral action to eliminate tariffs and support for the completion of the Doha Round, and through an aggressive bilateral free trade strategy that currently includes efforts to complete a Comprehensive Economic and Trade Agreement with the European Union, exploratory talks with India, and the implementation of recently concluded agreements with Colombia, Panama and Jordan.

With respect to this trade strategy, Budget 2010 implements the results of comprehensive consultations with Canadian industries to eliminate tariffs to lower their cost of production and allow them to invest in needed machinery and equipment. Such investment is critical to Canada's long-term prosperity. Free trade in manufacturing inputs and machinery and equipment are an important source of competitive strength for Canadian businesses. By reducing the cost of importing key factors of production, tariff relief encourages innovation and allows businesses to enhance their stock of capital equipment. This is of particular importance to the needs of small and medium-sized manufacturers that link to global supply chains and need to diversify their export markets.

A first phase of tariff relief, implemented in Budget 2009, has permanently eliminated tariffs applied on a broad range of machinery and equipment, providing average annual savings of $88 million.

Budget 2010 will implement a second phase of tariff relief by eliminating all remaining tariffs on manufacturing inputs and machinery and equipment (Chart 3.3.3). The majority of these 1,541 tariffs will be eliminated March 5, 2010, with the remainder being gradually eliminated by no later than January 1, 2015. When the second phase of tariff relief is fully implemented, more than $5 billion in imports will be liberalized, providing an additional $300 million in annual duty savings for Canadian business.

Budget 2010 eliminates 1,541 tariffs on industrial inputs and machinery and equipment

Chart 3.3.3
Tariff Relief on Machinery and Equipment and Industrial Inputs

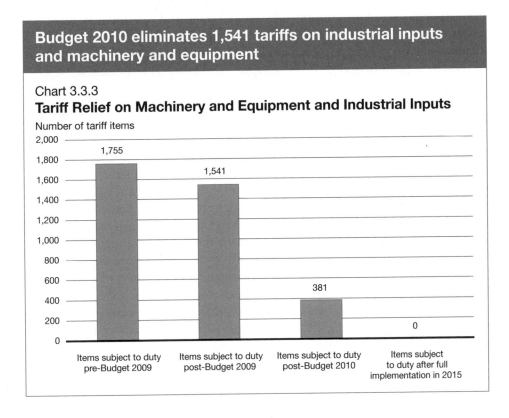

This historic step will position Canada as the first among its G20 partners to allow manufacturers to operate without the cost of tariffs on inputs and machinery and equipment. The elimination of tariffs on 1,541 items will also reduce customs compliance costs, allow for the simplification of the tariff structure and eliminate the administrative burden of complying with rules of origin and drawback regulations. This will make all of Canada a tariff-free zone for industrial manufacturers and a more attractive place for investors. This approach is superior to efforts by other countries that focus on location-specific free trade zones.

The initiative will increase investment and create jobs, improve innovation and productivity, lower prices for consumers and increase overall prosperity for Canadians. This tariff elimination is expected to result in the creation of up to 12,000 jobs over time.

The Government will continue working with Canadians to identify areas where further trade liberalization could take place.

Making Canada the Place to Do Business

As global markets recover competition will continue to intensify. This is why immediate action is needed to help Canada's manufacturing sector emerge from the global recession on stronger footing. The Budget 2010 Tariff Advantage will complement Canada's Tax Advantage and the solid reputation of our financial sector, making Canada the place to do business. In consultation with the Government, many firms indicated support for this measure with the following comments:

Tariff relief on the goods requested will allow (the company) to maintain domestic production levels and hopefully even repatriate some production back to Canada.

– A manufacturer in British Columbia

Elimination of the tariff is important to our manufacturing sector to help level the playing field against foreign competition…

– A manufacturer in Newfoundland and Labrador

Tariff relief would allow us to stabilize our domestic base by reducing costs and closing the gap between domestic and imported production.

– A manufacturer in British Columbia

Eliminating tariffs would have a significant and favourable impact on our cost structure and our competitiveness against foreign competitors who can perform these transformation processes in lower-cost jurisdictions.

– A manufacturer in Quebec

Such relief would reduce our production costs, making us more competitive against our competition (essentially foreign sources) and preserving our presence as a key employer in Ontario.

– A manufacturer in Ontario

Tariff relief would allow manufacturers to stabilize and expand domestic production and retain exports. …It will reduce the administrative burden and costs associated with obtaining, reviewing and maintaining certificates of origin. These costs can sometimes outweigh the benefits of preferential duty rates.

– A major Canadian manufacturing association

The Government is listening to Canadian manufacturers on how it can assist them in reducing costs and expanding production. International investors will also be paying attention to Canada's new approach to doing business.

Improving the Regulatory System and Reducing Red Tape

The Government has taken important steps to reduce the administrative and paperwork burden on Canadian businesses. In March 2009, the Government fulfilled its Budget 2007 commitment to reduce paperwork burden by 20 per cent under the Paperwork Burden Reduction Initiative. Almost 80,000 regulatory requirements and information obligations were eliminated by streamlining regulations, eliminating duplicate requirements and overlapping obligations, and reducing information requirements. As part of this initiative, the Government will introduce legislation to allow certain small excise remitters (those, other than tobacco licensees, with less than $10,000 in excise tax or duty monthly remittances) to file and remit semi-annually rather than monthly. With this change, most licensees will be able to file semi-annually rather than monthly, allowing these small businesses to invest more of their time in managing and growing their business.

Canadian businesses also say that more needs to be done to reduce the complexity of federal rules and structures. The Government is creating a new private sector Advisory Committee on Small Business and Entrepreneurship, which will report to the Government through the Minister of State (Small Business and Tourism) and provide advice on how to further improve business access to federal programs and information.

Reducing Red Tape and the Administrative Burden

Budget 2010 proposes several new initiatives to improve the federal regulatory system:

- **Red Tape Reduction Commission:** A commission, involving both Parliamentarians and private sector representatives, will be established to review federal regulations in areas where reform is most needed to reduce the compliance burden and provide specific recommendations for improvement.

- **Streamlining the Northern Regulatory Regime:** $11 million over two years will be provided to Indian and Northern Affairs Canada to accelerate the review process for resource projects in the North.

- **Telecommunications Sector:** The Government proposes to remove the existing restrictions on foreign ownership of Canadian satellites.

- **Advisory Committee on Small Business and Entrepreneurship:** A private sector committee will be created to provide advice on improving business access to federal programs and information.

Budget 2010 also proposes measures to reduce the administrative burden of the tax and tariff system:

- **Section 116:** Eliminating tax reporting under section 116 of the Income Tax Act for investments such as those by non-resident venture capital funds in a typical Canadian high-technology firm.

- **Disbursement Quota Reform:** Eliminating many of the disbursement quota requirements, which responds to calls from stakeholders in the charitable sector to reduce the administrative burden on charities so they may devote more of their time and resources to charitable activities.

- **Online Notices:** Issuing notices electronically, if authorized by a taxpayer, for those notices that can currently only be sent by ordinary mail. This will help reduce the volume of paper to be dealt with for both the Canada Revenue Agency and taxpayers.

- **Direct Sellers:** Simplifying Goods and Services Tax/Harmonized Sales Tax accounting for network sellers employing the commission-based model.

- **Reducing Customs Burden:** Eliminating tariffs on 1,541 tariff items, will reduce customs compliance costs, allow for the simplification of the tariff structure and eliminate the administrative burden of complying with rules of origin and drawback regulations related to imports under these tariffs.

Red Tape Reduction Commission

Reducing red tape for businesses is an ongoing challenge that requires continued attention. The Canadian Federation of Independent Business (CFIB) estimates that businesses in Canada currently spend over $30 billion each year complying with regulations. A number of provincial governments have previously undertaken work to reduce red tape. For example, British Columbia has eliminated more than 150,000 regulations since 2001, and has committed to maintaining a zero net increase in regulations through to 2012.

The Government of Canada will establish a new federal Red Tape Reduction Commission involving both Parliamentarians and private sector representatives to review federal regulations in areas where reform is most needed to reduce the compliance burden, especially on small businesses, while safeguarding the health and safety of Canadians. The Commission will be asked to provide specific recommendations on how to reduce unnecessary regulations and make the regulatory system more effective, so that small businesses can focus on investing and creating jobs. This approach will provide the strong leadership necessary to produce comprehensive and effective results.

Reducing the Administrative Burden of the Tax System

Budget 2010 proposes the following measures which will reduce the administrative burden of the tax system:

- **Section 116:** Narrowing the definition of taxable Canadian property will eliminate the need for tax reporting under section 116 of the Income Tax Act for many investments, improving the ability of Canadian businesses, including innovative high-growth companies that contribute to job creation and economic growth, to attract foreign venture capital.

- **Disbursement Quota Reform:** Eliminating many of the disbursement quota requirements responds to calls from stakeholders in the charitable sector to reduce the administrative burden on charities so they may devote more of their time and resources to charitable activities.

- **Online Notices:** Providing legislative authority to the Canada Revenue Agency (CRA) to issue notices electronically, if authorized by a taxpayer, for those notices that can currently only be sent by ordinary mail will help reduce the volume of paper to be dealt with, for both the CRA and taxpayers.

- **Direct Sellers:** Budget 2010 confirms the Government's intention to implement the Budget 2009 proposals to simplify Goods and Services Tax/Harmonized Sales Tax accounting for network sellers employing the commission-based model, and proposes enhancements and clarifications to better meet the needs of the industry.

More information on these proposals is available in Annex 5.

Administrative Improvements to the Scientific Research and Experimental Development Tax Incentive Program

Canada's Scientific Research and Experimental Development (SR&ED) Tax Incentive Program is one of the most advantageous systems in the industrialized world for research and development.

Following public consultations on the SR&ED Tax Incentive Program that were undertaken in 2007, Budget 2008 enhanced the support that this program provides for small and medium-sized businesses and extended the tax credit to certain expenditures incurred outside Canada. It also announced new funding for improvements to the administration of the SR&ED program in order to address challenges that were identified by stakeholders in the areas of accessibility, predictability and consistency. The Canada Revenue Agency (CRA) has taken steps to implement these measures. In November 2008, a new self-assessment tool and a new claim form and guide were introduced that are helping businesses determine the eligibility of their projects and making it easier for businesses to benefit from the SR&ED program. The CRA has also increased the number of technical reviewers who determine program eligibility and provide claimant services. The CRA is providing technical reviewers with more training and support, enhancing the quality assurance methodology, and reviewing the dispute resolution procedures.

In addition, as announced in January 2010, the CRA will begin to report quarterly, through its website, on the time it takes to review an SR&ED claim from start to finish. A new manual for CRA reviewers will become effective on April 1, 2010. This manual will emphasize how the CRA will work closely with claimants so that they may better understand the SR&ED program requirements and process.

The CRA continues to work with stakeholders to identify ways to improve the administration of the SR&ED program.

Strengthening Taxpayer Fairness

This Government is committed to treating taxpayers fairly. In 2007, the Canada Revenue Agency (CRA) introduced a strengthened Taxpayer Bill of Rights and, in 2008, a Taxpayers' Ombudsman was appointed. These measures built upon existing service standards, recourse and complaint resolution processes and taxpayer relief provisions, all of which are in place at the CRA. To help ensure that these rights are accessible and easily understood by all Canadians, the CRA will consult with key stakeholders, such as the Canadian Federation of Independent Business (CFIB), in order to identify ways in which transparency and accessibility can be strengthened.

Streamlining the Northern Regulatory Regime

The Government is committed to ensuring that a strong and prosperous North helps shape the future of our nation. Canada's Economic Action Plan included a number of investments in economic development, skills training, housing, and research infrastructure in support of the Government's Northern Strategy.

The resource potential in Canada's North is world-class, yet potential investors in northern resource projects face complex and overlapping regulatory processes that are unpredictable, costly and time-consuming. Streamlining the regulatory regime and removing barriers to private investment will support economic growth and help provide opportunities for Northerners by unlocking the resource potential in Canada's North, while at the same time protecting the environment.

Budget 2010 provides $11 million over two years to Indian and Northern Affairs Canada to support the acceleration of the review of resource projects in the North. These reforms will provide clarity and certainty for investors while ensuring that the environment is protected and that Canada's obligations under existing land claims agreements with Aboriginal groups are respected.

Increasing Competition and Foreign Investment in the Telecommunications Sector

The Government of Canada is committed to ensuring that Canadians can benefit from increased competition and investment in the telecommunications sector, which will lead to greater innovation and lower prices for consumers. Increasing foreign investment is an important way of strengthening market competition and attracting new capital and innovative ideas from abroad.

Consistent with the recommendations of the Competition Policy Review Panel, the Government is acting in Budget 2010 to remove the existing restrictions on foreign ownership of Canadian satellites. This will allow firms to access foreign capital and know-how and to invest in new and advanced technologies. The removal of restrictions will also allow Canadian firms to develop strategic global relationships that will enable them to participate fully in foreign markets.

Supporting Canadian Fisheries Access to International Markets

Access to international markets is essential to Canada's fish and seafood industry, which exports 85 per cent of its production. In 2010, the European Union introduced a new regulation which requires exporting countries to provide catch certificates attesting that marine fish and seafood products are legally harvested.

The Government is committed to ensuring that the Canadian fish and seafood industry maintains access to key markets around the world. Budget 2010 provides $7.2 million over two years to support the new Catch Certification Office. Through this office, Fisheries and Oceans Canada will issue certificates to exporters, ensuring that the Canadian fish and seafood industry remains competitive and maintains employment in both the harvesting and fish processing sectors.

Supporting Canada's Mining Sector

Canada's rich mineral resources represent significant economic opportunities. Promoting the exploration and development of these resources offers important benefits in terms of employment, investment and infrastructure, especially for rural and remote communities. The temporary 15-per-cent Mineral Exploration Tax Credit (METC) helps companies raise capital for mining exploration by providing an incentive to individuals who invest in flow-through shares issued to finance exploration. Canada's Economic Action Plan previously extended the temporary METC to flow-through share agreements entered into during the period from April 1, 2009 to March 31, 2010. Budget 2010 proposes to extend the credit for an additional year, to March 31, 2011.

It is estimated that the net cost of this extension will be $65 million over the next two fiscal years.

Supporting Canadian Agriculture

The Canadian agricultural sector is a key economic driver for rural communities across the country. Farmers also play a unique role by providing healthy, safe and nutritious food for families in Canada and around the world. Governments have helped the agriculture sector weather the turbulent economic conditions of the past year. Building on the investments made by federal, provincial and territorial governments under Growing Forward, the Government launched various initiatives in 2009 to help the sector adapt to pressures and improve its competitiveness. Canada's Economic Action Plan announced the $500-million Agricultural Flexibility Fund and the $50-million Slaughter Improvement Program. In recent months, the Government also took measures to promote access to foreign markets for Canadian agricultural products through the establishment of a Market Access Secretariat and extended support to the hog industry to assist with restructuring in response to new market realities facing the sector.

A More Competitive Cattle Sector

The cattle sector continues to face pressures. Budget 2010 announces three measures to ensure Canadian cattle producers continue to have access to competitive cattle processing operations in Canada.

Building on measures in Budget 2009, the Government will provide funding to support investments by Canadian cattle processing plants to help improve their operations. Funding available under the Slaughter Improvement Program will be increased by $10 million in 2010–11 to support the introduction of new, cost-effective technologies, and $25 million in 2010–11 will be targeted to cattle processing plants that handle cattle over 30 months of age.

The Government will also provide $40 million over three years to support the development and commercialization of innovative technologies related to the removal and use of specified risk materials to reduce handling costs and create potential revenue sources from these materials. These measures will be funded from the existing Agricultural Flexibility Fund.

Canadian Grain Commission

The Canadian Grain Commission plays a crucial role in establishing and ensuring standards of quality for Canadian grain. Through its grain quality assurance services, the Commission enables Canadian grain producers to access domestic and export markets. Rapidly changing global and domestic markets for grain require that the Commission become a more flexible institution. The Government remains committed to modernizing the Canadian Grain Act and the operations of the Canadian Grain Commission, and working with Canadian grain farmers to promote marketing freedom to address evolving needs of the sector. Budget 2010 provides $51.7 million over the next two years to support the operations of the Canadian Grain Commission.

Improving Canada's System of International Taxation

On December 10, 2008, the Advisory Panel on Canada's System of International Taxation released its final report. The Government expresses again its appreciation for the significant contribution that the members of the Panel, its secretariat and the tax community have made to the policy discussion.

The Panel noted that Canada's international tax system has served Canada well. At the same time, it put forward a number of recommendations for change. The Government is continuing to consider the report of the Panel as part of its ongoing assessment of the fairness and competitiveness of Canada's international tax rules for individuals and corporations that trade and invest across international borders. Over the last year, the Government has:

- Repealed section 18.2 of the Income Tax Act (ITA), which would have constrained in certain situations the deductibility of interest on debt used to acquire shares of a foreign affiliate. This change provides tax support for Canadian multinational firms undertaking foreign investment, particularly in the context of the current global financial environment.

- Signed, enacted or begun negotiations to update nine international tax treaties, thus improving trade opportunities with other nations, providing a more certain environment for investors, and facilitating tax information exchange for revenue authorities.

- Announced the signing of Canada's first tax information exchange agreement (TIEA) and that Canada is in the process of negotiating an additional 15 TIEAs, thus helping combat international tax evasion while, at the same time, opening up new business opportunities for Canadian corporations.

- Released, on December 18, 2009, a package of draft foreign affiliate rules for consultation, which introduced revised, simplified proposals designed to reduce uncertainty in the application of the tax law.

Consistent with this incremental approach to improving Canada's international tax rules, Budget 2010 includes proposals to facilitate investment, cut red tape and streamline the compliance process associated with the taxation of cross-border activity, and proposes to address other concerns in a fiscally responsible way. Specifically, Budget 2010 proposes to:

- Improve the ability of Canadian businesses, including innovative high-growth companies that contribute to job creation and economic growth, to attract foreign venture capital by narrowing the definition of taxable Canadian property, thereby eliminating the need for tax reporting under section 116 of the ITA for many investments. The Canadian Venture Capital Association has indicated, in making representations for changes of this nature, that "...a broader exemption...would make Canada a more attractive destination for equity investments by non-residents and, in particular, venture capital and private equity funds."

- Ensure taxpayers have an opportunity to apply for refunds of amounts withheld under section 105 of the Income Tax Regulations and section 116 of the ITA after a reassessment by the Canada Revenue Agency.

- Follow up on the commitment in Budget 2009 which stated that the Government would, in response to submissions by the Panel and others, review its outstanding proposals with respect to tax issues associated with foreign investment entities and non-resident trusts before proceeding with measures in this area. As a result of this review, the Government is initiating a consultation process for revised proposals on which commentary is welcomed and encouraged. The revised proposals would replace the outstanding proposals relating to foreign investment entities with several limited enhancements to the current ITA and substantially modify the outstanding proposals with respect to non-resident trusts in order to better target and simplify them.

Detailed information on Budget 2010's international tax proposals are contained in Annex 5.

These measures are estimated to provide tax relief of $30 million in 2010–11 and $25 million in 2011–12.

In addition, the Accounting Standards Board will require Canadian public companies to adopt the International Financial Reporting Standards (IFRS) as of 2011, which could help these companies better access international capital markets and reduce their cost of capital. In preparation for the adoption of IFRS, the Government will review the impact of IFRS on certain aspects of the tax system and, where necessary, make changes to ensure appropriate outcomes.

As part of the Economic Action Plan, the Government provided $170 million over two years through Natural Resources Canada to support market diversification and innovation initiatives, including research and demonstration projects on new forest products and initiatives to help forestry companies market innovative products internationally. More recently, in June 2009, the Government introduced the Pulp and Paper Green Transformation Program, with $1 billion available over three years to support investments by Canadian pulp and paper companies to improve the energy efficiency and environmental performance of their facilities.

Budget 2010 takes additional action to build on these promising initiatives by establishing the Next Generation Renewable Power Initiative, with $100 million over the next four years to support the development, commercialization and implementation of advanced clean energy technologies in the forestry sector. This initiative, which will be managed by Natural Resources Canada, will help create a more sustainable forestry sector while contributing to Canada's global leadership as a clean energy producer.

Clean Energy Generation—Tax Support

The tax system encourages investment in clean energy generation equipment through the provision of accelerated capital cost allowance (CCA). CCA Class 43.2 includes a variety of stationary equipment that generates or conserves energy by using renewable sources or fuels from waste, or by using fossil fuel efficiently. It allows the cost of eligible assets to be deducted for tax purposes at a rate of 50 per cent per year on a declining balance basis—which is faster than would be implied by the useful life of the assets.

Budget 2010 proposes to expand the eligibility for accelerated CCA under Class 43.2 to include:

- Heat recovery equipment used in a broader range of applications.

- Distribution equipment used in district energy systems that rely primarily on ground source heat pumps, active solar systems or heat recovery equipment.

These extensions will encourage investment in technologies that contribute to a reduction in greenhouse gas emissions and air pollutants, and increase the diversification of Canada's energy supply.

It is estimated that these measures will reduce federal revenues by a small amount in each of 2010–11 and 2011–12.

Great Lakes Action Plan

Millions of Canadians depend on the Great Lakes for their drinking water, for recreation and for jobs. Protecting ecosystem health and securing the water supply in the Great Lakes is an important responsibility shared by all orders of government, including the federal government. Cleaning up the Great Lakes is a key objective of our Government's Action Plan for Clean Water.

Under the *Canada-United States Great Lakes Water Quality Agreement,* both countries are committed to restoring environmental quality in areas identified as being most degraded. In June 2009, the Governments of Canada and the United States announced a commitment to strengthen and modernize the agreement to better address concerns resulting from pollution, invasive species and climate change.

Budget 2010 provides Environment Canada with $8 million per year ongoing to continue to implement its action plan to protect the Great Lakes. Through this new investment, the Government will continue working with its partners to address environmental restoration issues in the Areas of Concern and support Canada's commitments under international agreements.

Arctic Meteorological and Navigational Areas

Maritime traffic is expected to increase in the Arctic due to reduced ice coverage resulting in more navigable waters. Canada, as a sovereign and environmentally responsible polar nation, has committed to the International Maritime Organization to provide meteorological information and navigational data to facilitate the safe management of marine traffic in two well-defined Arctic areas that are substantially within Canadian territory. The areas include Canadian Arctic waters, such as the Northwest Passage, and adjacent waters north of Alaska and along part of the western coast of Greenland.

Budget 2010 provides $9.2 million over two years to Environment Canada and $2.2 million over two years to Fisheries and Oceans Canada to deliver meteorological and navigational services, respectively, in the Arctic to meet Canada's commitments to the International Maritime Organization in respect of these areas.

Community-Based Environmental Monitoring in the North

Effective environmental protection and responsible regulation require sound environmental monitoring to collect and interpret data on environmental change and the cumulative impacts of development. In the North, environmental monitoring is imperative to fulfill statutory requirements and commitments made under land claim agreements with Aboriginal groups.

Budget 2010 identifies $8 million over two years for Indian and Northern Affairs Canada to support community-based environmental monitoring, reporting and baseline data collection through the Northwest Territories Cumulative Impact Monitoring Program and the Nunavut General Monitoring Program.

Canadian Environmental Sustainability Indicators

The Canadian Environmental Sustainability Indicators initiative produces a coherent set of indicators on water quality, air quality and greenhouse gas emissions over time. Budget 2010 provides $18.4 million over two years to sustain the Government's annual reporting on environmental indicators. These indicators will satisfy Canada's legislative requirements to track environmental progress and serve as meaningful performance indicators for other types of regular reporting.

Positioning Canada's Nuclear Industry for Future Success

Atomic Energy of Canada Limited (AECL) is a federal Crown corporation which specializes in a range of advanced nuclear-energy products and services and works with Canada's diverse nuclear industry. Budget 2010 provides $300 million on a cash basis for AECL's operations in 2010–11 to cover anticipated commercial losses and support the corporation's operations, including the continued development of the Advanced CANDU Reactor, ensuring a secure supply of medical isotopes and maintaining safe and reliable operations at the Chalk River Laboratories.

The Government has initiated a restructuring process with respect to AECL to attract new investment and expertise, position the corporation for success in a changing global marketplace and create new opportunities for Canada's nuclear industry. Investors were invited to submit proposals for AECL's commercial reactor division in December 2009.

The Minister of Natural Resources will be reviewing these proposals, and assess how the corporation could best be restructured to meet the Government's objectives.

Modernizing Canada's Infrastructure

Modernizing Canada's Transportation Infrastructure

Efficient and modern transportation infrastructure is vital to Canada's competitiveness and long-term prosperity as well as the quality of life of its citizens. This is especially true given our geography and the importance of trade to our economy. In recent years, the Government has committed significant funding towards maintaining and advancing our transportation networks, including the roads, railways, bridges, marine services and ports that connect communities and facilitate the movement of people and goods across Canada.

Budget 2010 builds on these actions by announcing several initiatives aimed at modernizing our transportation infrastructure, including investments in passenger rail and ferry services, new resources to enhance aviation security in Canada, and funding to ensure the continued safety and reliability of bridges.

Marine Atlantic

Marine Atlantic provides a vital link between the Island of Newfoundland and the Canadian mainland. As an extension of the Trans-Canada Highway, Marine Atlantic's ferry services support tourism and the import and export of goods. In 2009, an estimated 27 per cent of all passengers, 50 per cent of all freight, and 90 per cent of all perishable goods between the Island of Newfoundland and the Canadian mainland were carried by Marine Atlantic.

Budget 2010 provides $175 million over the next two years to help renew Marine Atlantic's fleet and shore facilities and improve the quality and reliability of its services.

Ferry Services in Atlantic Canada

Ferry services enrich the transportation network in Atlantic Canada. The Government of Canada provides financial support to routes between Îles de la Madeleine, Quebec and Souris, Prince Edward Island; Saint John, New Brunswick and Digby, Nova Scotia; and Wood Islands, Prince Edward Island and Caribou, Nova Scotia. These ferries provide additional transportation options to passengers and for the shipment of freight.

Budget 2010 provides $28 million to support the operations of these ferry services.

Windsor-Detroit

The Windsor-Detroit border is the busiest commercial crossing in North America, through which over one-quarter of our merchandise trade with the U.S. passes. In 2007, the Government of Canada set out a strategy to advance the construction of a new crossing in the Windsor-Detroit corridor. Canada has worked in concert with the State of Michigan and its U.S. partners, with the U.S. federal administration, with the Province of Ontario and with the City of Windsor to move this project forward. Since 2007, the project has reached key milestones, culminating earlier this year in the issuance of a Request for Proposal of Interest for the development of the Detroit River International Crossing Project under a public-private partnership arrangement.

Budget 2010 provides $10 million over three years to Transport Canada to support the legal, financial and technical work required to advance this project.

The Jacques Cartier and Champlain Bridges Incorporated

The Jacques Cartier and Champlain Bridges Incorporated manages, operates and maintains bridges and other transportation infrastructure in the Greater Montréal Area: the Jacques Cartier and Champlain bridges, the Bonaventure Expressway, the federally owned section of the Honoré-Mercier Bridge, the Melocheville Tunnel and the Champlain Bridge Ice Control Structure. The Jacques Cartier and Champlain bridges are among the busiest in Canada, with almost 100 million vehicle crossings every year.

Budget 2010 provides $50.5 million over the next two years to The Jacques Cartier and Champlain Bridges Incorporated so that it has the financial resources to carry out capital expenditures required to maintain the safety of its bridges and ensure they continue to serve the needs of Montréal-area commuters.

Improving Border Efficiency

Canada's borders provide a gateway for approximately 100 million people and $400 billion in imported goods, which enter Canada by sea, air and land each year. Budget 2010 invests $87 million over two years to ensure the Canada Border Services Agency can continue to deliver efficient and secure border services. Funds will be used to invest in state-of-the-art equipment, such as vehicle and cargo scanning equipment, as well as upgraded information systems that underpin effective border operations. In order to streamline the movement of pre-screened, low-risk cargo and travellers, the Government will continue to enhance its trusted traveller and trader programs, such as Partners in Protection and NEXUS, to ensure that these Canada-United States initiatives are better coordinated and have fees that more closely reflect costs.

Ensuring Air Cargo Security

A large number of Canadian firms depend on timely and safe two-way trade with the rest of the world. An increasing share of that trade is shipped through air cargo. Canada, along with its major trading partners, is implementing measures to ensure an effective air cargo security regime. Budget 2010 provides Transport Canada with $37.9 million over two years to implement a comprehensive air cargo security program that will strengthen air cargo screening and the security of the supply chain. The program will monitor and respond to priority risks and evolving threats on a continuing basis.

Maintaining a Secure Air Travel Security System

The Canadian Air Transport Security Authority (CATSA) acts as Canada's front line for a secure aviation system. With 6,000 screeners at more than 80 designated airports across Canada, CATSA screened over 62 million pieces of baggage and 48 million passengers in 2009. The Government recently announced funding of $1.5 billion over five years for CATSA and Transport Canada to maintain security for Canada's air transportation system, to better align with international security requirements, and to keep up with recent U.S. measures.

To ensure that CATSA is fulfilling its mandate effectively, the Government has also announced that it will launch a full review into the spending, efficiency and structure of this Crown corporation. Details on the review will be forthcoming.

Air travel security is financed through the Air Travellers Security Charge (ATSC). The ATSC is intended to provide revenues that are roughly equivalent to expenses for air travel security over time. To fund new air travel security expenditures announced for CATSA and Transport Canada, the Government proposes to increase ATSC rates effective April 1, 2010.

Ensuring Maritime Safety

The Canadian Coast Guard plays a vital role in ensuring maritime safety. The Coast Guard provides search and rescue services on Canada's waters, which requires an operational fleet of hovercrafts. These vessels are used to conduct searches, transport ill or injured people, tow disabled vessels and provide logistical support during incidents.

Out of its Sea Island base near Vancouver, the Coast Guard operates two hovercrafts, one of which needs to be replaced. Budget 2010 provides $27.3 million over five years on a cash basis for a new hovercraft for the Coast Guard's Sea Island base.

Improving First Nations Infrastructure

Through the First Nations Water and Wastewater Action Plan, as well as an investment of $179 million over two years through Canada's Economic Action Plan, the Government has made significant progress in improving water conditions on reserves across Canada.

To build on this progress, Budget 2010 extends the First Nations Water and Wastewater Action Plan for two more years.

Every year, the Government invests over $1 billion in First Nations infrastructure, including improvements to drinking water and wastewater systems. Moving forward, the Government intends to place the financing system of on-reserve community infrastructure on a better footing. In particular, the Government will undertake a comprehensive review of its current approach to financing First Nations infrastructure. To be undertaken in partnership with First Nations representatives, the review will focus on ways to more effectively support access by First Nations to alternative sources of financing, and approaches to improve the life-cycle management of capital assets.

Strengthening the Financial Sector

Canada's financial sector has been widely acknowledged as being one of the strongest in the world. Well-capitalized financial institutions and sound regulation have meant that financial institutions in Canada were better able to weather the global financial crisis than those in many other countries. This strong foundation, along with the extraordinary support for access to financing provided as part of Canada's Economic Action Plan, helped to keep credit flowing to Canadian consumers and business throughout the crisis and helped Canada's financial sector improve its global competitive advantage.

Canada is playing a lead role in the international dialogue around strengthening the international financial system. As host of the G8 and G20 meetings this June, Canada will use its leadership role to continue to promote progress on the previously agreed international financial sector agenda.

Here at home, Budget 2010 introduces measures that will support Canada's strong and competitive financial sector, help businesses access the financing they need to support the recovery, and pursue a more forward-looking approach to protecting consumers of financial products and services.

Supporting Canada's Strong Financial Sector

Canada's financial regulatory regime is a model for other countries in many respects. However, our system can still be improved. One key gap that remains is the lack of a Canadian securities regulator. Capital markets are no longer regional but are increasingly national and international in nature. The global financial crisis has shown how important it is for all Canadians to have stable, well-functioning securities markets that earn their confidence.

All jurisdictions are invited and encouraged to join in this effort, which will build on the existing infrastructure and expertise of provincial and territorial securities regulators. In the meantime, the Government is moving forward with the majority of provinces and territories to establish a Canadian securities regulator. This new world-class national securities regulator will be implemented through the voluntary participation of provinces and territories.

The new Canadian securities regulator will provide:

- Better and more consistent protection for investors across Canada.
- Improved regulatory and criminal enforcement to better fight white collar crime.

- New information and tools to support the stability of the Canadian financial sector.

- Faster policy responses to emerging market trends.

- Simpler processes for business, resulting in lower costs for investors.

- More effective international representation and influence for Canada.

The Canadian securities regulator is targeted to be established within the next three years.

Key next steps include:

- Release of the draft Canadian securities bill this Spring;

- Referral of the draft securities bill to the Supreme Court of Canada for its opinion as to whether Parliament has the constitutional authority to enact and implement a federal securities regulatory regime;

- Delivery this Summer by the Canadian Securities Transition Office of an organizational and administrative transition plan; and

- Ongoing work on the rules and regulations that will complement the Canadian securities act.

We must also take advantage of and support the ongoing strong performance of Canada's financial services industry, which creates many high-quality and high-paying jobs. Initiatives such as the Toronto Financial Services Alliance's planned Global Integrative Risk Management Institute, which will identify and disseminate best practices in financial risk management, promise to play an important role in promoting Canada's experience and sound practices.

One of the lessons of the global financial crisis is that financial institutions need to have access to a variety of funding sources. The Government will help federally regulated financial institutions diversify their funding sources by introducing legislation setting out a framework for covered bonds. Covered bonds are debt instruments that are secured by high quality assets, such as residential mortgages. The legislation will increase legal certainty for investors in these debt instruments, thereby making it easier for Canadian financial institutions to access this low-cost source of funding.

Canada's housing market has been a source of strength for our country and a source of growing wealth for hard-working Canadians. The Government has recently taken a number of measured steps to support the long-term stability of Canada's mortgage and housing markets.

The adjustments made to the rules for government-backed mortgages in July 2008 and February 2010 will support healthy and stable growth in this important sector.

The Government will also propose measures to enhance the effectiveness of Canada Deposit Insurance Corporation's (CDIC) resolution tools by clarifying certain aspects of CDIC's bridge institution regime. In addition, the Government proposes to provide CDIC with the authority to establish new information and capabilities requirements for member institutions to improve CDIC's ability to quickly respond to the needs of insured depositors.

Extending Access to the Financing Needed to Support the Recovery

The Business Credit Availability Program (BCAP) is helping businesses find financing solutions to preserve jobs and fund growth through enhanced cooperation between private sector lenders and Export Development Canada and the Business Development Bank of Canada (BDC). This program is supported by new resources and flexibilities for these financial Crown corporations provided as part of Canada's Economic Action Plan. Through January 2010, the program has reached its target of providing at least $5 billion in direct lending and other types of financing support and facilitation at market rates to almost 9,000 businesses with viable business models whose access to financing would have otherwise been restricted. A recent report from The Conference Board of Canada concluded that having the Crown corporations work closely with private financial institutions under BCAP has helped build a bridge to more normal credit conditions.

Ensuring that businesses of all sizes have adequate access to financing to acquire vehicles and equipment will become increasingly important as the economic recovery matures. Access to financing has normalized for larger finance and leasing companies that can access capital markets directly. However, some smaller finance and leasing companies, although creditworthy, cannot obtain enough financing to meet the growing needs of their customers. These independent lenders provide specialized financing, often to smaller businesses, supplementing the credit available from banks and other large financing providers.

The Government is therefore creating the Vehicle and Equipment Financing Partnership as part of BCAP. This program will be funded and managed by BDC, with an initial allocation of $500 million in funding, in partnership with experienced lenders and investors in the private market for asset-based financing. The partnership will expand financing options for small and medium-sized finance and leasing companies, increasing the availability of credit at market rates for dealers and users of vehicles and equipment. Further details on this program will be announced in the coming weeks.

The Government will also introduce amendments to the Export Development Act to ensure that Export Development Canada has the flexibility to serve the needs of Canadian businesses in an evolving and increasingly complex international business environment.

Protecting Consumers

As users of financial services, consumers have a significant stake in almost all financial sector issues. As financial products and practices evolve, the impact on consumers needs to be monitored and their interests, at times, protected through regulatory action.

In Budget 2009, the Government enhanced consumer protection through measures dealing with credit cards and mortgage insurance. Also in Budget 2009, the Task Force on Financial Literacy was established to make recommendations to create a cohesive national strategy to improve financial literacy in Canada. This strategy will help Canadians make knowledgeable and confident decisions towards achieving their financial goals. The Task Force released a discussion paper on February 22, 2010 that will serve as the basis for discussion at the meetings it will hold in every province and territory in the coming weeks.

Proactive Consumer Protection

In this budget, the Government is proposing to take action to establish a more proactive and forward-looking approach to financial consumer issues and to address concerns of Canadians.

The Government is proposing to give the Financial Consumer Agency of Canada (FCAC) new responsibilities that leverage its existing role and marketplace proximity. The FCAC will increase its field testing and stakeholder engagement to provide valuable and timely information to the Government on financial consumer trends and emerging issues. This will also allow the Government to improve the effectiveness of regulatory initiatives, while ensuring that these initiatives are more responsive to the needs of financial consumers.

Enhancing Disclosure and Business Practices of Financial Institutions

The Government is also proposing additional steps to enhance the consumer protection framework for federally regulated financial institutions through the following measures:

- Prohibiting negative option billing in the financial sector. The Government will enact regulations to require financial institutions to offer products and services on an opt-in basis only, where consumers have sufficient disclosure about the terms and conditions before accepting.

- Standardizing the calculation and disclosure of mortgage pre-payment penalties. It is important that consumers have the information they need when making financial decisions, including when to pre-pay a mortgage. As such, the Government will bring forward regulations to bring greater clarity to the calculation of mortgage pre-payment penalties.

- Reducing the maximum cheque hold period. The Government is committed to ensuring affordable access to basic banking services. As consumers need timelier access to funds, the Government will make regulations to reduce the maximum cheque hold period to 4 days from the current 7 days and provide consumers access to the first $100 within 24 hours.

- Strengthening the dispute resolution framework. The Government already requires that institutions have procedures and personnel in place to address consumer complaints and that each institution also belong to a third-party dispute resolution body. However, there is a wide variation in terms of the procedures used. To ensure that consumers receive consistent treatment, the Government will require that banks belong to an approved third-party dispute handling body. Clear criteria will be established to govern the approval process. The Government will also work with the industry to establish minimum regulatory standards for institutions' internal complaints procedures. This will ensure fair, efficient and timely treatment of consumers' complaints and improve the effectiveness of the third-party dispute resolution process.

Strengthening Canada's Payments System

The Canadian payments system is a vital support to the economy, linking Canadians, merchants and financial institutions together and facilitating payment transactions through, for example, credit and debit card networks and clearing and settlement systems. Canada's domestic payments system has proven capable of meeting the needs of Canadians, even during the financial crisis.

On November 19, 2009 the Government released a proposed Code of Conduct for the Credit and Debit Card Industry in Canada that responds to issues raised by stakeholders in the debit and credit card markets. The Code, which was developed in consultation with market participants, aims to promote fair business practices and ensure that merchants and consumers clearly understand the costs and benefits associated with credit and debit cards.

The comment period closed on January 18, 2010, and the Government received comments from a significant number of stakeholders. The Code will be made available shortly for adoption by credit and debit card networks and their participants once it is finalized. The Government is proposing to amend the FCAC's mandate to enable it to monitor compliance with the Code. The Government will also propose legislation that will provide the Minister of Finance with the authority to regulate the market conduct of the credit and debit card networks and their participants, if necessary.

Given the importance of a safe and efficient payments system to consumers, merchants and payments system providers, the Government will appoint an independent Task Force to conduct a comprehensive review of the Canadian payments system and make recommendations to the Minister of Finance. The Task Force will review the safety, soundness and efficiency of the payments system; whether there is sufficient innovation in the system; the competitive landscape; whether businesses and consumers are being well served; and whether current payment system oversight mechanisms remain appropriate. The Task Force, which will be supported by a secretariat, is expected to be launched in the spring of 2010 and report to the Minister of Finance by the end of 2011.

Modernizing Canada's Currency

The Government is taking steps to modernize Canada's currency and protect against counterfeiting. The introduction of a new series of bank notes by the Bank of Canada will begin in 2011. These bank notes will have increased security features and will be printed on a polymer material, which lasts significantly longer than the current cotton-based paper, thereby reducing production costs and the impact on the environment. The Government is also planning to change the composition of the $1 and $2 coins using the Royal Canadian Mint's less expensive patented multi-ply plated steel technology.

Creating a Federal Framework for Credit Unions

Canada is home to a strong and vibrant credit union industry that provides financial services to millions of Canadian consumers and small businesses. To promote the continued growth and competitiveness of the sector and enhance financial stability, the Government will introduce a legislative framework to enable credit unions to incorporate and continue their operations as federal entities. Allowing credit unions to grow and be competitive on a national scale will broaden choices for consumers by helping credit unions to attract new members and improve services to existing members across provincial borders.

Combatting Money Laundering and Terrorist Financing

Budget 2009 announced the Government's commitment to bring forward new measures to safeguard the financial system from illicit financing emanating from outside of Canada. The new measures will enhance Canada's existing anti-money laundering and anti-terrorist financing (AML/ATF) regime by allowing targeted measures to be taken against jurisdictions and foreign entities that lack sufficient and effective AML/ATF controls.

Budget 2010 proposes further measures to ensure that the provisions of the Criminal Code that apply to serious crimes related to money laundering and terrosist financing can be invoked in cases of tax evasion prosecuted under Canada's tax statutes. The Government will aslo increase ongoing funding for the Financial Transactions and Reports Analysis Centre of Canada by a total of $8 million per year to help it combat money laundering and terrorist financing.

Renewal of Programs

Budget 2010 renews funding for a number of programs, including:

- $12 million over two years to Natural Resources Canada to renew the Targeted Geoscience Initiative, with a focus on developing new ways of exploring for deeper mineral deposits.

- $11 million over two years for the GeoConnections program, which provides consolidated geographic-related information to Canadians via the Internet.

- $11 million per year, ongoing for the Community Futures Program, which promotes community and economic development in rural Canada.

- $38 million over two years for federal programs under Canada's Invasive Alien Species Strategy to reduce the risk of invasive animal and plant species being introduced to Canada.

- $32 million over the next two years for the Regional and Remote Passenger Rail Services Contribution Program, which supports four remote and regional rail services: the Keewatin Railway in Manitoba; the Algoma Central Railway and the Ontario Northland Transportation Commission in Ontario; and Tshiuetin Rail Transportation in Quebec and Labrador.

- $285 million over two years for Aboriginal health programs in five key areas: the Aboriginal Diabetes Initiative; the Aboriginal Youth Suicide Prevention Strategy; maternal and child health; the Aboriginal Health Human Resources Initiative; and the Aboriginal Health Transition Fund.

Table 3.3.1

Building on a Strong Economic Foundation

	2009–10	2010–11	2011–12	Total
		(millions of dollars)		
Jobs Protection and Youth Employment Measures				
Work-sharing		101	5	106
Building skills for youth				
Youth internships		30		30
Canadian Youth Business Foundation	10			10
Youth at risk		30		30
Pathways to Education Canada		2	6	8
Better education outcomes for First Nations		15	15	30
Subtotal—Jobs Protection and Youth Employment Measures	10	178	26	214
Creating Economic Growth and Jobs Through Innovation				
Creating a more highly skilled workforce		5	10	15
World-leading research infrastructure				
Canadian High Arctic Research Station		1	2	3
TRIUMF		25	25	51
Supporting advanced research				
The research granting councils		32	32	64
Indirect costs of research		8	8	16
Genome Canada	75			75
Rick Hansen Foundation		5	5	9
Knowledge transfer and commercialization				
Supporting college innovation		15	15	30
National Research Council Canada regional innovation clusters		68	67	135
Diversifying the supply of medical isotopes		19	29	48
Canadian Space Agency		5	18	23
Promoting innovation by small and medium-sized businesses		15	25	40
International Science and Technology Partnerships		4	4	8
Supporting regional innovation				
Atlantic Canada Opportunities Agency		19	19	38

Table 3.3.1 *(cont'd)*

Building on a Strong Economic Foundation

	2009–10	2010–11	2011–12	Total
		(millions of dollars)		
Creating Economic Growth and Jobs through Innovation *(cont'd)*				
Canada Economic Development for Quebec Regions		15	15	29
Western Economic Diversification Canada		15	15	29
Subtotal—Creating Economic Growth and Jobs through Innovation	75	251	288	613
Encouraging Investment and Trade to Create Jobs and Growth				
Making Canada a tariff-free zone for manufacturers	17	210	230	457
Improving Canada's System of International Taxation		30	25	55
Improving the regulatory system and reducing red tape				
Red Tape Reduction Commission		4	4	8
Streamlining the Northern regulatory regime		6	5	11
Supporting Canadian fisheries access to international markets		4	4	7
Supporting Canada's mining sector		85	-20	65
Supporting Canadian agriculture				
A more competitive cattle sector		60	10	70
Canadian Grain Commission		24	28	52
Subtotal—Encouraging Investment and Trade to Create Jobs and Growth	17	422	286	725
Green Jobs and Growth				
Modernizing the regulatory system for major project reviews		2	3	5
Less cost recovery		-2	-3	-5
Participant funding—Aboriginal consultations		2	1	3
Supporting renewable energy in the forestry sector		25	25	50
Clean energy generation—tax support				
Great Lakes Action Plan		8	8	16
Arctic meteorological and navigational areas		4	8	11
Community-based environmental monitoring in the North		2	5	8

Table 3.3.1 *(cont'd)*

Building on a Strong Economic Foundation

	2009–10	2010–11	2011–12	Total
		(millions of dollars)		
Green Jobs and Growth *(cont'd)*				
Canadian Environmental Sustainability Indicators		10	9	18
Positioning Canada's nuclear industry for future success		253	2	255
Subtotal—Energy and the Environment		304	58	362
Modernizing Canada's Infrastructure				
Marine Atlantic		75	100	175
Ferry services in Atlantic Canada		25	3	28'
Windsor-Detroit		5	3	8
The Jacques Cartier and Champlain Bridges Incorporated		32	19	51
Improving border efficiency		40	47	87
Ensuring air cargo security		19	19	38
Ensuring maritime safety				
Improving First Nations infrastructure		165	165	331
Subtotal—Modernizing Canada's Infrastructure		361	357	717
Strengthening the Financial Sector				
Strengthening Canada's payments system		3	2	5
Combatting money laundering and terrorist financing		8	8	16
Subtotal—Strengthening the Financial Sector		11	10	21
Renewal of Programs				
Geological mapping		4	8	12
GeoConnections		5	6	11
Community Futures Program		11	11	22
Invasive species		19	19	38
Regional and remote passenger rail		16	16	32
Improving Aboriginal health		140	146	285
Subtotal—Renewal of Programs		194	206	400
Total—Building on a Strong Economic Foundation	102	1,721	1,230	3,053
Less: Funds existing in the fiscal framework		789	635	1,424
Net fiscal cost	102	932	595	1,628

Note: Totals may not add due to rounding.

3.4

Supporting Families and Communities and Standing Up for Those Who Helped Build Canada

Highlights

Budget 2010 takes action to support vulnerable Canadian families and communities by:

✓ Providing $6.6 million to enhance the existing Federal Victims Strategy, including facilitating access to Employment Insurance sickness benefits for families affected by a crime.

✓ Improving the taxation of the Universal Child Care Benefit so single parents receive comparable tax treatment to single-earner two-parent families.

✓ Providing $62 million to support Canada's elite athletes and encourage participation in amateur sport.

✓ Reforming the disbursement quota to reduce administrative complexity and better enable charities to focus their time and resources on charitable activities.

✓ Improving Registered Disability Savings Plans to allow more flexibility for contributions.

✓ Providing $45 million over three years for the Enabling Accessibility Fund to remove barriers for Canadians with disabilities.

✓ Providing $199 million to meet higher than expected funding needs in support of the settlement agreement with former students of the Indian residential school system.

✓ Providing $53 million to ensure further progress toward a prevention-focused approach to child and family services for First Nations children and parents.

✓ Reforming the Food Mail Program to improve access to affordable healthy food for Northerners.

Budget 2010 also stands up for those who helped build Canada by:

✓ Providing $2 million for a Community War Memorial Program.

✓ Improving access for military families to Employment Insurance parental and sickness benefits.

✓ Providing $10 million for the New Horizons for Seniors Program to support projects that focus on volunteering among seniors.

✓ Reaffirming the Government's commitment to ensure that Canada's retirement income system remains strong and efficient through spring consultations and a review of policy options at the May Finance Ministers' meeting.

T he quality of life enjoyed by Canadians rests in large part on the health of our families and communities. It reflects the efforts of the men and women who have helped build this country.

Supporting Families and Communities

The Government has taken action to strengthen communities across the country through investments in infrastructure, support for families and workers, and steps to make communities safer.

Budget 2010 builds on these actions. The budget introduces measures to protect Canadian families and communities, support the vulnerable, invest in the health of those living in the North and encourage participation in sport.

Protecting Canadian Families and Communities

Canadians want to feel safe and secure in their homes and communities. To that end, this budget provides additional resources for victims of crime, DNA processing and the Canadian Security Intelligence Service. The budget also provides funding to establish a new, independent civilian oversight organization for the RCMP.

Increasing Support for Victims of Crime

One of the most common frustrations that victims of crime report is that they feel excluded from the Canadian justice system. They want to be heard and respected. Canadians who have been the victim of a crime deserve to have a strong advocate within government. Budget 2006 announced the Federal Victims Strategy, which enhanced programming, and created the Federal Ombudsman for Victims of Crime. Building on this investment, Budget 2010 provides funding of $6.6 million over two years, to enhance support for victims of crime, including providing facilitated access to EI sickness benefits for eligible workers who have lost a family member as a result of a crime.

Strengthening Law Enforcement Tools

DNA is an important tool for Canadian law enforcement agencies, as it helps police across the country to identify the guilty and exonerate the innocent. Budget 2010 provides $14 million over two years to increase the ability to process DNA samples so that the results could be added to the National DNA Data Bank.

In order to improve the effective processing of forensic materials and help law enforcement more efficiently tackle crime, the Government will explore options for different delivery models, including potential privatization of the RCMP Forensic Laboratory Services. A new approach should improve the timeliness of processing samples, ensure sound financial administration and increase research and development in forensic science.

Canadian Security Intelligence Service

The Canadian Security Intelligence Service (CSIS) plays a leading role in protecting the national security interests of Canadians.

Budget 2010 provides CSIS with $28 million over two years to ensure its effective operation in the current global environment, which remains volatile and complex. This funding will help ensure the protection of Canada's national security interests and the safety of Canadians.

A New Review Mechanism for the RCMP

In response to concerns expressed by the public, provinces and territories, parliamentary committees and several major reports, including the Brown Task Force and the O'Connor Commission of Inquiry, the Government is taking action to enhance the independent review of RCMP actions. Budget 2010 provides $8 million over two years to establish a new organization. The creation of a new civilian independent review and complaints commission for the RCMP will contribute to the overall reform and modernization efforts underway at the RCMP.

Supporting the Vulnerable

Budget 2010 proposes several program and tax changes to improve support for the most vulnerable in our society and those who care for them. Also, improvements are proposed to the taxation of the Universal Child Care Benefit to better enable single parents to support their young children. In addition, significant reforms are proposed to the disbursement quota to reduce administrative complexity and better enable charities to focus their time and resources on charitable activities.

Improvements are also proposed to the Registered Disability Savings Plan to help parents and family members provide long-term financial security for a severely disabled child. Budget 2010 also proposes to extend the Enabling Accessibility Fund, which supports projects that allow the full participation of people with disabilities in their communities. As well, the budget provides support for First Nations child and family services, continues to address the legacy of residential schools and takes action to address violence against Aboriginal women.

Improving the Taxation of the Universal Child Care Benefit for Single Parents

The Universal Child Care Benefit (UCCB) is included in the income of the lower-income spouse or common-law partner in two-parent families. For single parents, the UCCB is included in their income and taxed at their marginal tax rate. As a result, a single-parent family can pay more tax on the same UCCB than a single-earner two-parent family with the same income.

Budget 2010 proposes to improve the taxation of the UCCB for single-parent families by allowing single parents to choose to include UCCB payments in their own income, or in the income of the dependant for whom an Eligible Dependant Credit is claimed, thereby providing treatment comparable to single-earner two-parent families. In most cases, the dependant would not be subject to tax. This change will ensure that single parents are not disadvantaged by their family status and will provide up to $168 in tax relief for single parents with one child under six in 2010.

It is estimated that this change will reduce federal revenues by a small amount in 2009–10, $5 million in 2010–11 and $5 million in 2011–12.

Helping Charities: Disbursement Quota Reform

The Government is proposing significant reforms to the disbursement quota to reduce administrative complexity and better enable charities to focus their time and resources on charitable activities.

The disbursement quota, introduced in 1976, was intended to ensure that a significant portion of a registered charity's resources is devoted to its charitable purposes. Many observers have noted that the disbursement quota has been unable to achieve its intended purpose, as it does not take account of the varying circumstances of individual charities. Stakeholders such as Imagine Canada have also noted that the disbursement quota imposes "an unduly complex and costly administrative burden on charities—particularly small and rural charities."

In recent years, the Canada Revenue Agency's ability to ensure the appropriateness of a charity's fundraising and other practices has been strengthened through the introduction of new legislative and administrative compliance measures and the provision of additional resources. These actions provide a more effective and direct means to fulfill many of the objectives of the disbursement quota.

Budget 2010 proposes to eliminate all disbursement quota requirements except those related to the requirement to annually disburse a minimum amount of investments and other assets not used directly in a charity's operations. This requirement is being updated to provide charitable organizations a greater ability to maintain reserves to deal with contingencies.

The reformed disbursement quota rules will apply to charities for fiscal years ending on or after March 4, 2010. These changes will have no fiscal impact.

Registered Disability Savings Plans (RDSPs)

Carry Forward of RDSP Grants and Bonds

The RDSP was introduced in Budget 2007 to better enable parents and others to ensure the long-term financial security of a child with a severe disability. The Government of Canada supports these plans by providing Canada Disability Savings Grants (CDSGs) and Canada Disability Savings Bonds (CDSBs).

In recognition of the fact that families of children with disabilities may not be able to contribute regularly to their plans, Budget 2010 proposes to allow a 10-year carry forward of CDSG and CDSB entitlements.

It is estimated that this change will cost $20 million in 2010–11 and $70 million in 2011–12.

Working With Provinces and Territories to Ensure the Success of the RDSP

The RDSP has been highly successful thanks in large part to the cooperation of provinces and territories in ensuring that RDSP benefits are not clawed back by reductions in social assistance payments.

A number of adults with disabilities have experienced problems in establishing a plan as the nature of their disability precludes them from entering into a contract. Questions of appropriate legal representation in these cases are a matter of provincial and territorial responsibility. In many provinces and territories, the only way that an RDSP can be opened for these individuals is for the individual to be declared legally incompetent and have someone named as their legal guardian—a process that can involve a considerable amount of time and expense on the part of concerned family members. In the event of delays, however, the proposed carry forward will preserve a beneficiary's entitlement to CDSGs and CDSBs, so that they are available when a plan is opened.

Some provinces, such as British Columbia, have instituted more streamlined processes to allow for the appointment of a trusted person, such as a parent or friend, to manage resources on behalf of a disabled individual. The Government of Canada encourages other provinces and territories to determine whether such streamlined processes would be appropriate for their jurisdiction.

Rollover of RRSP/RRIF Proceeds to an RDSP

An important concern for parents caring for a disabled child is to ensure that the child will be adequately provided for in the event that one or both parents die. Two key provisions assist parents in achieving financial security for their disabled child. The RDSP, which became available in 2008, helps parents and others save to ensure the long-term financial security of a child with a severe disability. In addition, under the current rules for Registered Retirement Savings Plans (RRSPs) and Registered Retirement Income Funds (RRIFs), a deceased individual's RRSP or RRIF proceeds may be rolled over, on a tax-free basis, to the RRSP or RRIF of a financially dependent infirm child or grandchild.

To give parents and grandparents more flexibility in providing for a disabled child's long-term financial security, Budget 2010 proposes to allow a deceased individual's RRSP or RRIF proceeds to be transferred, on a tax-free basis, to the RDSP of a financially dependent infirm child or grandchild.

It is estimated that this change will reduce federal revenues by a small amount in 2009–10 and 2010–11, and by $5 million in 2011–12.

Enabling Accessibility for Persons With Disabilities

In Budget 2007, the Government demonstrated its commitment to helping all Canadians, regardless of physical ability, to participate fully in their communities through the creation of the Enabling Accessibility Fund. The Fund has supported hundreds of community-based projects across Canada.

Budget 2010 builds on the success of this program by extending the Fund and providing an additional $45 million over the next three years. The budget expands eligibility for the program to include mid-sized projects, allowing for communities to undertake larger retrofit projects or foster partnerships for new facilities. Details will be announced by the Minister of Human Resources and Skills Development over the coming months.

Making Further Improvements to First Nations Child and Family Services

In 2007, the Government launched a prevention-focused approach to child and family services to ensure that more First Nations children and parents get the help they need to prevent crises that lead to family breakdown. Beginning with Alberta in 2007, the Government has signed tripartite agreements with First Nations partners and Nova Scotia, Saskatchewan, Quebec and Prince Edward Island. Budget 2010 commits $53 million over two years in order to ensure further progress.

Addressing the Legacy of Residential Schools

In 2005, an historic and unprecedented settlement agreement was reached between the Government of Canada and religious and Aboriginal organizations to address the legacy of Indian residential schools. Budget 2006 provided support for the Indian Residential Schools Settlement Agreement, including payments to former students.

Funding needs under the agreement have exceeded expectations. Recognizing this, Budget 2010 commits an additional $199 million over the next two years to ensure that necessary mental health and emotional support services continue to be provided to former students and their families, and that payments to former students are made in a timely and effective manner.

Taking Action to Address Violence Against Aboriginal Women

The Government is committed to ensuring that all women in Canada, including Aboriginal women, are safe and secure regardless of the community in which they live. Aboriginal women remain particularly vulnerable to violence and can face challenges in accessing the justice system, which should be protecting them. Budget 2010 invests $10 million over two years to address the disturbingly high number of missing and murdered Aboriginal women. Concrete actions will be taken to ensure that law enforcement and the justice system meet the needs of Aboriginal women and their families. The Minister of Justice will announce details in the coming months.

Investing in a Healthy North

Through its comprehensive Northern Strategy, the Government is making progress to help the North realize its true potential as a healthy, prosperous and secure region within a strong and sovereign Canada. Together with its partners, the Government is helping to create a vibrant Northern economy, with safe, healthy and prosperous communities.

Canada's Economic Action Plan took action to increase Northerners' access to skills training and education and to better housing. Budget 2010 builds on this action with strategic investments that will address key health care challenges for Northerners.

Improving Access to Healthy Food for Northerners

Consumption of nutritious food is a key component of a healthy lifestyle. In order to provide Northerners living in isolated communities with greater access to affordable healthy food, the Government has operated the Food Mail Program since the late 1960s. Over the past year, the Government has consulted Northerners in order to develop a more modern, efficient and cost-effective program.

Budget 2010 commits $45 million over two years to fund this new program. Including existing funding, this will bring the annual budget of the program to $60 million. The program will alleviate the costs of shipping healthy foods by air to isolated communities and include activities to encourage nutritious eating. The program will focus on supporting a basket of healthy foods that will be based on Canada's Food Guide, and will include a process for ensuring program sustainability. The Minister of Indian Affairs and Northern Development will announce further information on this new program in the coming months.

Territorial Health System Sustainability Initiative

To support the provision of timely access to quality health care in the North, the Government provides territories with long-term predictable funding through both the Canada Health Transfer and Territorial Formula Financing. In addition, in 2005, the Government provided the territories a five-year targeted fund to facilitate the transformation of territorial health systems to ensure greater responsiveness to Northerners' needs and improve community level access to services. Budget 2010 temporarily extends this supplementary funding by $60 million over two years to consolidate the progress made in reducing the reliance on outside health care systems and medical travel.

Encouraging Participation in Amateur Sport

Canadian athletes are ambassadors, both at home and on the world stage, through their dedicated performances and athletic endeavours. The Government recognizes the importance of sport and physical activity for all Canadians.

Budget 2010 provides $44 million for Canada's high performance athletes. This includes $10 million over two years to renew funding for the identification and development of elite athletes, and $34 million over two years to renew and enhance programs that support training and preparation for competition for both winter and summer elite athletes.

In the coming months, the Minister of State (Sport) will announce details on this new funding to ensure that it, as well as the existing funding, is targeted effectively and encourages private sector investment in elite athlete training. This funding will build on the success of Own the Podium.

Budget 2010 also provides:

- $10 million over two years to the Canadian Paralympic Committee to build on the successes of our Paralympians and continue to encourage persons with disabilities to actively participate in sport.

- $2 million over two years to Special Olympics Canada to help continue to enrich the lives of Canadians with an intellectual disability through sport and competition and prepare them for competition in Special Olympics events.

- $6 million over two years for ParticipACTION to enable the organization to promote more healthy lifestyles for Canadians through physical activity and fitness. This support will also highlight the inspirational work of Pierre Lavoie and his initiative, le Grand défi Pierre Lavoie, to promote healthy living and physical activity with school children across Canada.

133

Standing Up for Those Who Helped Build Canada

Budget 2010 recognizes the significant efforts of those who have helped to build our country and make it strong. The budget recognizes the efforts of Canadian forces and veterans, invests in seniors and affirms the Government's commitment to a strong and efficient retirement income system.

Community War Memorial Program

Budget 2010 provides $1 million per year for the Community War Memorial Program to partner with communities across our country who wish to build memorials to commemorate the achievements and sacrifices made by those who served our country.

This new program will work with communities and contribute a share of the capital costs for the construction of new cenotaphs and monuments that commemorate those who served Canada. Approved projects will have strong community support and will be erected in public places. Details of the Community War Memorial Program will be announced by the Minister of Veterans Affairs over the coming months.

Access to Employment Insurance Parental and Sickness Benefits for Military Families

The Employment Insurance (EI) program provides parental benefits to individuals who are adopting a child or caring for a newborn. For Canadian Forces members whose parental leave is deferred or interrupted because of military requirements, the Government will extend the period in which they are eligible by another 52 weeks.

The EI program also provides sickness benefits to eligible individuals who are unable to work because of sickness, injury or quarantine. In order to support the families of Canadian Forces members, the Government will provide facilitated access to EI sickness benefits for eligible workers who have lost a loved one as a result of a service-related injury.

Enhanced Support for Seniors

The New Horizons for Seniors Program provides funding to organizations that help ensure that seniors can benefit from, and contribute to, the quality of life in their communities through active living and participation in social activities.

Budget 2010 provides $10 million over two years to increase funding for the New Horizons for Seniors Program. The enhanced funding will support projects which focus on volunteering among seniors and ensuring that today's seniors can mentor the next generation of volunteers, passing on their valuable skills. It will also support projects that focus on raising awareness of financial abuse of seniors.

A Strong and Efficient Retirement Income System

A strong and efficient retirement income system provides Canadians with the confidence that their efforts to work and save will allow them to enjoy their retirement years.

The current government-supported retirement income system in Canada is recognized around the world by such organizations as the Organisation for Economic Co-operation and Development as a model that succeeds in reducing poverty among Canadian seniors and in providing high levels of replacement income to retired workers.

The Government, in collaboration with provinces and territories, is committed to maintaining a strong and efficient retirement income system to ensure that Canadians have the best available opportunities to save adequately and effectively for their retirement. In May 2009, the Minister of Finance, along with provincial and territorial Finance Ministers, launched a process to expand understanding of the issues. They received a report in December and are continuing their collaborative work, leading to a review of policy options at the next meeting of Finance Ministers in May 2010.

In preparation for the May meeting, the Government will undertake consultations with the public on the government-supported retirement income system, including the main issues in saving for retirement and approaches to ensuring the ongoing strength of the system. This process will be launched in March.

Ensuring Canada's Retirement Income System Is Strong

To ensure a strong and efficient retirement income system, the Government has taken significant actions, including:

- Ensuring the ongoing sustainability of the Canada Pension Plan with the completion of the Triennial Review with provinces and territories in May 2009.

- Introducing tax measures to improve rules for Registered Pension Plans (RPPs) and Registered Retirement Savings Plans (RRSPs), including:

  - Increasing the age limit for maturing pensions and RRSPs to 71 from 69.

  - Allowing more flexible phased retirement arrangements under defined benefit RPPs.

  - Increasing the pension surplus threshold for defined benefit RPPs to 25 per cent from 10 per cent.

- Introducing the Tax-Free Savings Account to increase tax-efficient savings opportunities for Canadians.

- Introducing pension income splitting to improve retirement income security for seniors and other pensioners.

- Announcing important changes to strengthen federally regulated private pension plans.

- Creating the Task Force on Financial Literacy, which recently launched its public consultation.

Table 3.4.1

Supporting Families and Communities and Standing Up for Those Who Helped Build Canada

	2009–10	2010–11	2011–12	Total
		(millions of dollars)		
Supporting Families and Communities				
Protecting Canadian Families and Communities				
Increasing support for victims of crime		3	3	7
Strengthening law enforcement tools		7	7	14
Canadian Security Intelligence Service		8	20	28
A new review mechanism for the RCMP		3	5	8
Subtotal—Protecting Canadian Families and Communities		21	35	56
Supporting the Vulnerable				
Improving the taxation of the Universal Child Care Benefit for single parents		5	5	10
Helping charities: disbursement quota reform				
Carry forward of RDSP grants and bonds		20	70	90
Rollover of RRSP/RRIF proceeds to an RDSP			5	5
Enabling accessibility for persons with disabilities		15	15	30
Making further improvements to First Nations child and family services		18	35	53
Addressing the legacy of residential schools		93	106	199
Taking action to address violence against Aboriginal women		5	5	10
Subtotal—Supporting the Vulnerable		155	241	397
Investing in a Healthy North				
Improving access to healthy food for Northerners		12	32	45
Territorial Health System Sustainability Initiative		30	30	60
Subtotal—Investing in a Healthy North		42	62	105

Table 3.4.1 *(cont'd)*

Supporting Families and Communities and Standing Up for Those Who Helped Build Canada

	2009–10	2010–11	2011–12	Total
		(millions of dollars)		
Encouraging Participation in Amateur Sport				
Elite athletes' development		5	5	10
Summer and winter elite athletes		17	17	34
Paralympics		5	5	10
Special Olympics		1	1	2
ParticipACTION		3	3	6
Subtotal—Encouraging Participation in Amateur Sport		31	31	62
Standing Up for Those Who Helped Build Canada				
Community War Memorial Program		1	1	2
Access to Employment Insurance parental and sickness benefits for military families		1	1	2
Enhanced support for seniors		5	5	10
Subtotal—Standing Up for Those Who Helped Build Canada		7	7	14
Total—Supporting Families and Communities and Standing Up for Those Who Helped Build Canada		257	376	633
Less: funds existing in the fiscal framework		35	35	70
Net fiscal cost		**222**	**341**	**563**

Note: Totals may not add due to rounding.

Honouring Canada's International Commitments

3.5

Highlights

Budget 2010 fulfills Canada's commitment to double international assistance by:

✓ Increasing the International Assistance Envelope, the principal means by which Canada allocates foreign aid, by $364 million, bringing it to $5 billion in ongoing annual support.

✓ Providing a further $800 million of loan resources and $40 million in subsidy resources to support concessional lending to the poorest countries through the International Monetary Fund's Poverty Reduction and Growth Trust.

C anada is a global leader and continuously demonstrates this by honouring its international commitments. The importance of accountability for promises will be a defining feature of Canada's G8 and G20 Summit year. Budget 2010 delivers on promised resources, and the Government will ensure Canada's contributions effectively address global challenges including the economic crisis, immediate and long-term recovery in Haiti, maternal and child health, as well as food security.

International Assistance

In 2002 Canada committed to double international assistance by 2010–11. Budget 2010 fulfills this commitment by increasing the International Assistance Envelope (IAE) by $364 million or 8 per cent, in 2010–11, bringing it to $5 billion (see Chart 3.5.1). There is no new fiscal impact from this measure. Furthermore, Canada has already met its commitment to double aid to Africa.

For planning purposes, the Government had provisioned for annual growth in the IAE of 8 per cent. With the achievement of the $5-billion aid target, future IAE spending levels will be capped at 2010–11 levels and will be assessed alongside all other government priorities on a year-by-year basis in the budget. Relative to the planning track in the September 2009 Update of Economic and Fiscal Projections, which assumed automatic ongoing growth for international assistance spending of 8 per cent per annum, this results in savings of $438 million in 2011–12, rising to $1.8 billion in 2014–15.

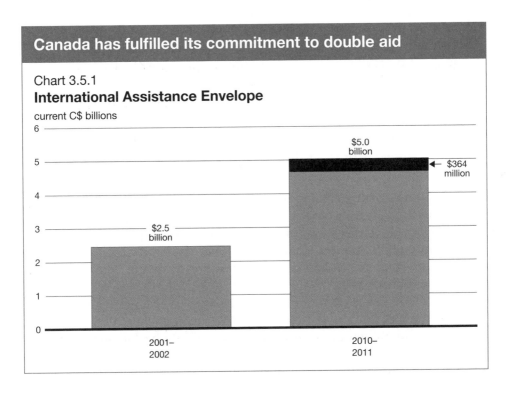

Canada has fulfilled its commitment to double aid

Chart 3.5.1
International Assistance Envelope

current C$ billions

Economic Crisis Recovery Efforts

The global economic crisis has had a serious impact on the poor, threatening to reverse years of development progress. At their Summits in Washington, London and Pittsburgh, G20 Leaders agreed to a range of measures to promote economic recovery, including a Framework for Strong, Sustainable and Balanced Growth. Under the Framework, G20 members will assess the mutual consistency of their policies and economic projections. The medium-term economic forecast submitted by Canada for this exercise is in Annex 4. Leaders also committed to ensuring that international financial institutions on the front lines of the crisis have the resources necessary to help developing countries.

Canada did its part and more. We have made available over US$22 billion to core institutions since January 2009. This includes:

- US$10 billion to the International Monetary Fund (IMF) to support additional balance of payments assistance in developing countries.

- US$4 billion in temporary capital to the Inter-American Development Bank (IDB) to help the bank bridge through the economic crisis. This innovation allowed the bank to immediately increase lending capacity by 45 per cent.

- Building on the success of its work with the IDB, Canada tripled its capital at the African Development Bank to US$2.6 billion for five years, allowing lending levels to increase by 75 per cent compared to pre-crisis forecasts. Along with other shareholders, Canada also agreed to triple its capital base at the Asian Development Bank to US$5.3 billion.

- Providing US$200 million as the anchor donor to the International Finance Corporation's Global Trade Liquidity Program, a multi-award-winning initiative that supports small and medium-sized enterprises' access to trade finance in the developing world.

In addition, Canada will provide a further $800 million in loan resources and $40 million in subsidy resources to support concessional lending to the poorest countries through the IMF's Poverty Reduction and Growth Trust. To follow through on our promise made at the G20 London Summit, the necessary resources will also be set aside within the IAE for upcoming capital and concessional resource increase negotiations at the World Bank and regional development banks.

Increased uncertainty resulting from the economic downturn has highlighted the need for countries to maintain open markets to ensure that a global recovery takes hold. This is why the G20 countries have committed to refrain from erecting new trade barriers and to promote open markets. The Government has done more than its part in respecting these important commitments by taking concrete actions to further open global markets. Canada's strong leadership in this area includes: unilateral tariff relief actions to support our manufacturers as well as global trade; the launch of ambitious trade and economic negotiations with the European Union; and the successful conclusion of free trade agreements with the European Free Trade Association, Colombia, Peru, Panama and Jordan.

Maternal and Child Health

Each year, more than 500,000 women lose their lives from causes related to pregnancy and childbirth and nearly 9 million children die before their fifth birthday. Despite the global community's promise to address these issues, as set out in the United Nations Millennium Development Goals, we are far off track. Many solutions are simple and affordable: training for health workers, vaccines, better nutrition and clean water. Canada will use its leadership at the 2010 G8 Summit in Muskoka to focus the world's attention on maternal and child health and will work to secure increased global spending on this priority.

Global Food Security

The global economic crisis has exacerbated the problem of food scarcity and price instability. In 2009, over 1 billion people were undernourished, more than at any time since 1970. At the G8 Summit in L'Aquila, Italy in July 2009, Leaders pledged to deliver a comprehensive package to address food security. Reinforcing Canada's reputation as a world leader in this critical sector, Canada was the first to announce a clear commitment with a three-year $600-million agriculture package—a doubling of our existing spending in this area. Of the total, $260 million is being provided through the World Bank to its Global Food Crisis Response Program and its new Global Agriculture and Food Security Program. Canada's contribution provides resources to enhance agricultural productivity and to improve long-term food security for poor and vulnerable populations.

Haiti

Canada has a long-standing and close relationship with Haiti. There are more than 100,000 people of Haitian origin living in Canada, and an estimated 6,000 Canadians were living in Haiti before the January 12 earthquake struck. Canadians were deeply affected by the tragedy, and they responded generously with personal donations to help victims begin to rebuild their shattered lives. Canadian civil society organizations also undertook significant emergency humanitarian efforts. The Government supported this response and immediately agreed to match eligible funds raised by private donations, estimated to be close to $130 million.

The Government took unprecedented action in responding to the crisis. Our rapid response mechanisms, including the dedicated Disaster Assistance Response Team, allowed us to get urgently needed relief supplies to Haiti, to deploy personnel to UN humanitarian agencies, and to provide cash contributions to key humanitarian partners in the immediate aftermath of the disaster. This was an important boost that assisted the overall Canadian and international response.

Recognition should in particular be given to the exemplary efforts of those Canadians deployed directly to Haiti and the Dominican Republic, including our aid officials and consular staff based in Port-au-Prince, over 2,000 Canadian Forces personnel, and members of the Royal Canadian Mounted Police.

Two weeks after the earthquake, Canada hosted the Montréal Conference with the Government of Haiti, where world leaders set in motion a joint approach to Haiti's reconstruction and development. Canada will continue to play a leadership role in the humanitarian and long-term response to the earthquake in Haiti. Our support includes a strong emphasis on the need for clear accountability of resources and results.

In 2009, Canada and others took action to cancel Haiti's bilateral debts. It is clear, however, that the country still faces an onerous debt burden with over $825 million owed to various international financial institutions. To address this issue, at the recent G7 Finance Ministers Meeting in Iqaluit, Canada led a consensus to forgive all Haitian debts to these institutions as soon as possible. G7 Ministers also agreed that reconstruction assistance should only be provided in grant form so as not to compromise the success of the country's long-term development efforts.

In order to sustain the Haitian economy during the reconstruction phase, the Government will take steps to ensure that trade is not unduly impacted. As such, the Government will ensure that Haitian exports to Canada continue to be eligible for tariff-free treatment.

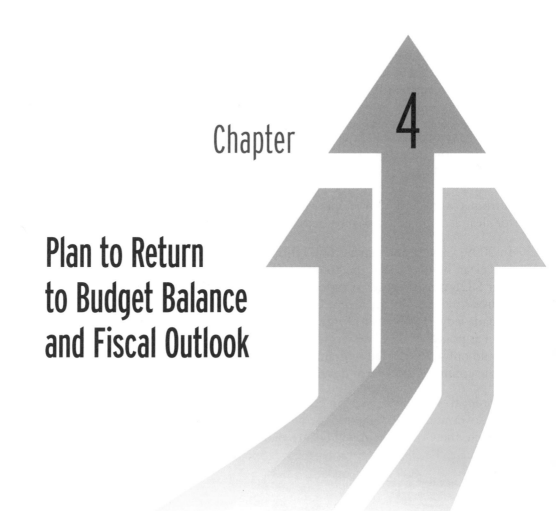

Chapter **4**

Plan to Return to Budget Balance and Fiscal Outlook

Highlights

✓ Budget 2010 outlines a three-point plan for returning to budgetary balance over the medium term and well before any other Group of Seven (G7) country.

- First, the Government will follow through with the "exit strategy" built into the Economic Action Plan. Temporary measures in the Action Plan will be wound down as planned.

- Second, the Government will restrain growth in spending through targeted measures. Towards achieving this objective, Budget 2010 proposes $17.6 billion in savings over five years.

- Third, the Government will undertake a comprehensive review of government administrative functions and overhead costs in order to identify opportunities for additional savings and improve service delivery.

✓ The Government will not raise taxes. The Government will not cut major transfers to persons and other levels of government.

✓ As a result of the planned wind-down of the Economic Action Plan and the spending growth restraint measures in this budget, the deficit is projected to be cut by almost half to $27.6 billion in 2011–12, and cut by two-thirds to $17.5 billion in 2012–13.

✓ The debt-to-GDP (gross domestic product) ratio is expected to peak at 35.4 per cent in 2010–11 and then fall to 35.2 per cent in 2011–12 and 31.9 per cent by 2014–15.

✓ Program spending as a share of GDP is expected to decline from 15.6 per cent in 2009–10 to 13.2 per cent in 2014–15.

Plan to Return
to Budget Balance

4.1

Introduction

Canada's Economic Action Plan is a significant and extraordinary response, taken in co-operation with other G20 governments, to the deepest synchronized global recession since World War II. The Action Plan was necessary because governments around the world recognized that the normal cyclical stabilizers—employment insurance programs, the tax system and monetary policy actions—may not have been sufficient to stabilize the economy, raising the risk of a systemic global economic collapse.

The Action Plan is organized around three guiding principles—that stimulus should be:

- Timely: to support the economy when private demand is weakest.

- Targeted: to businesses and families most in need.

- Temporary: to avoid long-term deficits.

All of these principles have been followed. The Action Plan is working. Positive economic signs are emerging. Canadians and businesses in Canada have received significant benefits. With this budget, the Government is starting to phase out specific elements of the stimulus as planned in the 2009 budget.

For example, millions of Canadian families took advantage of the Home Renovation Tax Credit before its expiry on January 31, 2010 and will be able to claim the credit when they file their 2009 income tax returns.

> *Overall, unprecedented policy efforts appear to have succeeded in limiting the severity of the downturn and fostering a recovery to a degree that was largely unexpected even six months ago. It is now time to plan the exit strategy from the crisis policies, even if its implementation will be progressive.*
>
> —Organisation for Economic Co-operation and Development, November 2009

The decision to phase out the stimulus measures as planned reflects the Government's belief that, over the lon term, the private sector is and should be the primary source of jobs and growth. Governments have an important role to play in creating the right conditions for Canadians and businesses to thrive.

This role includes:

- Minimizing the tax burden.

- Reducing disincentives to work and save.

- Supporting high-quality education, training and skills development.

- Promoting competitive trade and investment policies.

- Providing effective regulation and public services.

- Managing public finances responsibly.

As signs of stabilization and recovery in the economy increasingly emerge, the Government will refocus its attention on its long-term economic plan.

Canada entered the global recession in an enviable fiscal position. Canada's total government net debt-to-GDP ratio had declined to 23.5 per cent by 2007. Looking ahead, Canada's net debt burden is projected to increase by 5.9 percentage points between 2007 and 2014. This compares to expected increases of between 24.4 and 63.1 percentage points for other G7 nations (Chart 4.1.1).

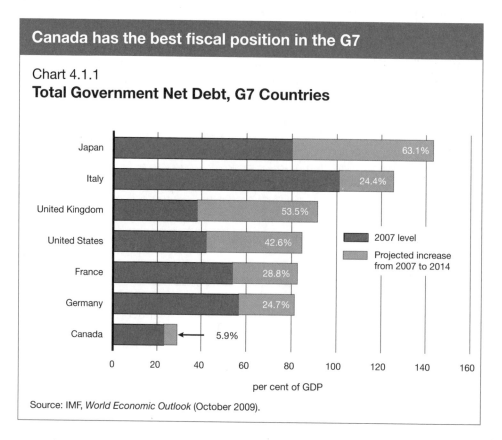

Canada has the best fiscal position in the G7

Chart 4.1.1
Total Government Net Debt, G7 Countries

Source: IMF, *World Economic Outlook* (October 2009).

Strong fiscal management, founded on the principle that governments should live within their means, is the cornerstone of the Government's economic plan. A balanced budget is not an end in itself. Rather, it is a means to better jobs and stronger, sustainable growth. Balancing the budget is the most direct way of ensuring that Canada's social infrastructure is sustainable for the long term.

- Returning to balanced budgets will minimize the amount of revenues absorbed by debt charges, thereby allowing ongoing investments in the areas that are critical to Canada's long-term growth and prosperity— infrastructure, education and training, science and technology, health care and elderly benefits.

- Returning to balanced budgets will provide Canadians and Canadian businesses with confidence that both their tax levels and public services are sustainable over the long term. This will also ensure fairness and equity toward future generations, by avoiding future tax increases or reductions in government services in the face of an aging population.

- By keeping debt levels low, the Government helps to keep interest rates low. High government debt in other countries has translated into higher borrowing costs for their economies. As investors become more concerned about rising debt loads around the globe, our strong fiscal position is helping insulate Canada from rising risk premiums and higher borrowing costs.

Budget 2010 Plan for Returning to Balance

To ensure that the economic recovery is secured, the Government will complete the implementation of the second year of Canada's Economic Action Plan so that recent positive economic growth is supported and jobs are maintained and created. Budget 2010 delivers on this commitment.

Budget 2010 sets out a three-point plan to bring the budget back to balance.

First, the Government will follow through on the "exit strategy" that is built into the Action Plan by ensuring that the temporary measures end as scheduled.

Second, the Government will put in place targeted measures to direct program spending growth now that will build over the medium term, when the recovery is secure. This will provide Canadians and Canadian businesses with certainty that the fiscal position of the Government is solid, that tax cuts are permanent and core program spending secure.

Third, the Government will undertake a comprehensive review of government administrative functions and overhead costs in order to identify opportunities for additional savings and improve service delivery. It will also continue with and augment a number of review processes, including strategic reviews.

In achieving this plan:

- The Government will not raise taxes. It will ensure that the costs of goods and services intended to be charged to recipients are recovered as appropriate.

- The Government will not cut major transfers to persons—including those for seniors and children and Employment Insurance. These important benefits for Canadians will not be reduced.

- The Government will not cut major transfers to other levels of government in support of health care and social services, Equalization and the gas tax transfer to municipalities. The federal government will do its share to fund these essential services.

Ending the Economic Action Plan on Time

Governments around the world are working together to stimulate their economies through significant short-term expenditures. These actions have been endorsed internationally, but with an emphasis on the need for sustainable medium-term fiscal plans. At the Pittsburgh Summit in September 2009, G20 Leaders committed to follow through on their stimulus plans in the near term, while preparing strategies to wind down stimulus and improve their fiscal positions as the recovery is established.

Canadians expect federal, provincial and municipal governments to work together to stimulate the economy and create and maintain jobs. But they also expect governments to return to balanced budgets as quickly as possible once the recovery takes hold. That is why many elements of the Economic Action Plan are time-limited. For the most part, funds are only available through March 2011.

Allowing the temporary elements of the Action Plan to wind down, as scheduled, is the first step in the Government's plan to return to balance over the medium term. This alone will cut the budget deficit almost in half between 2009–10 and 2011–12. The Government is starting to phase out specific elements of the stimulus, as planned in the 2009 budget.

- In December, the Government set a deadline of January 29, 2010, for partner authorities to secure firm commitments to implement projects. This deadline was set to allow for projects to be completed by March 31, 2011. Projects with partner authorities have now been finalized. In areas where funds were not committed, these have been reallocated to other priorities.

- On January 31, 2010, the Home Renovation Tax Credit came to an end after successfully boosting activity in the home renovation sector. Canadians will see the benefits upon filing their 2009 income tax returns.

Targeted Measures

The second element of the Government's plan to bring the budget back to balance is to put in place targeted measures to reduce the rate of growth of spending that will build over the medium term. Budget 2010 announces $17.6 billion in savings measures over the next five years. Each of these spending growth restraint measures is described below.

Restraining Growth in National Defence Spending

In recent years, the Government has made major, necessary investments in the country's military capabilities in support of the *Canada First* Defence Strategy, the Government's long-term vision for the Canadian Forces. The *Canada First* Defence Strategy is a long-term commitment to modernize the Canadian Forces. The strategy sets out key objectives of growing the forces, recapitalizing air, land and naval fleets and other major equipment, restoring infrastructure, and ensuring the Canadian Forces are ready to deploy in the defence of Canada and Canada's interests both at home and abroad. The *Canada First* Defence Strategy continues to point the way forward for Canada's military.

In addition to incremental funding received for deployed operations, National Defence's annual expenses have increased from $15 billion in 2005–06 to $18 billion in 2008–09. In 2008–09, National Defence spending represented approximately one-fifth of total government direct program spending on an annual basis. These investments have strengthened the Canadian Forces and produced tangible results, as most recently demonstrated by the Afghanistan mission, support for relief efforts in Haiti, and the provision of security at the 2010 Winter Olympics in Vancouver.

The Government remains committed to continuing to build the Canadian Forces into a first-class, modern military. However, as part of measures to restrain the growth in overall government spending and return to budget balance in the medium term, the Government will slow the rate of previously planned growth in the National Defence budget. Budget 2010 reduces growth in National Defence's budget by $525 million in 2012–13 and $1 billion annually beginning in 2013–14. Defence spending will continue to grow but more slowly than previously planned (Chart 4.1.2).

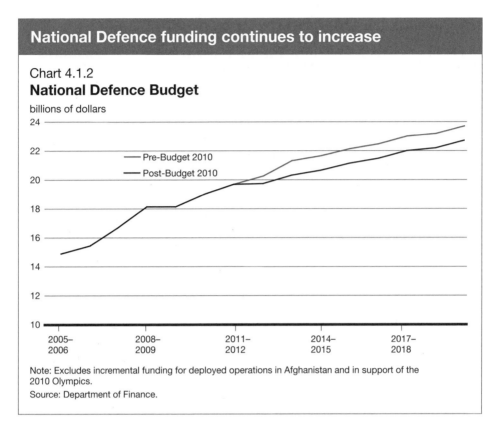

National Defence funding continues to increase

Chart 4.1.2
National Defence Budget

billions of dollars

Pre-Budget 2010
Post-Budget 2010

2005–2006　2008–2009　2011–2012　2014–2015　2017–2018

Note: Excludes incremental funding for deployed operations in Afghanistan and in support of the 2010 Olympics.
Source: Department of Finance.

By implementing this measure beginning in 2012–13, the Government will ensure that it does not adversely affect military operations during the current Afghanistan mission, and that National Defence has sufficient time to adjust its long-term expenditure plans. The Government is confident that the long-term objectives of the *Canada First* Defence Strategy can be achieved and that the Canadian Forces will continue to fully meet its three key roles: defending Canada, defending North America and contributing to international peace and security.

National Defence has already begun work on a comprehensive strategic review to ensure its resources are fully aligned with the priorities set out in the *Canada First* Defence Strategy. This review will identify measures necessary to implement the Budget 2010 decision.

International Assistance Envelope

In 2002, Canada committed to double international assistance by 2010–11. Budget 2010 fulfills this commitment by increasing the International Assistance Envelope (IAE) by $364 million, or 8 per cent, in 2010–11, bringing it to $5 billion (Chart 4.1.3).

For planning purposes, the Government had provisioned for annual IAE growth of 8 per cent. With the achievement of the $5-billion aid target, future IAE spending levels will be capped at 2010–11 levels and will be assessed alongside all other government priorities on a year-by-year basis in the budget. Relative to the planning track that was assumed in the September 2009 Update of Economic and Fiscal Projections, which assumed automatic ongoing growth for international assistance spending of 8 per cent per annum, this results in savings of $438 million in 2011–12, rising to $1.8 billion by 2014–15.

International assistance remains a priority for the Government. Honouring the commitment to double our international assistance budget by 2010–11 will mean significant new ongoing resources to allow Canada to respond to global challenges with strong leadership, including support for reconstruction in Haiti and our G8 and G20 Summit priorities. More details on these initiatives can be found in Chapter 3.5.

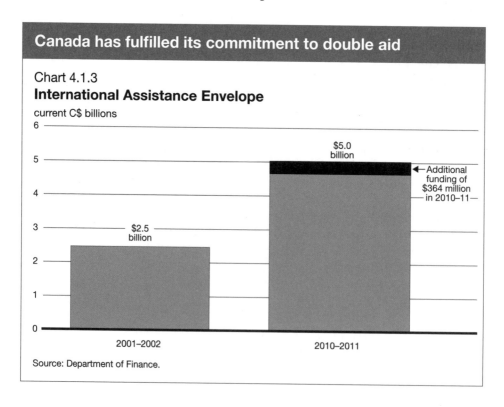

Canada has fulfilled its commitment to double aid

Chart 4.1.3
International Assistance Envelope
current C$ billions

Source: Department of Finance.

Containing the Administrative Cost of Government

The Government is also proposing to reduce the rate of growth of its operating expenditures and improve efficiency while lowering the rate of growth in the size and operations of the public service.

The Government will lead by example, introducing legislation to freeze the salaries of the Prime Minister, Ministers, Members of Parliament and Senators for 2010–11, 2011–12 and 2012–13. It will also freeze the overall budget of Ministers' offices and calls on Members of both Houses of Parliament to do the same. It will also maintain the freeze at 2008–09 levels on departmental spending on travel, conferences and hospitality.

This budget proposes two further significant actions to reduce the growth in operating expenses.

- For 2010–11, departmental budgets will not be increased to fund the 1.5-per-cent increase in annual wages for the federal public administration. Employees will continue to see their wages increase as set out in collective agreements and the Expenditure Restraint Act, which is in effect through 2011. However, departments will be required to reallocate from the remainder of their operating budgets to fund these increases.

- For 2011–12 and 2012–13, operating budgets of departments, as appropriated by Parliament, will be frozen at 2010–11 levels. Departmental spending is appropriated through the Main and Supplementary Estimates. The Government tabled the 2010–11 Main Estimates on March 3, 2010. The spending in the Main Estimates is generally consistent with the program expenses set out in the budget. However, the Estimates do not take into account measures announced in Budget 2010 or expected adjustments to fund cost pressures related to essential services, payments that arise from liabilities and other contingencies. An allowance for these adjustments is included in the fiscal framework. Treasury Board will set departmental operating spending levels for 2011–12 and 2012–13 at 2010–11 amounts, adjusted to reflect the expiration of operating budget authorities to deliver the Economic Action Plan. Practically speaking, salary and operating budgets of departments will be frozen at their 2010–11 levels in 2011–12 and 2012–13.

While the Department of National Defence will be subject to the overall operating budget constraint, the Defence escalator will continue to apply over those years, such that the Defence budget will continue to increase.

The Government expects that other federal organizations, for which expenses are not appropriated by Parliament (for example, enterprise Crown corporations), will follow suit and freeze their operating expenses.

Given the constraints on departments' operating budgets, the Government will engage with public sector bargaining agents and will assess measures taken by other jurisdictions in Canada to ensure that total costs of compensation are reasonable, the organization of work is effective, technology is used appropriately to drive productivity, and the federal public service maintains its reputation for excellence. The Government will also continue to examine ways in which all compensation costs, including benefits, could be better managed.

Actions to reduce growth in operating expenses proposed in this budget are projected to save $0.3 billion in 2010–11, $0.9 billion in 2011–12 and $1.8 billion in 2012–13, as reflected in Table 4.1.1 below.

Review of Government Operations

The third element of the Government's plan to return the budget to balance is to undertake, continue with, and in some cases augment, a number of review processes aimed at reducing costs while improving efficiency. Over time this should result in a reduction in the size of the public service.

- Strategic reviews, through which departments assess all their programs and identify 5 per cent of the lowest-priority and lowest-performing ones, will continue. Strategic reviews are carried out under the leadership of the President of the Treasury Board. Over the first two years of the strategic review exercise, almost $1.0 billion has been identified in ongoing annual savings. This budget proposes savings in respect of the 2009 round of strategic reviews that reach $287 million in 2012–13. To maximize savings in future strategic reviews, departments will no longer be asked as a matter of course to suggest reinvestments of strategic review savings. Detailed outcomes of the 2009 round of strategic reviews are provided in Annex 2.

- The Government will undertake a comprehensive review of government administrative functions and overhead costs in order to identify opportunities for additional savings and improve service delivery. Simplification of processes and delivery mechanisms will improve access to government services and reduce costs of program delivery. The Government will report on the results of this review in the 2011 budget.

- The Government will ensure that, as part of its ongoing assessment processes of grants and contributions, including renewal of program terms and conditions, the funding provided to organizations is tied to furthering government priorities and achieving results for Canadians.

- The Corporate Asset Management Review is continuing, consistent with the Budget 2009 commitment. The Review assesses selected assets under the leadership of the Minister of Finance, with a view to improve their efficiency and effectiveness and ensure that resources of the Government are employed in ways that focus on the priorities of Canadians. Reviews consider a wide set of options for the future of selected assets, including the status quo, amendments to current mandates or governance, and divestment. A systematic review of corporate assets is a normal part of good governance and contributes to the ongoing reallocation of financial resources from low to high priorities in order to maximize economic benefits to taxpayers.

- The Government is proceeding with a reduction of 245 Governor in Council (GiC) positions. This reduction represents 9.1 per cent of the approximately 2,700 positions covered by the GiC review announced in the 2009 budget. This streamlining exercise will provide for more effective governance and operations and strengthen the management of Canada's federal agencies, boards, commissions and Crown corporations.

In addition to the expenditure restraint announced above, this budget introduces a number of measures intended to protect the integrity of the Canadian tax system. The introduction of these measures will yield $355 million in savings in 2010–11, rising to $625 million by 2014–15. These measures are detailed in Chapter 3 and Annex 5.

In total, Budget 2010 savings measures amount to $17.6 billion in savings. Table 4.1.1 outlines these major actions. As a result of the actions taken in this budget, average annual growth in direct program spending after the expiry of the Economic Action Plan will slow to 1.3 per cent.

Table 4.1.1

Budget 2010 Savings Measures—Expected Savings

	2009– 2010	2010– 2011	2011– 2012	2012– 2013	2013– 2014	2014– 2015	Total
			(millions of dollars)				
Restraining growth in National Defence spending				525	1,000	1,000	2,525
International Assistance Envelope			438	869	1,337	1,842	4,486
Containing the administrative cost of government		300	900	1,800	1,800	2,000	6,800
2009 strategic reviews		152	248	287	288	288	1,262
Tax fairness—closing tax loopholes	20	355	440	500	565	625	2,505
Total	**20**	**807**	**2,026**	**3,981**	**4,990**	**5,755**	**17,578**

Note: Totals may not add due to rounding.

Budget 2010 Plan for Returning to Balance: Results

Chart 4.1.4 shows the projected deficit for this fiscal year and the next five years. This projection takes into account the wind-down of the Economic Action Plan, the savings from direct program spending growth restraint outlined above, the impact of the new actions outlined in Chapter 3, and the impact of recent economic developments on government revenues and expenses, as described later in this chapter.

- The deficit is projected to be cut by almost half from $53.8 billion in 2009–10 to $27.6 billion in 2011–12. This significant drop in the deficit for the most part reflects the Government's commitment to make certain that Action Plan stimulus measures expire as scheduled on March 31, 2011.

- The deficit is projected to be cut by two-thirds from $53.8 billion in 2009–10 to $17.5 billion in 2012–13.

The projected deficit in 2009–10 of 3.5 per cent of GDP is considerably below the deficits recorded in previous recessions of 5.6 per cent of GDP in 1992–93 and 7.6 per cent of GDP in 1982–83. By 2014–15, the deficit measured in relation to the size of the economy is projected to be 0.1 per cent of GDP (Chart 4.1.5).

Rapid decline in deficits

Chart 4.1.4
Federal Budgetary Deficit

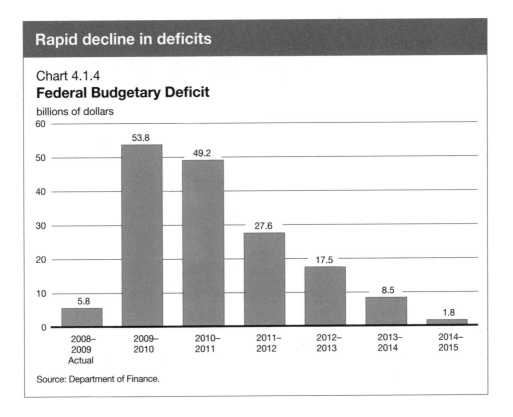

billions of dollars

Source: Department of Finance.

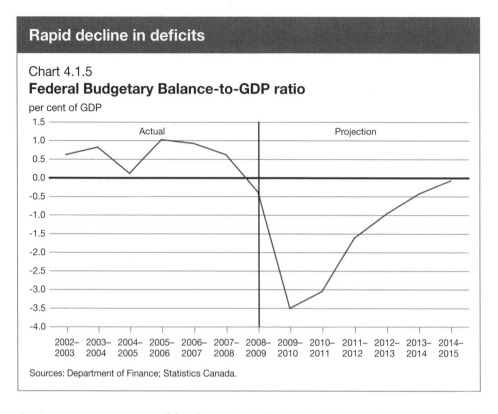

Rapid decline in deficits

Chart 4.1.5
Federal Budgetary Balance-to-GDP ratio

per cent of GDP

Actual | Projection

Sources: Department of Finance; Statistics Canada.

An important measure of fiscal sustainability is the debt burden as measured by the debt-to-GDP ratio. Reductions in the debt burden in recent years have provided Canada with the flexibility to put in place measures to support the economy that are sustainable. Chart 4.1.6 shows that the federal debt, measured in relation to the size of the economy, is projected to increase from 29 per cent of GDP in 2008–09—the lowest debt ratio in 29 years— to a peak of 35.4 per cent in 2010–11. The debt ratio over this year and next will be about equal to the ratio in 2005–06, when the Government recorded a $13.2-billion surplus. In 2011–12, following the expiry of the measures in the Economic Action Plan, the debt ratio is projected to fall once more to 35.2 per cent of GDP, and to continue to fall to 31.9 per cent of GDP by 2014–15.

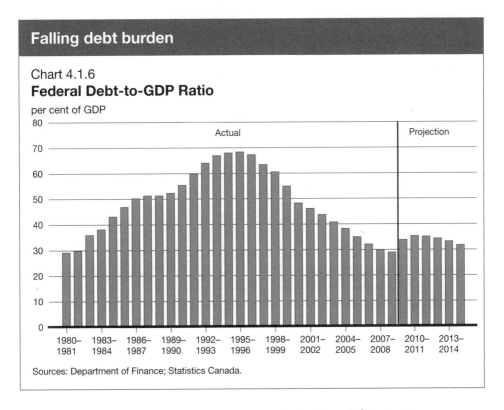

Falling debt burden

Chart 4.1.6
Federal Debt-to-GDP Ratio

per cent of GDP

Sources: Department of Finance; Statistics Canada.

The total government net debt-to-GDP ratio in Canada[1] is the lowest of all G7 countries and will continue to be so over the medium term (Chart 4.1.7). In fact, by 2014, Canada's debt-to-GDP ratio is expected to be proportionately much lower than in other G7 countries than it is now.

---

[1] Includes federal, provincial-territorial and local governments, as well as the Canada Pension Plan and the Québec Pension Plan.

Canada's fiscal advantage

Chart 4.1.7
Total Government Net Debt-to-GDP Ratio
per cent of GDP

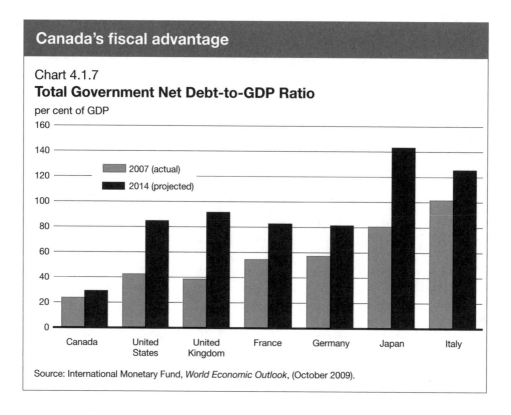

Source: International Monetary Fund, *World Economic Outlook*, (October 2009).

Fiscal Planning Framework

4.2

Fiscal Outlook Before the Measures Proposed in Budget 2010

Table 4.2.1 provides a summary of the changes in the fiscal projections since the September 10, 2009 Update of Economic and Fiscal Projections. Although budget measures have been presented over two years, this section provides a five-year forecast as part of the Government's medium-term economic plan. In the Update, underlying budgetary deficits of $55.9 billion in 2009–10, $45.3 billion in 2010–11, $27.4 billion in 2011–12, $19.4 billion in 2012–13, $11.2 billion in 2013–14 and $5.2 billion in 2014–15 were projected.

Table 4.2.1

Summary of Changes in the Fiscal Outlook Since the September 2009 Update of Economic and Fiscal Projections

	2009–2010	2010–2011	2011–2012	2012–2013	2013–2014	2014–2015
	(billions of dollars)					
September Update budgetary balance	-55.9	-45.3	-27.4	-19.4	-11.2	-5.2
Decisions since the September Update	-0.1	-0.5	-0.1	-0.1	-0.1	-0.1
Impact of economic and fiscal developments						
Budgetary revenues	-2.7	-2.0	-2.3	-2.5	-2.5	-2.1
Budgetary expenses[1]	5.0	-1.1	1.0	1.4	1.4	0.9
Total economic and fiscal developments	2.3	-3.1	-1.2	-1.1	-1.1	-1.3
Revised status quo budgetary balance	**-53.7**	**-48.9**	**-28.7**	**-20.6**	**-12.5**	**-6.6**

Note: Totals may not add due to rounding.

[1] A positive number implies a decrease in spending and an improvement in the budgetary balance. A negative number implies an increase in spending and a deterioration in the budgetary balance.

The status quo budgetary balance (before actions in this budget) has been revised to deficits of $53.7 billion in 2009–10, $48.9 billion in 2010–11, $28.7 billion in 2011–12, $20.6 billion in 2012–13, $12.5 billion in 2013–14 and $6.6 billion in 2014–15.

The revision reflects both the cost of decisions taken by the Government since the September Update and the impact of economic changes.

The cost of decisions taken since the September Update amount to $500 million in 2010–11 and $100 million per year in 2009–10 as well as in 2011–12, 2012–13, 2013–14 and 2014–15. These costs include the Government's December 2009 commitment to provide one-time protection payments to Newfoundland and Labrador, Prince Edward Island, Nova Scotia, New Brunswick, Manitoba and Saskatchewan totalling $525 million. This measure ensures that no province experiences a decline in its combined entitlements under the Canada Health Transfer, Canada Social Transfer and Equalization in 2010–11. In addition, it reflects the fiscal impact of the extension of certain Employment Insurance benefits to the self-employed, funding for repairs to the Atomic Energy of Canada Limited's isotope facility, and an increase to the pension surplus threshold. Additional funds have also been provided for the ecoENERGY Retrofit – Homes program.

While the economic outlook has been revised up in the near term, revenues have been weaker than expected to date in 2009–10. As well, a lower than projected take-up in the Insured Mortgage Purchase Program (IMPP) has lowered projected interest earnings of the Government. This results in a corresponding reduction in debt charges. As a result, revenues are projected to be somewhat lower than projected in the September Update through 2014–15. Revenues are revised down by $2.7 billion in 2009–10, $2.0 billion in 2010–11, $2.3 billion in 2011–12, $2.5 billion in 2012–13, $2.5 billion in 2013–14 and $2.1 billion in 2014–15.

In 2009–10 budgetary expenses, which include program expenses and public debt charges, are projected to be $5.0 billion below the level estimated in the September Update. This results from a change in the profile of Economic Action Plan spending, as some spending initially planned for 2009–10 is now expected to take place in 2010–11. In addition, savings have been realized due to the upward valuation of the General Motors of Canada Inc. shares the Government acquired as part of its support to the auto industry. In 2010–11, budgetary expenses are projected to be higher than projected at the time of the September Update, largely reflecting the shift of some spending under the Economic Action Plan into 2010–11. Starting in 2011–12, budgetary expenses are projected to be lower than projected at the time of the September 2009 Update. This is due to significantly lower projected debt charges, which more than offset higher projected Employment Insurance (EI) benefits (reflecting higher average benefits and the extension of certain EI benefits to the self-employed). Lower projected public debt charges reflect both lower forecast interest rates and a lower projected take-up of the IMPP.

In total, economic and fiscal developments since the September Update have led to a decrease of $2.3 billion in the projected budgetary deficit for 2009–10, and to projected increases in the budgetary deficit of $3.1 billion in 2010–11, $1.2 billion in 2011–12, $1.1 billion in 2012–13, $1.1 billion in 2013–14 and $1.3 billion in 2014–15.

Fiscal Cost of Measures Proposed in Budget 2010

Table 4.2.2 sets out the impact of measures proposed in this budget. The reductions proposed in Budget 2010 result in cumulative savings of $17.6 billion over five years.

Table 4.2.2
Fiscal Outlook

	2009–2010	2010–2011	2011–2012	2012–2013	2013–2014	2014–2015
	(billions of dollars)					
Status quo budgetary balance (before budget measures)	-53.7	-48.9	-28.7	-20.6	-12.5	-6.6
Return to budget balance— savings measures						
Restraining growth in National Defence spending	0.0	0.0	0.0	0.5	1.0	1.0
International Assistance Envelope	0.0	0.0	0.4	0.9	1.3	1.8
Containing the administrative cost of government	0.0	0.3	0.9	1.8	1.8	2.0
2009 strategic reviews	0.0	0.2	0.2	0.3	0.3	0.3
Tax fairness—closing tax loopholes	0.0	0.4	0.4	0.5	0.6	0.6
Subtotal—savings measures	0.0	0.8	2.0	4.0	5.0	5.8
Measures proposed in this budget[1]						
Building on a strong economic foundation	-0.1	-0.9	-0.6	-0.7	-0.8	-0.7
Supporting Families and Communities and Standing Up for Those Who Helped Build Canada	0.0	-0.2	-0.3	-0.2	-0.2	-0.2
Subtotal—policy measures	-0.1	-1.1	-0.9	-0.9	-1.0	-0.9
Total (net savings)	-0.1	-0.3	1.1	3.1	4.0	4.8
Budgetary balance (after Budget measures)	-53.8	-49.2	-27.6	-17.5	-8.5	-1.8

Note: Totals may not add due to rounding.

[1] A positive number implies a decrease in spending and an improvement in the budgetary balance. A negative number implies an increase in spending and a deterioration in the budgetary balance.

Savings proposals are designed to build over the medium term as the economy recovers. The cost of proposed new policy measures totals $1.1 billion in 2010–11 and about $0.9 billion per year thereafter.

As a result of the expiration of the Economic Action Plan and the measures in this budget, the deficit is projected to decline by almost half over the next two years, to $27.6 billion in 2011–12, and by two-thirds to $17.5 billion in 2012–13. In 2014–15, the deficit is projected to be $1.8 billion.

Summary Statement of Transactions

Table 4.2.3 provides a summary of the Government's financial position, including the cost of measures and the savings proposed in Budget 2010.

Expressed as a share of the economy, budgetary revenues are projected to increase from a low of 14.0 per cent of GDP in 2009–10 to 15.2 per cent of GDP in 2014–15. This increase reflects the impact of the economic recovery. In contrast, savings measures proposed in this budget are expected to lower the ratio of program spending to GDP from 15.6 per cent in 2009–10 to 13.2 per cent in 2014–15. As a result, the federal deficit is projected to be 0.1 per cent of GDP in 2014–15.

The federal debt-to-GDP ratio (accumulated deficit) stood at 29.0 per cent in 2008–09, down significantly from its peak of 68.4 per cent in 1995–96. The debt ratio is expected to increase to 35.4 per cent in 2010–11, the second year of the Economic Action Plan, before declining steadily to 31.9 per cent in 2014–15.

Table 4.2.3

Summary Statement of Transactions
(Including Budget 2010 Measures)

		Projection					
	2008–2009	2009–2010	2010–2011	2011–2012	2012–2013	2013–2014	2014–2015
	(billions of dollars)						
Budgetary revenues	233.1	213.9	231.3	249.0	266.5	282.7	296.5
Program expenses	207.9	237.8	249.2	241.4	245.2	251.4	257.7
Public debt charges	31.0	29.9	31.3	35.3	38.9	39.8	40.6
Total expenses	238.8	267.7	280.5	276.7	284.0	291.2	298.3
Budgetary balance	-5.8	-53.8	-49.2	-27.6	-17.5	-8.5	-1.8
Federal debt	463.7	517.5	566.7	594.3	611.9	620.3	622.1
Per cent of GDP							
Budgetary revenues	14.6	14.0	14.4	14.8	15.0	15.2	15.2
Program expenses	13.0	15.6	15.6	14.3	13.8	13.5	13.2
Public debt charges	1.9	2.0	2.0	2.1	2.2	2.1	2.1
Budgetary balance	-0.4	-3.5	-3.1	-1.6	-1.0	-0.5	-0.1
Federal debt	29.0	33.9	35.4	35.2	34.4	33.3	31.9

Note: Totals may not add due to rounding.

175

Outlook for Budgetary Revenues

Table 4.2.4

**Revenue Outlook
(Including Budget 2010 measures)**

	2008–2009	2009–2010	2010–2011	2011–2012	2012–2013	2013–2014	2014–2015
				Projection			
				(billions of dollars)			
Income taxes							
Personal income tax	116.0	108.2	117.0	124.5	133.3	141.9	150.6
Corporate income tax	29.5	22.3	25.5	28.9	29.5	31.6	33.2
Non-resident income tax	6.3	4.9	5.5	5.9	6.4	6.9	7.0
Total income tax	151.8	135.4	148.0	159.4	169.3	180.3	190.8
Excise taxes/duties							
Goods and Services Tax	25.7	25.8	27.3	28.8	30.5	32.1	33.7
Customs import duties	4.0	3.4	3.4	3.5	3.7	3.8	4.1
Other excise taxes/duties	10.0	10.1	10.3	10.3	10.3	10.3	10.4
Total excise taxes/duties	39.8	39.3	41.0	42.7	44.4	46.3	48.3
Total tax revenues	191.6	174.7	188.9	202.0	213.7	226.6	239.1
Employment Insurance premium revenues	16.9	16.6	17.6	20.0	22.6	25.2	26.6
Other revenues	24.6	22.6	24.8	27.0	30.3	30.8	30.8
Total budgetary revenues	233.1	213.9	231.3	249.0	266.5	282.7	296.5
Per cent of GDP							
Personal income tax	7.3	7.1	7.3	7.4	7.5	7.6	7.7
Corporate income tax	1.8	1.5	1.6	1.7	1.7	1.7	1.7
Goods and Services Tax	1.6	1.7	1.7	1.7	1.7	1.7	1.7
Total tax revenues	12.0	11.4	11.8	12.0	12.0	12.2	12.2
Employment Insurance premium revenues	1.1	1.1	1.1	1.2	1.3	1.4	1.4
Other revenues	1.5	1.5	1.5	1.6	1.7	1.7	1.6
Total	14.6	14.0	14.4	14.8	15.0	15.2	15.2

Note: Totals may not add due to rounding

Personal income tax revenues—the largest component of budgetary revenues—are projected to decline by $7.8 billion, or 6.7 per cent, to $108.2 billion in 2009–10. This primarily reflects the impact of tax relief measures, notably the increases in the basic personal amount and personal income tax bracket thresholds, the enhancement of the Working Income Tax Benefit and the Home Renovation Tax Credit, as well as the impact of the weaker economy. Personal income tax revenues are projected to rise by 8.1 per cent in 2010–11, reflecting the resumption of growth in personal income, as well as the end of the Home Renovation Tax Credit. From 2011–12 onwards, personal income tax revenues are projected to grow on average by 6.5 per cent per year, reflecting the progressive nature of the income tax system combined with growth in the personal income tax base.

Corporate income tax revenues are expected to decline by $7.2 billion, or 24.3 per cent, to $22.3 billion in 2009–10, reflecting a projected decline in corporate profits, refunds of taxes paid in previous years and a 0.5-percentage-point reduction in the general corporate income tax rate in 2009. Corporate income tax revenues are projected to increase by 14.1 per cent in 2010–11 and 13.7 per cent in 2011–12, lifted by a recovery in profits, but partly offset by the carry-forward of losses recorded during the recession, as well as ongoing tax relief. Growth in corporate income tax revenues is projected to moderate to 2.0 per cent in 2012–13, largely due to the decline in the general corporate income tax rate to 15 per cent in 2012 and other tax relief measures, as well as a moderation in profit growth. Growth in corporate income tax revenues is projected to average 6.0 per cent in 2013–14 and 2014–15.

Non-resident income tax revenues are expected to decline by 22.3 per cent to $4.9 billion in 2009–10, reflecting the drop in corporate profits in 2009, as well as the impact of the phase-out of the withholding tax on non-arm's length payments of interest to the U.S. under the Fifth Protocol to the Canada-U.S. Tax Treaty. Non-resident income tax revenues are projected to rise by 13.3 per cent in 2010–11 as the economy recovers, and then to grow at an average rate of 6.2 per cent over the remainder of the forecast period.

Goods and Services Tax (GST) revenues are projected to be flat in 2009–10, reflecting weak growth in consumption. Consistent with a projected recovery in consumption in 2010–11, growth in GST revenues is projected to average 5.5 per cent over the remainder of the projection period.

Customs import duties are projected to decline by 15.4 per cent to $3.4 billion in 2009–10, reflecting a decline in imports combined with tariff relief for machinery and equipment announced in Budget 2009. Customs import duties are projected to decline a further 1.4 per cent in 2010–11, reflecting tariff relief on manufacturing inputs and machinery and equipment announced in this budget. Growth in customs import duties is projected to average 5.3 per cent through 2014–15.

Other excise taxes and duties are projected to rise by 0.6 per cent to $10.1 billion in 2009–10, and then rise to $10.3 billion in 2010–11.

Employment Insurance (EI) premium revenues are projected to decline by 1.6 per cent in 2009–10, reflecting a decline in employment. The EI premium rate was kept stable in 2009 and 2010 at $1.73 per $100 of insurable earnings. When the temporary freeze of EI premiums is lifted in 2011, premium rates will be set by an independent arm's length Crown corporation, the Canada Employment Insurance Financing Board (CEIFB). Under the EI financing regime passed into law in Budget 2008, the CEIFB will set EI premium rates in order to balance the EI program over time, subject to a 15-cent limit on annual changes. Based on current economic projections, it is expected that the deficits incurred by the EI program during the recession will be paid back by 2014. Consistent with the Government's commitment in Budget 2009, the CEIFB will not be mandated to recover any EI deficits resulting from the $2.9 billion in benefit enhancements announced in Budget 2009.

Other revenues include those of consolidated Crown corporations, net gains/losses from enterprise Crown corporations, foreign exchange revenues, returns on investments and revenues from the sales of goods and services. These revenues are volatile, owing partly to the impact of exchange rate movements on the Canadian-dollar value of foreign-denominated interest-bearing assets and to net gains/losses from enterprise Crown corporations. Other revenues are projected to decline by 8.1 per cent in 2009–10, due in part to a decline in revenues under the Atlantic Offshore Revenue Accounts, reflecting lower oil prices as well as a decline in offshore production. This decline in revenues is offset by a corresponding decline in projected transfers to Newfoundland and Labrador and Nova Scotia under the Atlantic Offshore Accords, such that there is no net impact on the budgetary balance. Other revenues are projected to rise by 9.6 per cent in 2010–11, by 9.0 per cent in 2011–12 and by 12.1 per cent in 2012–13, largely reflecting rising interest rates, along with measures introduced in this budget to reduce the interest rate paid by the Government on tax overpayments by corporations. Other revenue growth is then projected to slow to 1.8 per cent in 2013–14 and remain largely unchanged in 2014–15, reflecting the winding down of the Insured Mortgage Purchase Program.

The revenue projections include foregone revenues of $12 million over two years due to the extension by one year, to May 2011, of the current fee waiver for firearms licence renewals or upgrades.

Recovery from the recession

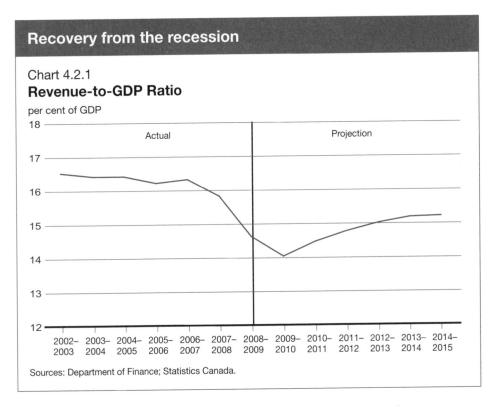

Chart 4.2.1
Revenue-to-GDP Ratio

per cent of GDP

Sources: Department of Finance; Statistics Canada.

Chart 4.2.1 shows that revenues as a share of GDP are projected to fall to 14.0 per cent in 2009–10. The projected decline in the revenue ratio reflects tax relief measures announced in previous budgets, as well as the impact of automatic fiscal stabilizers, which lower collections when the economy slows in order to dampen the impact of the recession. The revenue ratio is expected to increase to 15.2 per cent in 2014–15 as the economy recovers.

Outlook for Program Expenses

Table 4.2.5

**Program Expense Outlook
(Including Budget 2010 Measures)**

| | 2008–2009 | Projection | | | | | |
		2009–2010	2010–2011	2011–2012	2012–2013	2013–2014	2014–2015
				(billions of dollars)			
Major transfers to persons							
Elderly benefits	33.4	35.0	36.7	38.6	40.7	42.9	45.2
Employment Insurance benefits[1]	16.3	22.4	22.6	19.6	18.8	18.4	18.4
Children's benefits	11.9	12.3	12.7	13.2	13.4	13.4	13.5
Total	61.6	69.7	72.0	71.4	72.9	74.8	77.1
Major transfers to other levels of government							
Federal transfers in support of health and social programs	33.3	35.7	37.1	38.7	40.7	42.7	44.7
Fiscal arrangements[2]	15.2	16.1	16.4	16.8	17.7	18.6	19.5
Alternative Payments for Standing Programs	-3.0	-2.7	-2.9	-3.1	-3.3	-3.5	-3.7
Canada's cities and communities	1.0	2.0	2.0	2.0	2.0	2.0	2.0
Other[3]	0.0	0.3	4.3	1.9	0.0	0.0	0.0
Total	46.5	51.4	56.8	56.3	57.1	59.8	62.4
Direct program expenses							
Transfer payments	30.2	39.8	39.4	33.7	33.6	32.8	32.1
Capital amortization	4.1	4.4	4.6	4.9	5.1	5.3	5.4
Other operating expenses	20.6	20.8	21.5	22.9	24.2	25.2	25.8
Operating expenses subject to freeze	44.9	51.8	54.9	52.2	52.4	53.5	54.8
Total	99.8	116.8	120.4	113.7	115.2	116.7	118.2
Total program expenses	**207.9**	**237.8**	**249.2**	**241.4**	**245.2**	**251.4**	**257.7**

Table 4.2.5 *(cont'd)*

Program Expense Outlook
(Including Budget 2010 Measures)

	Projection						
	2008–2009	2009–2010	2010–2011	2011–2012	2012–2013	2013–2014	2014–2015
Per cent of GDP							
Major transfers to persons	3.8	4.6	4.5	4.2	4.1	4.0	3.9
Major transfers to other levels of government	2.9	3.4	3.5	3.3	3.2	3.2	3.2
Direct program expenses	6.2	7.6	7.5	6.7	6.5	6.3	6.1
Total program expenses	13.0	15.6	15.6	14.3	13.8	13.5	13.2

Note: Totals may not add due to rounding

1 EI benefits include EI regular benefits, sickness, maternity, parental, compassionate care, fishing and work-sharing benefits, and employment benefits and support measures. These represent 90 per cent of total EI program expenses. The remaining EI costs relate mainly to administration costs.

2 Fiscal arrangements include Equalization, Territorial Formula Financing, the Youth Allowances Recovery and statutory subsidies.

3 Includes transfer protection and transitional payments.

Table 4.2.5 provides an overview of the projections for program expenses by major component, including the cost of measures proposed in this budget. Program expenses consist of major transfers to persons, major transfers to other levels of government and direct program expenses.

Major transfers to persons consist of elderly, Employment Insurance (EI) and children's benefits.

Growth in elderly benefits, which include Old Age Security and the Guaranteed Income Supplement, is expected to average about 5 per cent annually over the planning period due to increases in the seniors' population and consumer price inflation, to which benefits are fully indexed. The Government makes ongoing efforts to ensure that all those who are eligible for these programs receive payments.

EI benefits are projected to increase by 37.2 per cent to $22.4 billion in 2009–10. This large increase is due to higher unemployment, growth in average weekly benefits, and significant measures to support Canadians affected by the recession. These measures include enhanced EI benefits, a significant increase in funding for training, and the temporary extension of benefits for long-tenured workers enacted on October 25, 2009. EI benefits are projected to remain high in 2010–11, at $22.6 billion, as a small decline in unemployment is largely offset by an increase in costs associated with the extension of benefits for long-tenured workers. EI benefits are projected to decline by 13.2 per cent in 2011–12, as the level of unemployment declines and as the temporary enhancements under the Economic Action Plan are phased out. EI benefits are projected to decline gradually over the remainder of the projection period.

Children's benefits, including the Canada Child Tax Benefit and the Universal Child Care Benefit, are projected to increase moderately over the forecast horizon, largely reflecting increases to the National Child Benefit supplement and Canada Child Tax Benefit related to Budget 2009 measures and projected temporary reductions in personal income.

Major transfers to other levels of government include transfers in support of health and social programs as well as Equalization. Transfers are projected to grow at current legislated rates over the forecast period. Also included in major transfers are amounts for transitional assistance for the provinces of Ontario and British Columbia, related to their respective decisions to adopt the Harmonized Sales Tax framework.

Direct program expenses include operating expenses for National Defence and other departments, transfers administered by departments for farm income support, natural resource royalties paid to provinces, student financial assistance and expenses of Crown corporations. The projected growth in direct program expenses reflects the impact of past budget measures, as well as initiatives announced in Budget 2010.

Within direct program expenses, transfers administered by departments are projected to decline over the projection period. This reflects the expiration of Economic Action Plan measures and changes to the International Assistance Envelope proposed in this budget.

Expenses for capital projects are not being constrained in this budget. Amounts for capital expenses are presented on an accrual basis. The Government will carefully manage capital expenses and capital assets. However, in general and as a matter of principle, the Government will not run down the stock of capital assets to eliminate the deficit, as this only results in deferring spending to future years.

Other direct program expenses include costs for employee pensions and other benefits, non-wage expenses of National Defence and accrual amounts for items such as the allowance for bad debt. Employee pension and other benefits are not subject to the general operating budget freeze. However, as noted above, the Government will continue to examine ways in which these costs can be better managed and will engage with public sector bargaining agents to ensure that total costs of compensation are reasonable. The National Defence budget is being adjusted as described above.

As described earlier in this chapter, operating budgets of departments and Crown corporations, as appropriated by Parliament, are being adjusted in 2010–11 and then frozen at 2010–11 levels for both 2011–12 and 2012–13. The budgetary impact of the operating budget freeze is shown in Table 4.1.1.

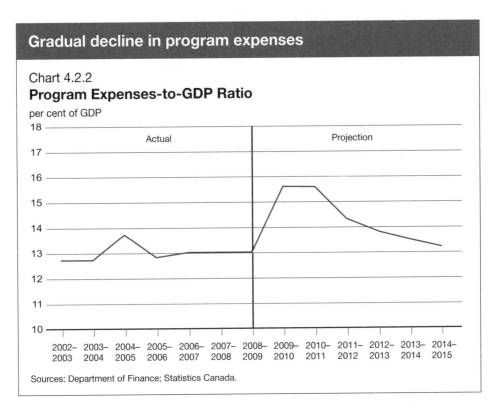

Gradual decline in program expenses

Chart 4.2.2
Program Expenses-to-GDP Ratio
per cent of GDP

Sources: Department of Finance; Statistics Canada.

Chart 4.2.2 shows program expenses as a share of GDP. The Economic Action Plan will strengthen Canada's economy and support Canadians, and will result in a temporary increase in the program expenses-to-GDP ratio.

The Government remains committed to focused and disciplined spending, and will ensure that spending as a share of GDP, after 2010–11, declines over the medium term. As a result of the actions taken in this budget, average annual growth in direct program spending after the expiry of the Economic Action Plan will slow to 1.3 per cent.

In 2014–15, the program expenses-to-GDP ratio is projected to fall to about 13 per cent. This would bring the program spending ratio in line with spending ratios in the 2006–07 to 2008–09 period. Achieving this would also be consistent with the Government's commitment in *Advantage Canada* to keep the rate of growth in program spending, on average, below the rate of growth in the economy.

Financial Source/Requirement

The budgetary balance is presented on a full accrual basis of accounting, recording government liabilities and assets when they are incurred or acquired, regardless of when the cash is paid or received.

In contrast, the financial source/requirement measures the difference between cash coming in to the Government and cash going out. This measure is affected not only by the budgetary balance but also by the Government's non-budgetary transactions. These include changes in federal employee pension accounts; changes in non-financial assets; investing activities through loans, investments and advances; changes in other financial assets and liabilities; and foreign exchange activities.

Table 4.2.6

The Budgetary Balance, Non-Budgetary Transactions and Financial Source/Requirement

	Projection						
	2008–2009	2009–2010	2010–2011	2011–2012	2012–2013	2013–2014	2014–2015
	(billions of dollars)						
Budgetary balance	-5.8	-53.8	-49.2	-27.6	-17.5	-8.5	-1.8
Non-budgetary transactions							
Pensions and other accounts	5.0	5.6	5.6	5.4	5.0	4.7	4.5
Non-financial assets	-2.9	-3.3	-3.6	-3.3	-3.3	-3.1	-2.8
Loans, investments and advances							
Enterprise Crown corporations	-20.0	-28.3	-6.3	-5.4	-3.7	-5.6	-5.9
Insured Mortgage Purchase Program	-54.2	-9.0	4.5	3.3	2.4	40.2	12.8
Other	-0.3	3.7	-0.7	-0.5	-0.4	-0.3	-0.3
Total	-74.5	-33.6	-2.6	-2.7	-1.7	34.3	6.6
Other transactions	-11.9	14.0	5.2	5.2	3.9	6.7	3.2
Total	-84.3	-17.3	4.6	4.6	3.9	42.6	11.5
Financial source/ requirement	**-90.1**	**-71.1**	**-44.6**	**-23.0**	**-13.6**	**34.1**	**9.7**

Note: Totals may not add due to rounding.

As shown in Table 4.2.6, significant financial requirements are projected from 2009–10 to 2012–13 ($71.1 billion in 2009–10, $44.6 billion in 2010–11, $23.0 billion in 2011–12 and $13.6 billion in 2012–13), followed by financial sources of $34.1 billion in 2013–14 and $9.7 billion in 2014–15. The requirements mainly reflect the budgetary balance. Financial requirements also arise because of direct lending to certain Crown corporations and government initiatives to support access to financing under the Extraordinary Financing Framework.

The large increase in market debt associated with the Insured Mortgage Purchase Program does not affect federal debt or the federal government's net debt as the borrowings are offset by an increase in revenue-earning assets. Other borrowings undertaken to strengthen the financial system are also offset by interest-earning assets.

The financial source associated with pensions and other accounts is expected to be $5.6 billion in 2009–10. Pensions and other accounts include the activities of the Government of Canada's employee superannuation plans, as well as those of federally appointed judges and Members of Parliament. Since April 2000, the net amount of contributions less benefit payments related to post-March 2000 service has been invested in capital markets. Contributions and payments pertaining to pre-April 2000 service are recorded in the pension accounts. The Government also sponsors a variety of future benefit plans, such as health care and dental plans and disability and other benefits for war veterans and others.

Financial requirements for non-financial assets include the cash outlay for the acquisition of new tangible capital assets, proceeds from the net losses or gains of tangible capital assets, the amortization of existing tangible assets, losses on the disposal of tangible capital assets, the change in inventories, and prepaid expenses. In the calculation of the budgetary balance, the acquisition of new capital assets is not included; only the amortization of existing tangible assets is included. In the calculation of the financial source/requirement, this is reversed. A net cash requirement of $3.3 billion is estimated for 2009–10.

Loans, investments and advances include the Government's investments in enterprise Crown corporations, such as Canada Mortgage and Housing Corporation (CMHC), Canada Post Corporation, Export Development Canada and the Business Development Bank of Canada (BDC). They also include loans, investments and advances to national and provincial governments and international organizations, and for government programs. The requirements projected from 2009–10 to 2012–13 under this category are the result of the Government's decision to purchase mortgages under the Insured Mortgage Purchase Program of CMHC. The increase in loans also reflects the Government's commitment to meet all the borrowing needs of CMHC, BDC and Farm Credit Canada through direct lending in order to reduce overall borrowing costs and support a well-functioning Government of Canada securities market.

Risks to the Fiscal Projections

Risks associated with the fiscal projections primarily relate to risks to the Canadian economic outlook and volatility in the relationship between fiscal variables and the underlying economic activity to which they relate.

Tables illustrating the sensitivity of the budget balance to a number of economic shocks are provided later in this chapter. These tables are generalized rules of thumb that provide a guide to the impact of changes in economic assumptions on the fiscal projections. Even if the economic outlook were known with certainty, there would still be risks associated with the fiscal projections because of the uncertainty in the translation of economic developments into spending and tax revenues. The following are the key sources of uncertainty:

- The corporate income tax projections in this chapter assume a sharp rise in corporate losses. The income tax system allows corporations to use certain losses to reduce taxable income in the 3 preceding years or the 20 following years. As a result, there is considerable uncertainty around the timing of the application of these losses, in addition to uncertainty as to the size of the losses.

- There is considerable uncertainty around the timing of the recovery in markets following the sharp decline in the S&P/TSX Composite Index over the latter months of 2008 and early 2009. In addition, there is significant uncertainty as to how these fluctuations in the market will affect market-related income and, in turn, personal and corporate income tax revenues.

- On the expense side, the extent to which departments and agencies do not fully use all of the resources appropriated by Parliament varies from year to year and can materially affect the fiscal outcome. In addition, during the course of the fiscal year, departments and agencies often incur liabilities for which no payments are made. These liabilities are recognized throughout the year and are updated following the close of the fiscal year as part of the normal year-end accrual adjustments. Changes in estimates of liabilities can be significant.

Sensitivity of the Budget Balance to Economic Shocks

Changes in economic assumptions affect the projections for revenues and expenses. The following tables illustrate the sensitivity of the budgetary balance to a number of economic shocks:

- A one-year, 1-percentage-point decrease in real GDP growth driven equally by lower productivity and employment growth.

- A decrease in nominal GDP growth resulting solely from a one-year, 1-percentage-point decrease in the rate of GDP inflation.

- A sustained 100-basis-point increase in all interest rates.

These sensitivities are generalized rules of thumb that assume any decrease in economic activity is proportional across income and expenditure components.

Table 4.2.7

Estimated Impact of a One-Year, 1-Percentage-Point Decrease in Real GDP Growth on Federal Revenues, Expenses and Budgetary Balance

	Year 1	Year 2	Year 5
	(billions of dollars)		
Federal revenues			
Tax revenues			
Personal income tax	-1.7	-1.8	-2.2
Corporate income tax	-0.3	-0.4	-0.4
Goods and Services Tax	-0.3	-0.3	-0.4
Other	-0.2	-0.2	-0.3
Total tax revenues	-2.5	-2.7	-3.3
Employment Insurance premiums	-0.1	-0.2	-0.3
Other revenues	0.0	0.0	0.0
Total budgetary revenues	-2.6	-2.9	-3.6
Federal expenses			
Major transfers to persons			
Elderly benefits	0.0	0.0	0.0
Employment Insurance benefits	0.6	0.6	0.7
Children's benefits	0.0	0.0	0.0
Total	0.6	0.6	0.7

Table 4.2.7 *(cont'd)*

Estimated Impact of a One-Year, 1-Percentage-Point Decrease in Real GDP Growth on Federal Revenues, Expenses and Budgetary Balance

	Year 1	Year 2	Year 5
	(billions of dollars)		
Other program expenses	-0.2	-0.2	-0.4
Public debt charges	0.0	0.1	0.5
Total expenses	0.5	0.5	0.8
Budgetary balance	**-3.1**	**-3.4**	**-4.4**

Note: Numbers may not add due to rounding.

A 1-percentage-point decrease in real GDP growth reduces the budgetary balance by $3.1 billion in the first year, $3.4 billion in the second year and $4.4 billion in the fifth year.

- Tax revenues from all sources fall by a total of $2.5 billion in the first year, $2.7 billion in the second year and $3.3 billion in the fifth year. Personal income tax revenues decrease as employment and wages and salaries fall. Corporate income tax revenues fall as output and profits decrease. GST revenues decrease as a result of lower consumer spending associated with the fall in employment and personal income.

- EI premiums decrease as employment and wages and salaries fall.

- Expenses rise, mainly reflecting higher EI benefits (due to an increase in the number of unemployed) and higher public debt charges (reflecting a higher stock of debt due to the lower budgetary balance).

Table 4.2.8

Estimated Impact of a One-Year, 1-Percentage-Point Decrease in GDP Inflation on Federal Revenues, Expenses and Budgetary Balance

	Year 1	Year 2	Year 5
	(billions of dollars)		
Federal revenues			
Tax revenues			
Personal income tax	-1.7	-1.4	-1.5
Corporate income tax	-0.3	-0.4	-0.4
Goods and Services Tax	-0.3	-0.3	-0.4
Other	-0.2	-0.2	-0.3
Total tax revenues	-2.5	-2.3	-2.6
Employment Insurance premiums	-0.1	-0.2	-0.3
Other revenues	-0.1	-0.1	-0.1
Total budgetary revenues	-2.6	-2.5	-2.9
Federal expenses			
Major transfers to persons			
Elderly benefits	-0.2	-0.4	-0.5
Employment Insurance benefits	-0.1	-0.1	-0.1
Children's benefits	-0.1	-0.1	-0.1
Total	-0.4	-0.6	-0.7
Other program expenses	-0.4	-0.4	-0.8
Public debt charges	-0.3	0.0	0.2
Total expenses	-1.1	-0.9	-1.3
Budgetary balance	**-1.6**	**-1.5**	**-1.6**

Note: Numbers may not add due to rounding.

A 1-percentage-point decrease in nominal GDP growth resulting solely from lower GDP inflation (assuming that the Consumer Price Index moves in line with GDP inflation) lowers the budgetary balance by $1.6 billion in the first year, $1.5 billion in the second year and $1.6 billion in the fifth year.

- Lower prices result in lower nominal income and, as a result, personal income tax, corporate income tax and GST revenues all decrease, reflecting declines in the underlying nominal tax bases. For the other sources of tax revenue, the negative impacts are similar under the real and nominal GDP shocks. EI premium revenues decrease marginally in the price shock in response to lower earnings. However, unlike the real GDP shock, EI benefits do not rise since unemployment is unaffected by price changes.

- Partly offsetting lower revenues are the declines in the cost of statutory programs that are indexed to inflation, such as elderly benefit payments and the Canada Child Tax Benefit, as well as federal wage and non-wage expenses. Payments under these programs are smaller if inflation is lower. Public debt charges decline in the first year due to lower costs associated with Real Return Bonds, then rise due to the higher stock of debt.

Table 4.2.9

**Estimated Impact of a Sustained 100-Basis Point Increase
in All Interest Rates on Federal Revenues,
Expenses and Budgetary Balance**

	Year 1	Year 2	Year 5
	(billions of dollars)		
Federal revenues	0.9	1.1	1.4
Federal expenses	1.9	3.1	4.4
Budgetary balance	**-1.0**	**-2.1**	**-3.0**

An increase in interest rates decreases the budgetary balance by $1.0 billion
in the first year, $2.1 billion in the second year and $3.0 billion in the
fifth year. The decline stems entirely from increased expenses associated
with public debt charges. The impact on debt charges rises through time
as longer-term debt matures and is refinanced at higher rates. The impact
on debt charges also rises due to the higher stock of debt. Moderating
the overall impact is an increase in revenues associated with the increase in
the rate of return on the Government's interest-bearing assets, which are
recorded as part of non-tax revenues. The lower sensitivity to interest rates
of expenses and revenues relative to previous estimates reflects decreased
borrowing and returns on investments related to the Government's
Extraordinary Financing Framework initiatives, notably the Insured
Mortgage Purchase Program. The greater sensitivity of the budgetary
balance to interest rates reflects the larger budgetary deficit.

Chapter **5**

Canada's Economic Action Plan:
A Fifth Report to Canadians

Highlights

✓ Canada's Economic Action Plan is delivering a $62-billion shot in the arm to the economy.

✓ By the end of this month, most of the $37 billion in planned 2009–10 federal and provincial/territorial stimulus will have flowed into the economy.

✓ Since July 2009, over 135,000 jobs have been created across the country.

✓ For 2010–11, the Action Plan will deliver a further $19 billion in federal stimulus spending, complemented by $6 billion in stimulus funding from provinces, territories, municipalities and other partners.

✓ 92 per cent of 2010–11 funding has been committed.

✓ The Government has commitments in place for almost 16,000 projects across the country under the Economic Action Plan. Over 12,000 of these projects have begun or have been completed.

✓ Canadians are benefiting from permanent tax relief. As well, millions of Canadian families took advantage of the temporary Home Renovation Tax Credit.

✓ Due to unprecedented demand under the ecoENERGY Retrofit – Homes program, the Government is allocating a further $80 million to support additional retrofits by Canadian homeowners. In total, the Government has provided $585 million to the program under the Economic Action Plan.

✓ The Government is providing exceptional support for the unemployed, with total Employment Insurance (EI) payments up by more than $6 billion from last year. Enhancements to EI are flowing and continue to be available.

✓ The Government has committed all of the funding available for projects under the $4-billion Infrastructure Stimulus Fund.

✓ Almost all of the $500 million available under the Recreational Infrastructure Canada program has been committed to almost 2,000 projects across the country to build and upgrade hockey arenas, soccer fields, swimming pools and other community-based recreational facilities. Over 1,500 projects are already underway or completed.

✓ Over 3,500 projects are underway to improve social housing and First Nations housing across the country.

✓ Under the Knowledge Infrastructure Program, work has begun on 361 projects and an additional 20 projects have been completed.

Overview

Canada's Economic Action Plan has helped Canadians through the worst global recession since the 1930s and is now contributing to an economic recovery. While a global recovery is now underway, it remains fragile. At home, too many Canadians remain out of work. For these reasons, the Government will complete the implementation of the Economic Action Plan.

At their recent meeting in Iqaluit, Nunavut, Group of Seven (G7) finance ministers and central bank governors were in broad agreement on the need for continued stimulus spending. The International Monetary Fund (IMF) also recently stressed the importance of fully implementing stimulus plans.

> *We need to continue to deliver the stimulus to which we are mutually committed and begin to look ahead to exit strategies and move to a more sustainable fiscal track, consistent with continued recovery.*
>
> — G7 Chair's Summary, The Honourable Jim Flaherty, Minister of Finance,
> G7 Meeting of Finance Ministers and Central Bank Governors,
> Iqaluit, Nunavut, February 6, 2010
>
> *Due to the still-fragile nature of the recovery, fiscal policies need to remain supportive of economic activity in the near term. The fiscal stimulus planned for 2010 should be fully implemented.*
>
> — IMF, *World Economic Outlook Update*, January 2010

For 2010–11, the Economic Action Plan will provide $19 billion in federal stimulus spending. This funding will be complemented by a further $6 billion in stimulus by provinces, territories, municipalities and other partners. In total, over $25 billion in stimulus will be provided to Canadians next year under the Action Plan.

Just as it is important to complete the implementation of the Action Plan to protect jobs and secure the recovery, it is equally important that the stimulus wind down as planned, in order to ensure that the federal government's fiscal position is sustainable and that the budget is returned to balance. The Home Renovation Tax Credit, which ended as scheduled on January 31, 2010, is one example of a stimulus measure that has benefited millions of Canadian families. This approach underscores the Government's fundamental belief that the private sector is the engine of growth and wealth creation. The role of government is to provide the infrastructure, programs and services for a prosperous economy and society at levels of taxation that are competitive and sustainable for the long term.

Canada's Economic Action Plan

Canada's Economic Action Plan continues to be timely and effective. The Action Plan protects Canadian jobs and incomes by delivering a $62-billion shot in the arm to the economy (Table 5.1). Taxes have been reduced, EI benefits have been extended for the unemployed, thousands of infrastructure projects are underway across the country, significant support has been provided for science and technology, industries and communities, and extraordinary actions have been taken to improve access to financing. The Economic Action Plan is an investment in jobs now and in our future prosperity. The Action Plan is:

- **Reducing the Tax Burden for Canadians**: Providing Canadians with significant, permanent personal income tax relief and Canadian businesses with the lowest overall tax rate on new business investment among the major industrialized economies.

- **Helping the Unemployed**: Providing more resources for EI benefits to support those who have lost their jobs and providing the training required to help Canadians get the additional skills they need for the jobs of tomorrow and to get back to work. This includes providing additional benefits to long-tenured workers. The Government has also enacted measures to provide additional support for the self-employed.

- **Building Infrastructure to Create Jobs**: Providing new infrastructure and housing funding to create jobs across Canada and ensure Canada emerges from the economic downturn with a more modern and greener infrastructure, as well as an expanded capacity to provide affordable housing to lower-income Canadians. These projects are moving forward and benefiting workers and the economy across the country.

- **Creating the Economy of Tomorrow**: Improving infrastructure at colleges, universities, federal laboratories and research facilities, introducing additional support for graduate students and internships, and supporting research and technology leadership in Canada.

- **Supporting Industries and Communities**: Supporting local economies and protecting jobs in regions, communities and sectors that have been most affected by the economic downturn.

- **Improving Access to Financing and Strengthening Canada's Financial System**: Ensuring the continued stability of the Canadian financial system and improving access to financing for Canadian households and businesses.

Table 5.1

Canada's Economic Action Plan

	2009–10	2010–11	Total
	(millions of dollars—cash basis)		
Reducing the Tax Burden for Canadians	3,020	3,180	6,200
Helping the Unemployed	2,852	4,167	7,019
Building Infrastructure to Create Jobs	8,312	7,696	16,007
Creating the Economy of Tomorrow	2,139	1,880	4,018
Supporting Industries and Communities	11,768	2,231	13,998
Total federal stimulus measures	**28,090**	**19,152**	**47,242**
Assumed provincial and territorial actions	8,441	5,978	14,419
Total Economic Action Plan stimulus	**36,531**	**25,131**	**61,661**

Notes: Totals may not add due to rounding. This table reflects adjustments to infrastructure and other funding as described later in this chapter.

Managing the Economic Action Plan

The Government is actively managing the implementation of the Economic Action Plan to ensure that Canadians benefit from the Plan now, when they need it most. Toward this end, and to help Canadians make their homes more energy efficient, the Government is allocating a further $80 million to finance up to 60,000 additional retrofits under the ecoENERGY Retrofit – Homes program. This is in addition to the $205 million provided through the Clean Energy Fund, which was announced in the December 2009 Fourth Report to Canadians. In total, the Economic Action Plan has provided $585 million for energy-saving home retrofits.

Timely Implementation

The implementation of Canada's Economic Action Plan is on track. Virtually all of the 2009–10 funding for the Economic Action Plan is committed and is expected to be spent in that fiscal year—an estimated $28 billion in federal stimulus for the Canadian economy.

Thirty days before the start of the 2010–11 fiscal year, 92 per cent of 2010–11 funding has been committed (Table 5.2). As a result, significant support has been and will continue to be provided to Canadians.

Table 5.2

Progress in Implementing the Economic Action Plan

	2009–10		2010–11	
	Stimulus Value	Stimulus Committed	Stimulus Value	Stimulus Committed
	(billions of dollars)	(per cent)	(billions of dollars)	(per cent)
Reducing the Tax Burden for Canadians	3.0	100	3.2	100
Helping the Unemployed	2.9	100	4.2	100
Building Infrastructure to Create Jobs	8.3	100	7.7	92
Creating the Economy of Tomorrow	2.1	100	1.9	85
Supporting Industries and Communities	11.8	99	2.2	67
Total—Federal Support	**28.1**	**100**	**19.2**	**92**

Notes: Figures are presented on a cash basis. Totals may not add due to rounding.

Over the past year, a great deal has been achieved. Elements of the Economic Action Plan that are directly controlled by the federal government are either already in place or on track to be rolled out in 2010–11. For example:

• Enhanced EI benefits are flowing and continue to be available.

• Many federal infrastructure projects have begun, with a number of projects completed. Work on many projects will continue in 2010–11.

• The Working Income Tax Benefit is fully implemented. Canadians will be able to benefit from it when they file their 2009 income tax returns.

• The Home Renovation Tax Credit (HRTC) has benefited millions of Canadian families, who will be able to claim the credit on their 2009 income tax returns. The HRTC ended as scheduled on January 31, 2010.

The Government has also secured agreements over the past year to enable provinces, territories, municipalities and private sector partners to implement measures for 2009–10 and 2010–11 that are a shared responsibility. Provincial and territorial governments are delivering:

- Enhanced EI training programs.

- Enhanced training for workers who are not eligible for EI. These programs are underway.

- Significant infrastructure and social housing spending.

Economic Action Plan funds have been committed to almost 16,000 projects across the country, of which over 12,000 have begun or have been completed. Projects underway or completed include:

- Close to 4,800 provincial, territorial and municipal infrastructure projects, including over 1,500 Recreational Infrastructure Canada projects and about 1,000 accelerated Building Canada projects.

- 1,270 projects to renovate and repair federal buildings.

- Over 200 projects to enhance the accessibility of Crown-owned buildings for persons with disabilities.

- 381 projects to improve infrastructure at colleges and universities across the country.

- 170 projects to modernize federal laboratories.

- Over 3,500 social housing and First Nations housing projects which are underway.

- 242 projects to improve small craft harbours.

- Over 1,000 projects to assist communities hardest hit by the recession through the Community Adjustment Fund.

- 96 cultural infrastructure projects.

- More than 130 projects to upgrade facilities at National Parks and National Historic Sites.

- 58 First Nations infrastructure projects.

The Government has made considerable progress in implementing the Economic Action Plan. One objective of the Action Plan was to create or maintain 220,000 jobs by the end of 2010. The Action Plan is on track. In the first year of implementation, an estimated 130,000 jobs have been created or maintained as a result of the Economic Action Plan.

In addition, over 160,000 Canadians are benefiting from the work-sharing program. Overall this has contributed to the net creation of over 135,000 jobs recorded in Canada since July 2009. Annex 1 provides a review of the economic impact of the Action Plan to date.

Reducing the Tax Burden for Canadians

The tax reductions in Canada's Economic Action Plan are an essential part of the Government's effort to stimulate the economy and to create or maintain jobs. Lower taxes help ease the financial pressure on individuals, families and businesses and help build a solid foundation for future economic growth. Lower taxes also stimulate individual spending, which helps to protect and create jobs. The tax reductions in the Action Plan reinforce the Government's ambitious agenda of tax relief aimed at creating a tax system that improves standards of living and fuels job creation and investment in Canada.

The Government took early significant action in the October 2007 Economic Statement, anticipating the prospect of a weaker global economy. It put in place broad-based permanent tax reductions that are sustainable for the future. As a result of these actions, Canada is better positioned than most countries to withstand the effects of today's global economic challenges.

Actions taken by the Government since 2006, including those in the Economic Action Plan, will reduce taxes on individuals, families and businesses by an estimated $220 billion over 2008–09 and the following five fiscal years. Of this amount, the tax relief in the Economic Action Plan totals more than $20 billion.

Table 5.3

Economic Action Plan Measures to Reduce the Tax Burden for Canadians

	2008–09	2009–10	2010–11	Total
	(millions of dollars)			
Personal income tax relief for all taxpayers	470	1,885	1,950	4,305
Increases to the National Child Benefit supplement and the Canada Child Tax Benefit		230	310	540
Enhancing the Working Income Tax Benefit	145	580	580	1,305
Targeted relief for seniors	80	325	340	745
Total—accrual and cash value	**695**	**3,020**	**3,180**	**6,895**

Notes: Totals may not add due to rounding. The Canada Child Tax Benefit and the National Child Benefit supplement are considered expenditures for budgetary purposes and thus should not be included in calculations of total tax relief.

Tax Relief for Individuals and Families

The Economic Action Plan introduced significant new personal income tax reductions that have provided relief, particularly for low- and middle-income Canadians, as well as measures to help Canadians purchase and improve their homes. For example:

- The amount of income that Canadians can earn before paying federal income tax was further increased, and the top of the two lowest income tax brackets was increased so that Canadians can earn more income before being subject to higher tax rates.

- The Working Income Tax Benefit, first introduced in Budget 2007, has been effectively doubled. This enhancement lowers the "welfare wall" by further strengthening work incentives for low-income Canadians already in the workforce and encouraging other low-income Canadians to enter the workforce.

- The level at which the National Child Benefit supplement for low-income families is fully phased out and the level at which the Canada Child Tax Benefit begins to be phased out have been raised, providing a benefit of up to $436 per year for a family with two children. Additional monthly benefits under these programs began to be paid to families with children in July 2009.

- The Age Credit amount was increased by $1,000 to provide tax relief to low- and middle-income seniors. This means additional annual tax savings of up to $150 per year for low-income seniors.

- To assist first-time home buyers, Canada's Economic Action Plan provided a tax credit of up to $750 as well as additional access to their Registered Retirement Savings Plan savings to purchase or build a home.

Tax relief for individuals and families announced in Canada's Economic Action Plan is now fully implemented, and Canadians are realizing its benefits.

The Home Renovation Tax Credit provided an estimated 4.6 million Canadian families with up to $1,350 in tax relief on eligible renovation projects. Canadians will be able to claim the credit when they file their 2009 income tax returns.

Actions the Government has taken since 2006 are providing important stimulus to the economy and creating jobs, with almost $160 billion in tax relief for individuals and families over 2008–09 and the following five fiscal years. Key actions include:

- All Canadians—even those who do not earn enough to pay personal income tax—are benefiting from the 2-percentage-point reduction in the Goods and Services Tax (GST) rate. Maintaining the GST Credit level while reducing the GST rate by 2 percentage points translates into more than $1.1 billion in GST Credit benefits annually for low- and modest-income Canadians, making purchases more affordable for these Canadians.

- All taxpayers are benefiting from the reduction in the lowest personal income tax rate to 15 per cent from 16 per cent.

- The Tax-Free Savings Account, introduced in Budget 2008, is improving incentives to save through a flexible, registered general-purpose account that allows Canadians to earn tax-free investment income.

- The Government has also introduced relief measures targeted to help families, students, seniors and pensioners, workers, persons with disabilities, and communities.

Tax Relief for Canadian Businesses

A competitive business tax system is essential for creating an environment that encourages new investment, growth and job creation in Canada. The Economic Action Plan builds on corporate income tax reductions to help position Canadian businesses to weather the effects of the current global economic challenges, maintain and create jobs, and emerge from the economic downturn even stronger. Key measures include:

- To help businesses adopt newer technology at a faster pace, a temporary two-year 100-per-cent capital cost allowance (CCA) rate for computers acquired after January 27, 2009 and before February 1, 2011 was introduced.

- To help businesses in manufacturing and processing industries restructure and retool to position themselves for long-term success, the temporary 50-per-cent straight-line accelerated CCA rate for investments in manufacturing or processing machinery and equipment was extended to include investments undertaken in 2010 and 2011. Manufacturers and processors were already benefiting from this measure, which was first introduced in Budget 2007 and extended in Budget 2008.

- To help small businesses retain more of their earnings for reinvestment, expansion and job creation, the amount of small business income eligible for the reduced federal income tax rate was further increased to $500,000 effective January 1, 2009, following a previous increase to $400,000 from $300,000 as of January 1, 2007.

- To support mineral exploration activity across Canada, the temporary Mineral Exploration Tax Credit was extended to March 31, 2010.

All of the business tax measures in the Economic Action Plan have been fully implemented.

The Government has introduced significant tax relief for Canadian businesses since 2006, including measures in the Economic Action Plan, that total more than $60 billion over 2008–09 and the following five fiscal years. Key actions include:

- Substantial, broad-based tax reductions that are lowering the federal general corporate income tax rate from 22.12 per cent (including the corporate surtax) in 2007 to 15 per cent in 2012. These tax reductions include the elimination of the corporate surtax in 2008 for all corporations and the reduction in the federal general corporate income tax rate to 18 per cent as of January 1, 2010.

- A reduction of the federal income tax rate applying to qualifying small business income to 11 per cent in 2008.

- Alignment of CCA rates for a number of assets to better reflect their useful life—this both reduces the tax burden on investment and ensures neutral tax treatment of different capital assets, encouraging investment to flow to its most productive uses.

- Elimination in 2006 of the federal capital tax, a particularly damaging tax for business investment, and the introduction in 2007 of a temporary financial incentive to encourage provinces to eliminate their general capital taxes and to eliminate or replace their capital taxes on financial institutions with a minimum tax. All provincial general capital taxes will be eliminated by 2012.

Early actions taken by this Government as well as the measures included in Canada's Economic Action Plan are positioning Canadian businesses to emerge stronger and better equipped to compete globally as the economy recovers.

As a result of federal and provincial business tax changes, this year Canada will have an overall tax rate on new business investment[1] that is the lowest in the G7 and below the average of the Organisation for Economic Co-operation and Development (OECD) (Chart 5.1). By 2012, Canada will also have the lowest statutory corporate income tax rate in the G7. The competitiveness of our business tax system encourages new investment in Canada, including direct investment from abroad.

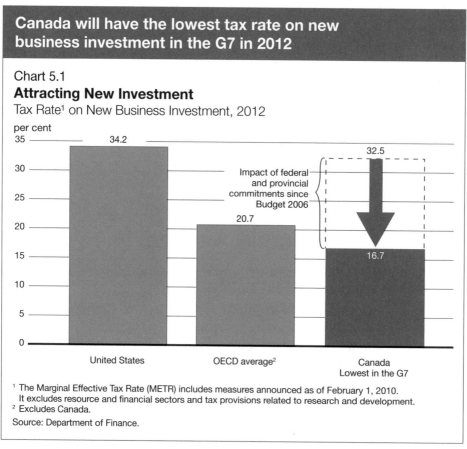

Canada will have the lowest tax rate on new business investment in the G7 in 2012

Chart 5.1
Attracting New Investment
Tax Rate[1] on New Business Investment, 2012

per cent

- United States: 34.2
- OECD average[2]: 20.7
- Canada (Lowest in the G7): 16.7
- 32.5 (Impact of federal and provincial commitments since Budget 2006)

[1] The Marginal Effective Tax Rate (METR) includes measures announced as of February 1, 2010. It excludes resource and financial sectors and tax provisions related to research and development.
[2] Excludes Canada.
Source: Department of Finance.

Improving the competitiveness of the Canadian tax system requires collaboration among all governments to help Canadian businesses compete globally as the economy recovers. Provinces and territories have also taken action to enhance Canada's business tax advantage. These actions are helping Canada build a strong foundation for future economic growth, job creation and higher living standards for Canadians.

---

[1] The marginal effective tax rate (METR) on new business investment takes into account federal, provincial and territorial statutory corporate income tax rates, deductions and credits available in the corporate tax system and other taxes paid by corporations, including provincial capital taxes and retail sales taxes on business inputs. The methodology for calculating METRs is described in the 2005 edition of *Tax Expenditures and Evaluations* (Department of Finance).

Table 5.4

Reducing the Tax Burden for Canadians

	2009–10		2010–11	
	Stimulus Value	Stimulus Committed	Stimulus Value	Stimulus Committed
	(millions of dollars)			
Personal income tax relief for all taxpayers	1,885	1,885	1,950	1,950
Increases to the National Child Benefit supplement and the Canada Child Tax Benefit	230	230	310	310
Enhancing the Working Income Tax Benefit	580	580	580	580
Targeted relief for seniors	325	325	340	340
Total	**3,020**	**3,020**	**3,180**	**3,180**

Reference:

Tax Measures to Support Housing and Business

Home Renovation Tax Credit	3,000	3,000	–	–
Increasing withdrawal limits under the Home Buyers' Plan	15	15	15	15
First-Time Home Buyers' Tax Credit	175	175	180	180
Extending the Mineral Exploration Tax Credit	70	70	-15	-15
Increase in the income limit for the small business tax rate	45	45	80	80
Temporary 100-per-cent capital cost allowance rate for computers	340	340	355	355
Temporary accelerated capital cost allowance rate for manufacturing or processing machinery and equipment[1]	–	–	–	–

[1] Businesses will benefit from the extension of this measure, first introduced in Budget 2007 and extended in Budget 2008, starting in 2011–12.

Helping the Unemployed

Canadians have felt the impacts of the global economic slowdown. Canada's Economic Action Plan includes $7 billion over two years to support those workers most affected and help them access opportunities through skills development and training. The Government has delivered over $2.9 billion in support for the unemployed in 2009–10 and will provide a further $4 billion in 2010–11.

Table 5.5

Helping the Unemployed

	2009–10	2010–11	Total
	(millions of dollars)		
Strengthening benefits for Canadian workers	1,115	1,550	2,665
Enhancing the availability of training	919	986	1,905
Maintaining low Employment Insurance premium rates	818	1,631	2,449
Total—accrual and cash value	**2,852**	**4,167**	**7,019**

Note: Totals may not add due to rounding.

Over the course of the recession, the Employment Insurance (EI) program has provided Canadians with needed temporary support. Total EI expenditures are expected to be $6 billion higher in both 2009–10 and 2010–11 than they were last year (Chart 5.2).

The EI premium rate will remain at $1.73 per $100 in insurable earnings in 2010, the lowest level since 1982. This represents projected relief of $11.1 billion over 2009 and 2010 for Canadian workers and their employers relative to what would have been the case had rates been set at the break-even level over these two years. This fiscal cost excludes the additional $2.9 billion for enhanced EI benefits and training announced in Budget 2009.

When the temporary freeze of EI premiums is lifted in 2011, premium rates will be set by an independent arms's length Crown corporation, the Canada Employment Insurance Financing Board (CEIFB). Under the EI financing regime announced in Budget 2008, the CEIFB will set EI premium rates in order to balance the EI program over time, subject to a 15-cent limit on annual changes. Consistent with the Government's commitment in Budget 2009, the CEIFB will not be mandated to recover any EI deficits resulting from the benefit and training enhancements announced in Budget 2009.

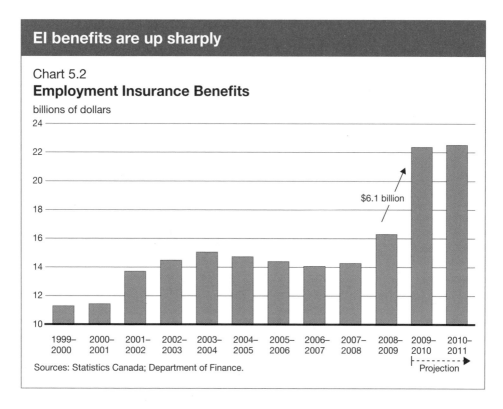

EI benefits are up sharply

Chart 5.2
Employment Insurance Benefits

billions of dollars

$6.1 billion

Sources: Statistics Canada; Department of Finance.

Projection

Canada's Economic Action Plan took immediate and decisive action to protect jobs and help Canadians directly affected by the global recession. At the same time, the Government has maintained a focus on the economy of the future by contributing to the development of a skilled, flexible and knowledgeable workforce. These initiatives will continue to support jobs and training through 2010–11:

- An extra five weeks of EI benefits have already been provided to over 512,583 EI claimants. This extension of benefits will remain available to workers making EI claims up to September 11, 2010.

- More than 8,445 long-tenured workers are receiving additional benefits in order to participate in long-term training. The intake for workers participating in this program will continue until May 29, 2010. In addition, the Government has provided further assistance to more than 500,000 long-tenured workers by making between 5 to 20 weeks of additional benefits available to those who have paid into EI for years.

- In January 2010, over 160,000 Canadians were participating in approximately 5,900 work-sharing agreements (Chart 5.3).

- Payments have been made to more than 15,000 claimants under the Wage Earner Protection Program.

- The Government has responded to the needs of Canada's self-employed workers by providing on a voluntary basis EI special benefits, including maternity, parental, sickness and compassionate care benefits, to the self-employed. The self-employed can now register for the EI program to gain access to these benefits.

- The Government provided $750 million to the provinces and territories in 2009–10 in support of training and skills development programs, benefiting more than 122,000 Canadians, and will provide a further $750 million in 2010–11.

- It is expected that current projects under the enhanced Targeted Initiative for Older Workers will provide additional support to over 5,400 older workers.

- Over 3,500 summer jobs were created as a result of additional support provided to the Canada Summer Jobs Program in 2009–10. A similar number of additional jobs are expected to be created this summer.

- Training and skills development support will be provided to more than 11,500 Aboriginal Canadians through Aboriginal Skills and Employment Partnerships and the Aboriginal Skills and Training Strategic Investment Fund.

- Apprenticeship Completion Grants have already been provided to almost 16,000 apprentices who completed their apprenticeship training and obtained their certification in any of the designated Red Seal trades.

- Support is being provided to implement the Pan-Canadian Framework for the Assessment and Recognition of Foreign Qualifications.

- Funding is currently supporting almost 300 youth internships in not-for-profit and community service organizations through the YMCA and YWCA.

The number of Canadian workers benefiting from work-sharing has increased sixfold since the beginning of 2009

Chart 5.3
Canadian Workers Participating in Work-Sharing Agreements

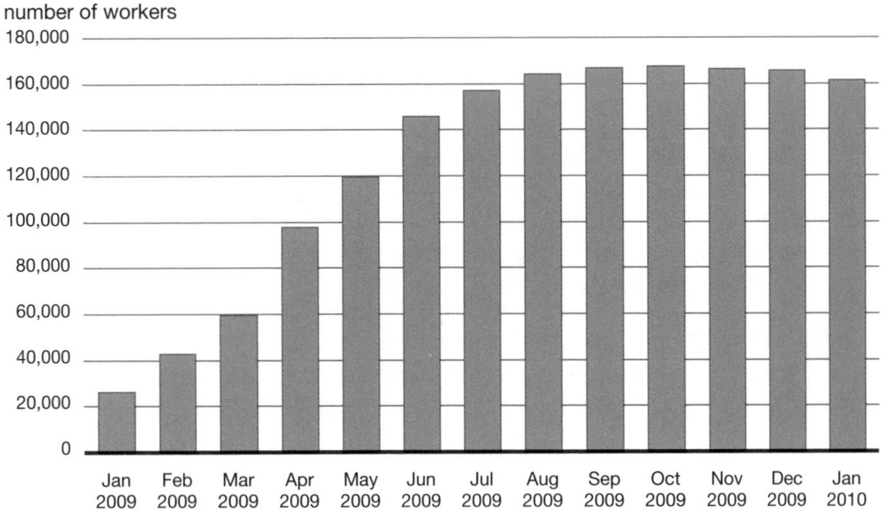

number of workers

Source: Human Resources and Skills Development Canada.

211

Enhanced Work-Sharing

Nova Agri Inc.

Nova Agri Inc. of Centreville, Nova Scotia, farms more than 2,000 acres of rich soil in the Annapolis Valley. This farming organization, consisting of 40 full-time employees and 150 seasonal workers, has experienced some difficult times in the last year due to substantially reduced crop yields during the 2008 growing season. In addition, the global economic downturn added extra strains, as the company began seeing a downward trend in product pricing coupled with rising production costs. Like many businesses, Nova Agri Inc. considered temporary layoffs to reduce costs. However, through open discussions with its employees, the company was presented with an alternative option—the Government of Canada's work-sharing program. Nova Agri Inc.'s work-sharing agreement with 18 participating employees began in January 2009 and ran until June 2009, a shorter time than anticipated. Since the company ended its participation in the program, Nova Agri Inc. is back to normal operations and is doing well.

Through Work-Sharing, we were able to keep our key staff during a tough time. We were able to maintain the integrity of our workforce skills. This allowed us to continue delivering quality products and customer service with complete respect to our employees and customers. I would recommend the program to any company that is experiencing a temporary reduction in business activities.

— Allie Craswell, Director of Supply Chain
Nova Agri Inc.

Northern Uniform Service

Northern Uniform Service, based in Sudbury, Ontario, has been serving the retail and wholesale laundry market in Ontario since 1901 and now meets the uniform rental needs of customers. Staying in business for over 100 years has required both commitment and the ability to adapt to changing times. However, like many other companies in Ontario and across Canada, the downturn in the economy has had a negative impact on Northern Uniform Service's business. Since April 2009, 48 employees from Northern Uniform Service have been benefiting from work-sharing.

We would have had to lay people off. We have been able to avoid layoffs because of this program. It really helped workers. Without the program, they would have had to give up one fifth of their earnings. Now, through the Work-Sharing program, employees get benefits. It's a little less money, but they don't feel like they have to go out and get a five-day job. Replacing a job is just not that easy.

— Paul Stewart, General Manager
Northern Uniform Service

Enhanced Work-Sharing *(cont'd)*

MODUS Modular Structures Inc.
MODUS Modular Structures Inc., located in Swift Current, Saskatchewan, is a leading provider of high-performance modular structures for demanding environments. Deployed in hundreds of locations across Canada, MODUS modular structures have been relied on by schools, telecommunications, and oil and gas industries, to meet their needs in even the most rigorous conditions.

MODUS Modular Structures Inc.'s work-sharing agreement began July 12, 2009 and ended December 14, 2009. It was supposed to be a 52-week agreement—scheduled to end in July 2010, but MODUS was able to end the agreement earlier since they were back up to full production.

When the economic downturn affected our enterprise client, they suspended a 460-unit project which was less than fifty percent completed at the time. Staff reduction resulted as we tried to rectify the contract with our client under strained economic conditions. Work-Sharing allowed us to keep the doors open and keep essential staff. Some staff members continued to seek out new opportunities while others were kept to expand and enhance the re-growth we knew would come. With the change in the economy and by diversifying our customer base, we would need to ramp up production again and keeping employees with key skills was imperative. Keeping 37 people employed allowed us to be ready for new projects and the restart of the previous project. This program also put us in position to rehire many of the staff that were laid off.

We are one of a few organizations in the Swift Current area that incorporated the Work-Sharing agreement into their survival strategy. Work-Sharing has had a vast impact on the community of Swift Current and surrounding area.

— Tanja MacIsaac, Business Manager
MODUS Modular Structures Inc.

Table 5.6

Helping the Unemployed

	2009–10		2010–11	
	Stimulus Value	Stimulus Committed	Stimulus Value	Stimulus Committed
	(millions of dollars)			
An extra five weeks of EI benefits	575	575	575	575
EI—long-tenured workers (Career Transition Assistance Initiative)	250	250	250	250
EI—long-tenured workers (extension of regular benefits)	165	165	600	600
EI—work-sharing	100	100	100	100
Wage Earner Protection Program	25	25	25	25
EI training programs	500	500	500	500
Strategic Training and Transition Fund	250	250	250	250
Canada Summer Jobs Program	10	10	10	10
Federal public service student employment program	10	10	10	10
YMCA-YWCA	15	15	–	–
Targeted Initiative for Older Workers	12	12	28	28
Apprenticeship Completion Grant	40	40	40	40
Foreign Credential Recognition program	20	20	30	30
Aboriginal Skills and Employment Partnerships	12	12	68	68
Aboriginal Skills and Training Strategic Investment Fund	25	25	50	50
Aboriginal Human Resources Development Strategy	25	25	–	–
Keeping Employment Insurance rates frozen for 2010	818	818	1,631	1,631
Total	**2,852**	**2,852**	**4,167**	**4,167**

Building Infrastructure to Create Jobs

Canada's Economic Action Plan provides approximately $16 billion over two years to modernize a broad range of infrastructure including our roads, bridges, public transit, parks and water treatment facilities, and to support home ownership, help stimulate the housing sector and improve housing across Canada. These investments are helping to create and maintain jobs across Canada for the benefit of all Canadians, and will ensure the country emerges from the economic downturn with a more modern and greener infrastructure.

Table 5.7

Building Infrastructure to Create Jobs

	2008–09	2009–10	2010–11	Total
	(millions of dollars)			
Immediate Action to Build Infrastructure				
Investments in provincial, territorial and municipal infrastructure		1,705	4,042	5,747
Investments in First Nations Infrastructure		230	285	515
Investments in federal infrastructure projects		485	265	750
Subtotal—Building Infrastructure		2,421	4,591	7,013
Stimulating Housing Construction				
Support for home ownership and the housing sector	530	2,840	425	3,795
Investments in social housing for Canadians		1,025	1,050	2,075
Subtotal—Stimulating Housing Construction	530	3,865	1,475	5,870
Total—accrual value	530	6,286	6,066	12,883
Total—cash value		8,312	7,696	16,007
Total with provincial contributions—cash value		10,726	12,674	23,400

Notes: Totals may not add due to rounding. The accrual value may be somewhat smaller because some of these expenditures relate to construction and renovation costs of federal assets (for which only depreciation is recorded on a budgetary basis) and loans to third parties (where there is a budgetary impact only in the event that there is a risk of loss).

Infrastructure and housing projects are underway across the country. Virtually all funds earmarked for these investments have been committed. Thousands of infrastructure and housing projects have begun, and more will begin in 2010–11, creating significant new direct employment in the construction and manufacturing industries.

Building Infrastructure

Investments in Provincial, Territorial, and Municipal Infrastructure

Through Canada's Economic Action Plan, the Government has worked closely with each province and territory to greenlight projects and get work underway. In the 2009 and 2010 construction seasons, the Government has committed close to $5.5 billion in stimulus funding towards close to 7,000 projects. This includes all of the funding available for projects under the Infrastructure Stimulus Fund. Provinces, territories, municipalities and other partners are also contributing towards these projects, thereby generating a total investment in public infrastructure of more than $14 billion at a critical time.

To date, work has begun or has been completed on close to 4,150 projects that are worth over $7 billion. As the 2010 construction season gets underway, these totals will continue to grow.

In addition to providing significant new funding for provincial, territorial and municipal infrastructure, the Government has taken steps to expedite approvals for Building Canada initiatives announced in Budget 2007, so that more work gets started in the 2009 and 2010 construction seasons. With accelerated approvals under the Building Canada initiatives, the Government committed a total of more than $10 billion towards 8,032 provincial, territorial and municipal infrastructure projects since the launch of Canada's Economic Action Plan. These investments will extend beyond 2010–11.

Every region of the country is benefiting from investments in various types of provincial, territorial and municipal infrastructure that are being generated thanks to Canada's Economic Action Plan.

Accelerating Existing Provincial, Territorial and Municipal Infrastructure Initiatives under Building Canada

Specific actions taken since January 27, 2009 include:

- Streamlining the process required for securing federal approval of infrastructure projects.

- Announcing over $2.8 billion in federal funding towards close to 100 major projects that are worth more than $9.4 billion. This funding is coming from the Major Infrastructure Component of the Building Canada Fund.

- Fully committing the funding available under the Communities Component of the Building Canada Fund, including the top-up announced in Canada's Economic Action Plan. This represents $1.5 billion in federal funding to support close to 1,400 infrastructure projects in smaller communities (i.e., those with populations of less than 100,000 people). When combined with funding from provinces and municipalities, these projects represent a total investment of $4.6 billion.

- Transferring $689 million to provinces and territories through the Provincial/Territorial Base Funding Initiative. Most provinces and territories agreed to take advantage of this federal offer to accelerate payments and are thus receiving in 2009–10 and will receive in 2010–11 funding that was originally to be provided during the final three years of the initiative (2011–12, 2012–13 and 2013–14).

New Provincial, Territorial and Municipal Infrastructure Initiatives

Infrastructure Stimulus Fund: Working in partnership with provinces, territories and municipalities, the Government has committed all of the funding available for projects under the $4-billion Infrastructure Stimulus Fund. Close to 4,000 projects, representing a total investment of almost $10 billion, are benefiting from assistance from the Infrastructure Stimulus Fund.

More and more projects are getting underway. Based on reporting by provinces and territories, work has started or has been completed on more than 1,700 projects. This includes contracting, engineering, environmental work and construction. Close to 300 projects have been completed.

Canada's Economic Action Plan: Working for Canadians

Examples of Infrastructure Stimulus Fund Projects

British Columbia

The Princeton Regional Library project involves relocating the library into an existing 3,000-square-foot building in the heart of the downtown core, adjacent to the revitalized town square. Work to refurbish the space includes interior and exterior renovations, as well as electrical and mechanical upgrades. Approximately $200,000 in federal funding is being provided to this project.

Alberta

The Government of Canada is providing close to $1 million through the Infrastructure Stimulus Fund to help the Town of Sedgewick replace eight blocks of sewer main, including service lines to the curb and the street-level asphalt. This project, now underway, is expected to cost $3 million.

Saskatchewan

The Morin Creek Tributary Bridge project in Meadow Lake advanced thanks to $133,333 in federal funding from the Infrastructure Stimulus Fund. This $400,000 project, which is now complete, replaced an existing timber bridge with a new concrete bridge. The more modern bridge will increase its carrying capacity and improve trucking efficiency on the provincial road network.

Manitoba

The Western Manitoba Centennial Auditorium in Brandon is one of the city's main cultural venues. Thanks to $250,000 from the Infrastructure Stimulus Fund, the Auditorium is having its lighting system upgraded and the building's entrance replaced. The new entry way will improve access to the building and modernize its overall appearance, while correcting safety concerns associated with the current entrance.

Ontario

The Mount Pleasant Village Mobility Hub in Brampton will facilitate inter-regional connections to the Greater Toronto Area and beyond for commuter rail, bus rapid transit and conventional transit users, as well as pedestrians, cyclists and drivers. The project includes the creation of bus layover areas, shelters and amenities that will encourage and facilitate alternative modes of travel; and the restoration and incorporation of an historic Canadian Pacific Railway station as a cultural feature. This $23-million project is benefiting from $7.7 million in federal funding.

Canada's Economic Action Plan: Working for Canadians

Examples of Infrastructure Stimulus Fund Projects *(cont'd)*

Quebec
Through the Infrastructure Stimulus Fund, the Government of Canada is providing more than $800,000 to refurbish an indoor pool and cultural centre in Beauceville. The cost of this project totals approximately $2.4 million.

New Brunswick
A pavement rehabilitation project on Route 17 (Whites Brook) was completed in September 2009. It will prolong the life of the existing pavement structure and is improving safety. The total cost of the project is approximately $1.84 million and the Government of Canada is contributing $918,000 under the Infrastructure Stimulus Fund.

Nova Scotia
More than $1.15 million from the Infrastructure Stimulus Fund is going towards refurbishing Route 236 in Princeport. The work, now complete, involved 7.9 kilometres of new paving, which will help extend the life of the road and lower maintenance costs for motorists.

Prince Edward Island
The Heritage Park and Gardens project in Summerside will provide a vital pedestrian link along the city's waterfront. Gardens and trees, more walking paths and lighting in Heritage Park are all part of the improvements the Park will offer residents and tourists alike. The project will also extend the boardwalks along the shoreline to enhance biking and walking. More than $300,000 in federal funding is being provided to this project.

Newfoundland and Labrador
The Route 220 project in St. Lawrence included the replacement of the asphalt and ditch work along a section of the road. The work also involved building new culverts, and installing a guide rail and better highway signage. This $2-million project has improved the driving surfaces and is making the roads safer for both drivers and pedestrians. Federal funding of $1 million is being provided to this project.

The Territories
The Nahanni Range Road project in Watson Lake, Yukon, was completed in September 2009, with a contribution of $44,280. This project upgraded the existing road to alleviate safety and secure access concerns for mining properties, as well as the general public.

Infrastructure: Funding Commitments Across Canada

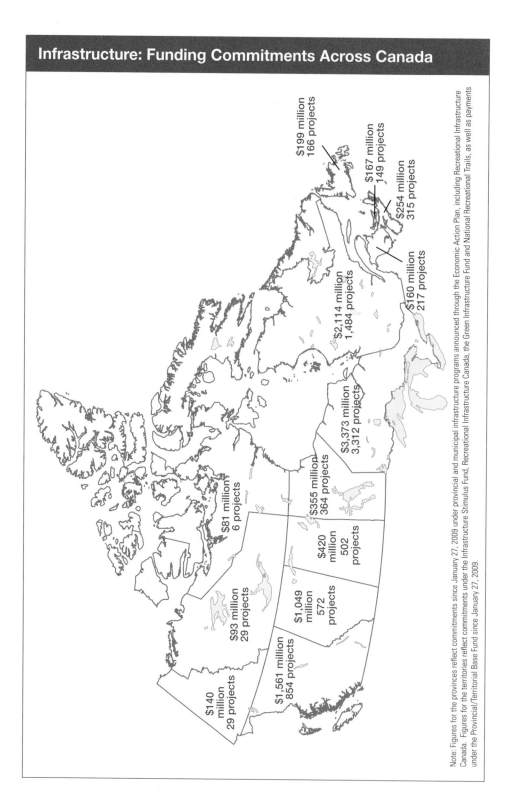

$199 million
166 projects

$167 million
149 projects

$254 million
315 projects

$2,114 million
1,484 projects

$160 million
217 projects

$3,373 million
3,312 projects

$355 million
364 projects

$81 million
6 projects

$420 million
502 projects

$93 million
29 projects

$1,049 million
572 projects

$1,561 million
854 projects

$140 million
29 projects

Note: Figures for the provinces reflect commitments since January 27, 2009 under provincial and municipal infrastructure programs announced through the Economic Action Plan, including Recreational Infrastructure Canada. Figures for the territories reflect commitments under the Infrastructure Stimulus Fund, Recreational Infrastructure Canada, the Green Infrastructure Fund and National Recreational Trails, as well as payments under the Provincial/Territorial Base Fund since January 27, 2009.

Green Infrastructure Fund: More than half of the $1 billion of federal funds available over five years under the Green Infrastructure Fund has been committed and the Government is continuing to evaluate other proposals. Provinces, territories, municipalities and the private sector are also contributing funding towards Green Infrastructure Fund projects, thereby bringing the total investment to more than $1.4 billion. To date, 16 projects have been announced.

Canada's Economic Action Plan: Working for Canadians

Examples of Green Infrastructure Fund Projects

- $71 million for the Mayo B hydro generation facility and Carmacks-Stewart transmission line in the Yukon.

- $130 million for the Northwest Transmission Line in British Columbia.

- $134.3 million to upgrade wastewater treatment in seven Ontario communities, primarily in the Great Lakes and St. Lawrence watershed—Red Rock, Owen Sound, South Dundas, Cornwall, Halton Region, Timmins and Kirkland Lake.

- $170.8 million to improve the treatment of organic waste, reduce landfill waste and generate green energy in Greater Montréal, Rivière-du-Loup and the city of Québec.

- $11 million to support improvements to the existing South End Water Pollution Control Centre in Winnipeg, Manitoba, to deal with wastewater during peak periods (e.g., heavy downpours), and protect the health of the Red River and Lake Winnipeg.

National Recreational Trails: Canada's Economic Action Plan provided $25 million in funding to the National Trails Coalition to help build and renew recreational trails for walking, running, cross-country skiing and biking, as well as snowmobile and all-terrain vehicle trails. The Coalition and its partners committed to at least matching the federal contribution. Approximately 500 projects, with a total value of $60 million, have been selected for funding. Of these projects, 100 have already been completed and work on the remaining projects will be completed by March 31, 2010.

Recreational Infrastructure Canada: Hockey arenas, soccer fields, tennis courts and swimming pools provide Canadians and their families with the benefits of physical activity and community-based experience.

The Economic Action Plan provides $500 million over two years for the Recreational Infrastructure Canada (RInC) program, supporting the construction of new facilities and upgrades to existing ones across the country.

To date, virtually all funding has been committed to almost 2,000 projects across the country, of which over 1,500 projects are already underway or completed, creating significant new economic activity in all parts of Canada.

Canada's Economic Action Plan: Working for Canadians

Examples of Recreational Infrastructure Canada (RInC) Projects

Arena Renovation and Expansion (Lambton, Quebec)
In partnership with the municipality of Lambton and the province of Quebec, the Government of Canada has committed $141,785 out of total project costs of $425,350 to upgrade the Lambton arena.

Baseball Fields (Port Alberni, British Columbia)
The city of Port Alberni will receive $620,000 from the federal government to convert existing sports fields into baseball fields and upgrade related facilities. This $1,865,000 project will create 76 person-months of employment.

Soccer Field Enhancements (Clarenville, Newfoundland and Labrador)
The Town of Clarenville, in partnership with the Clarenville Area Recreation Association and the Clarenville Area Soccer Association, received $50,000 in financial assistance to construct a clubhouse and to develop an oval track around an existing soccer field. This project has created 12 person-months of employment.

Arena Renovations (Point Edward, Ontario)
The village of Point Edward received $1 million in federal funding in support of the renovation of the Point Edward Memorial Arena. The extensive renovation project encompassed electrical, structural and mechanical upgrades including electrical re-wiring; replacement of existing lighting; masonry improvements; roof reinforcement; and accessibility upgrades including the installation of ramps and the addition of washrooms on the building's main level. This project created approximately 100 person-months of employment in construction-related industries.

Public-Private Partnerships (P3s): PPP Canada Inc. successfully completed its first call for project applications to the P3 Fund in October 2009. Twenty applications were received from provincial and territorial governments as well as Indian and Northern Affairs Canada. Six applications were for municipal projects. Projects ranged in size from $45 million to $500 million in capital costs and represented eight different infrastructure sectors.

PPP Canada Inc. will commit over $100 million in 2010 to projects that demonstrate leadership in P3 procurement. The first project announcement will take place in the coming weeks. Further announcements based on Round 1 applications are expected later this spring. PPP Canada Inc. will launch its second call for project applications in mid-2010.

PPP Canada Milestones

October 31, 2009—First call for project applications completed.

February 2010—Projects reviewed and prioritized.

Spring 2010—First project announcements anticipated.

Mid-2010—Second call for project applications.

First Nations Infrastructure

The Government of Canada provides financial support to First Nations to develop and maintain community infrastructure on reserve. This infrastructure is critical for the delivery of basic services to First Nations communities.

The Economic Action Plan provided $515 million over two years to support infrastructure projects in three priority areas: schools, water and wastewater projects, and health and police facilities in First Nations communities. Virtually all of these funds have now been committed, and construction is moving ahead.

Investments in 2009–10 have sparked job creation and economic development on reserve and in remote and rural First Nations communities:

- $81 million invested in 9 school projects underway.

- $70 million invested in 11 water and wastewater projects underway or completed.

- $68 million invested in health service infrastructure, with 24 major projects underway or completed.

- $12 million invested in policing projects, 14 of which are underway or completed.

Canada's Economic Action Plan: Working for Canadians

Investing in Schools and Water Infrastructure

Birch Narrows, Saskatchewan (school): Through the Economic Action Plan, $20 million has been invested to build a new school for the Birch Narrows Dene Nation in Saskatchewan to accommodate future growth of the community. Through this partnership, the Government of Saskatchewan will cover approximately 20 per cent of the total costs, while the First Nation has committed $1 million towards the project.

Construction of this school project is just over 50 per cent complete and has already had a positive impact on the community through employment of local labour.

Dene Tha', Alberta (water and wastewater): $12 million is being invested through the Economic Action Plan to build a new facility. The Dene Tha' First Nation is located 812 kilometres north west of Edmonton. Construction began in August 2009 with completion scheduled for March 2011.

This project is creating economic benefits for local businesses and employment opportunities for First Nation members and Aboriginal-owned companies.

Investing in Critical First Nations Health Infrastructure

Fort Hope Nursing Station: Located in Ontario, this $9.4-million project will expand the existing nursing station, built in 1984, to better meet the needs of the current population. Construction is anticipated to be complete in June 2010.

Fort Chipewyan Health Centre: Located in Alberta, this centre will replace the existing nursing station, which was built in 1981. Construction has begun and is anticipated to be complete in March 2011. The project is valued at $15 million.

God's Lake Narrows Nursing Residence: God's Lake Narrows is located 1,037 kilometres north east of Winnipeg with an on-reserve population of approximately 1,400 residents. The construction of this nursing residence will help recruit and retain nurses working in the community. The project is valued at $695,000. Construction has begun and is anticipated to be complete in February 2011.

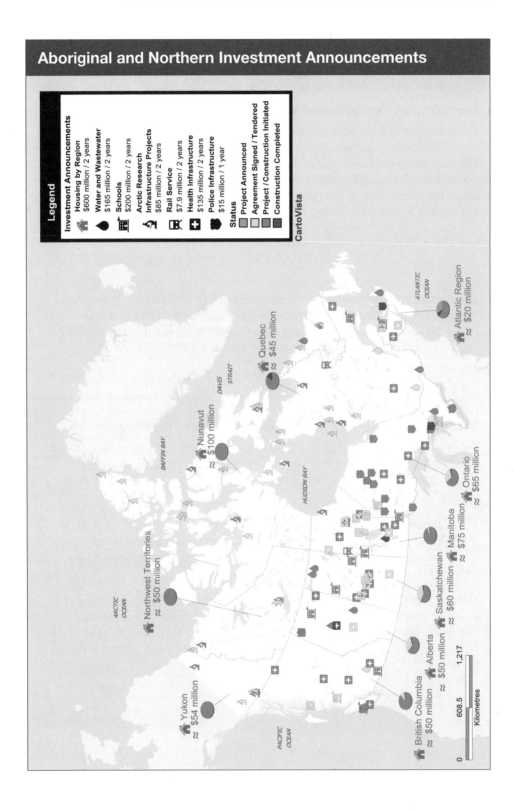

Aboriginal and Northern Investment Announcements

Legend

Investment Announcements

Housing by Region
$600 million / 2 years

Water and Wastewater
$165 million / 2 years

Schools
$200 million / 2 years

Arctic Research
Infrastructure Projects
$85 million / 2 years

Rail Service
$7.9 million / 2 years

Health Infrastructure
$135 million / 2 years

Police Infrastructure
$15 million / 1 year

Status

Project Announced

Agreement Signed / Tendered

Project / Construction Initiated

Construction Completed

CartoVista

Atlantic Region
≈ $20 million

ATLANTIC OCEAN

Quebec
$45 million

DAVIS STRAIT

Nunavut
$100 million

BAFFIN BAY

HUDSON BAY

Ontario
≈ $65 million

Northwest Territories
≈ $50 million

ARCTIC OCEAN

Manitoba
≈ $75 million

Saskatchewan
≈ $60 million

Alberta
≈ $50 million

Yukon
$54 million

British Columbia
≈ $50 million

PACIFIC OCEAN

0   608.5   1,217

Kilometres

Funding to Upgrade and Modernize Federal Infrastructure

Federal infrastructure projects, including faster and more reliable passenger rail services, safer bridges and highways, refurbished harbours for small crafts and more efficient border crossings, are now underway, creating jobs across the country.

VIA Rail: Canada's Economic Action Plan provides funding for a wide range of projects designed to modernize rail passenger services through improvements to infrastructure, locomotives, passenger cars, stations, and related facilities.

The infrastructure upgrades to the Montréal-Toronto line are the single largest project being undertaken by VIA Rail under the Economic Action Plan. This project will provide new segments of third main line track to permit passenger trains to overtake slower moving freight trains. Contractors are working through the winter at Brockville, Gananoque, Marysville, Grafton, Cobourg and Oshawa to prepare the substructure for the new track and bridges.

Canada's Economic Action Plan: Working for Canadians

VIA Rail

Canada's Economic Action Plan funding is being used to upgrade 75 of the passenger cars used on VIA Rail's western transcontinental train. Since their last major rebuilding, these cars have accumulated over one million miles in service between Toronto and Vancouver.

As part of this project, VIA Rail is overhauling the mechanical systems of all 75 passenger cars and refurbishing the interiors of 45 of the 75 passenger cars with new carpets, upholstery and wall coverings. A firm from British Columbia has been hired to paint the interior of the cars while VIA employees undertake the mechanical and refurbishing work.

This project allowed VIA Rail to call back 21 employees who had been laid off and kept an additional 29 employees at work. A total of approximately 65 person-years of employment are being created by this project, which will take two years to complete.

Remote Passenger Rail Services: Canada's Economic Action Plan includes projects on the Keewatin Railway and Tshiuetin Rail Transportation. These First Nations-owned companies provide service to remote Aboriginal communities with funding from the federal government. The Economic Action Plan provides two years of funding to upgrade various capital assets. Work completed to date includes rail line upgrades, a new station unloading ramp and rail car purchases.

Federal Bridges: Canada's Economic Action Plan includes projects at the following bridges:

- **The Champlain Bridge in Montréal:** The Jacques Cartier and Champlain Bridges Incorporated, a Crown corporation, is implementing a comprehensive 10-year post-tensioning program of the Champlain Bridge in Montréal. This work will ensure that this bridge, the busiest in Canada, remains safe for its users. At this time, it is expected that all repairs planned for 2009–2010 will be completed by the end of March 2010, right on schedule.

- **The Blue Water Bridge in Sarnia:** This strategic investment in additional lanes, plaza enhancement and other improvements will allow the bridge to respond to the steady growth in commercial traffic and to support the introduction of programs such as Free and Secure Trade and NEXUS, as well as new Canada Border Service Agency requirements. It will help improve the safety and efficiency of Canada's second busiest commercial crossing and is expected to have regional economic development benefits. The necessary financial agreements were finalized on July 23, 2009, and construction began in late August 2009. All jobs created will be private sector jobs in the construction, engineering and manufacturing sectors.

- **The Peace Bridge in Fort Erie:** This strategic investment will help facilitate the flow of commercial goods across one of Canada's top three border crossings. Engineering and planning work on the Peace Bridge project began in July 2009 and construction activities are scheduled to begin in March 2010. Federal funds for the project have begun flowing to the bridge authority. It is anticipated that by the time the project work is completed in the summer of 2010, it will have generated approximately 50 direct and indirect full-time jobs.

- **National Capital Region Interprovincial Bridges:** The cities of Ottawa and Gatineau are linked by five interprovincial crossings, including the Alexandra Bridge and the Chaudière Crossing. A major rehabilitation of the Alexandra Bridge started in April 2009, creating approximately 60 jobs. Contracts for rehabilitation work on the Chaudière Crossing were awarded in October 2009 and mobilization for the rehabilitation of the arches started in January 2010.

- **Kingston and Burlington Bridges**: The LaSalle Causeway in Kingston and the Burlington Lift Bridge provide passage for essential commercial traffic both on land and water. The Burlington Lift Bridge provides passage for around 1,000 cargo-carrying vessels each year. Work on the Burlington Lift Bridge started in January 2010. Rehabilitation work on the LaSalle Causeway began in November 2009 with completion scheduled for May 2010.

Federal Buildings: The Economic Action Plan committed significant funds to repair and renovate the federal government's building portfolio. A total of 324 repair and renovation projects have already been completed and over 900 projects worth over $128 million are currently underway.

Canada's Economic Action Plan: Working for Canadians

Federal Buildings—Examples of Repair and Renovation Projects

Heritage Building (Red Deer, Alberta)
The project included the removal of an old steam boiler and the installation of eight smaller humidification units throughout the tenant space. The work also generated lasting benefits for the environment by eliminating the need for water treatment and chemicals into the local watershed and doing away with nitrogen dioxide emissions that were generated by the old boiler system. The new system also improved energy efficiency within the building, and construction waste from the project was recycled or stored for future use. This was all achieved without changing the heritage characteristics of the building.

Parking and Loading Deck Repairs (Woodstock, New Brunswick)
The project consisted of installing a new membrane over the entire parking roof area, constructing a new vault around an electrical transformer, and correcting a slope in the parking roof to prevent water pooling. The investment also permitted the installation of new wheelchair ramps, making the building much more accessible.

Government Conference Centre (Ottawa, Ontario)
The project included roof replacement and repainting of the exterior windows. The project contributes to the restoration of an important heritage site.

In addition, funding was provided to enhance the accessibility of Crown-owned buildings for persons with disabilities. To date, 40 projects have been completed and over 175 projects worth about $16 million are currently underway. For 2010–11, a preliminary list of projects is currently being reviewed by Public Works and Government Services Canada. Priority continues to be given to facilities where services are provided directly to Canadians. Projects include:

- Improvements for the visually impaired such as signage in braille.

- Power door openers, voice identification in elevators, and interior and exterior ramps and primary access doors to improve access for persons with physical disabilities.

Most of these projects are contracted through Public Works and Government Services Canada's private sector building management service provider. To date, the service provider has contracted nearly 600 vendors for the Economic Action Plan investments alone, who in turn contract a large number of sub-contractors, including small and medium-sized enterprises, from coast to coast to deliver this program.

The Economic Action Plan also provided $2 million over two years for the development of a comprehensive plan to secure the future of the historic Manège Militaire in the city of Québec. The results of public consultations were released in October and a real property consultant has been selected to conduct a feasibility and profitability study. The recommendations from this study were received in December and the Government is currently reviewing the report and is firmly committed to the reconstruction of this historic site.

Alaska Highway: On sections of the Alaska Highway from Summit Lake, British Columbia to the Yukon border, deck repairs to eight bridges were completed, 28 kilometres of asphalt road surface was repaved, and an intersection was rebuilt to make it safer. These investments totalled $12 million and were all completed on budget and during the short northern summer construction period. Additional work to stabilize erosion and install new culverts will be completed by March.

Twinning of the Trans-Canada Highway in Banff National Park:
The project involves two separate design/build tenders, one for the Icefields
Interchange and a second for the twinning of eight kilometres of the
Trans-Canada Highway between the Interchange and the Alberta-British
Columbia border. The site preparation is complete along with the fencing,
the wildlife overpass, the paving in the vicinity of Lake Louise Village and
aggregate crushing. For the twinning of the highway to the border with
British Columbia, soil investigations and crushing for sub-base aggregate is
complete, and a second request for detailed tender bids was issued in early
January and will close in March 2010. Design and construction is expected
to begin in the spring of 2010.

Small Craft Harbours: Implementation of the Small Craft Harbours
Accelerated Infrastructure Program has progressed more quickly than
anticipated. To date, 242 repair, maintenance, and dredging projects
representing $177 million are in the engineering or tendering processes,
under construction, or have been completed. Some funding for 2010–11
projects was advanced to 2009–10, bringing total funding to be spent in
2009–10 at existing harbours to $112 million. It is expected that a further
$88 million will be spent in 2010–11.

Construction of Nunavut's first small craft harbour in Pangnirtung, Nunavut
is progressing and approximately $5 million will be spent in 2009–10. Some
work planned for 2009–10 will be completed in 2010–11 due to unforeseen
delays. As a result, $12 million is now expected to be spent in 2010–11.

**Canada's Economic Action Plan:
Working for Canadians**

Accelerated Repair and Maintenance of Small Craft Harbours

The newly constructed commercial fishing wharf at Seldom on Fogo Island
in Newfoundland and Labrador provides for improved fish landing and
vessel berthage capacity in this active fishing community. A contract for
$1.14 million was awarded to Trident Construction Limited on June 19, 2009,
and the project was completed on December 22, 2009.

Aviation Security: Canada's Economic Action Plan provides funding for the deployment of new, advanced, and internationally compatible screening equipment as well as supplies funding for the jobs associated with maintaining, operating and managing this equipment. Funding from the Economic Action Plan, however, not only creates jobs related to screening operations; it also serves to increase levels of security and efficiency at airports across Canada.

Federal Contaminated Sites: The Government is accelerating work to assess and remediate federal contaminated sites, with over $153 million worth of projects underway or completed. This work is helping to create jobs and economic activity in communities across Canada, while contributing new green spaces and cleaner bodies of water and soils, and enabling long-term development. Departments have selected over 220 projects for accelerated remediation and will conduct over 2,000 site assessments in 2009–10 and 2010–11.

For example, the Department of National Defence is receiving $16 million over two years to undertake accelerated remediation and risk management activities at the 5 Wing Goose Bay Canadian Air Forces base located in Happy Valley-Goose Bay, Newfoundland and Labrador.

Stimulating Housing Construction

To stimulate Canada's construction industry and protect and create jobs, the Government is providing significant support for home ownership and renovations. It is also making investments to renew Canada's social housing and improve municipal housing–related infrastructure.

Supporting Home Ownership and Jobs in Housing Construction

The housing industry is an important source of economic activity and job creation in Canada, as it promotes demand for building materials and other goods and services. For many Canadians, their homes are the most important investment of their lives.

Canadians who undertook eligible renovations to their homes before February 1, 2010 were entitled to receive up to $1,350 in tax relief from the temporary Home Renovation Tax Credit introduced last year in Canada's Economic Action Plan. An estimated 4.6 million families in Canada will claim the credit on their 2009 tax returns.

Canada's Economic Action Plan has provided additional tax support to first-time home buyers, who benefit from greater access to their Registered Retirement Savings Plan savings to purchase or build a home, as well as up to $750 in tax relief from the First-Time Home Buyers' Tax Credit.

Canada's Economic Action Plan: Working for Canadians

Supporting Home Renovation Activity

The temporary Home Renovation Tax Credit (HRTC) has provided timely stimulus to the Canadian economy while boosting energy efficiency and the value of Canada's housing stock. The HRTC has provided an estimated 4.6 million Canadian families with up to $1,350 in tax relief on eligible renovation projects.

There is a clear public consensus that the HRTC has been a powerful incentive for Canadians to invest in their homes—thereby supporting employment in the construction industry.

We estimate that the tax credit likely bolstered renovation activity by an additional $4.3 billion above what it would have been over January 2009 to January 2010—which represents a 0.3% boost to real GDP. As a result, renovation investment was one of the first components of the Canadian economy to fully bounce back from the economic downturn … Were it not for government economic stimulus, renovation investment would have been materially weaker in 2009 … The renovation stimulus measure helped to support a Canadian economic recovery through increasing demand for housing-related goods and services at a time when most other areas of the economy remain weak.

— *TD Economics Observation*, February 17, 2010

I think there's no question it's increased economic activity, it's created jobs, it's definitely shown consumer confidence in renovating their homes, and I think it's done a lot of good for the industry and for consumers … it obviously has kept the industry stronger in these tough times and in job creation as well.

— Canadian Home Builders' Association.
House of Commons Standing Committee on Finance, November 3, 2009

I think this is a great idea. Anything that is getting people to spend money when they normally wouldn't and gives them a break at the same time is good. We are seeing money pumping into the economy for buying materials and other things and it all gets passed down the line, right down to the truck driving and transport industry.

— Mark Buyan of MB Home Improvements & Construction
(Penticton, British Columbia).
Penticton Western News, January 7, 2010

Canada's Economic Action Plan: Working for Canadians

Supporting Home Renovation Activity *(cont'd)*

Manufacturers in Manitoba have been getting a shot in the arm from an unlikely source—the federal home renovation tax credit program, which is bolstering sales and saving jobs. The chief executive (Craig McIntosh) of Acrylon Plastics, which manufactures PVC window frames, said the home renovation tax credit program has sent window-frame sales into record-setting territory for the Winnipeg company. "The renovation side (of the housing market) just really took off in April and May and it hasn't slowed down at all ... It was a record November for us." Before last spring, when the impact of the two-month-old federal HRTC program really started to be felt, Acrylon had been girding for the worst ... Then along came the HRTC program ... For firms like Acrylon, it was the perfect tonic ... "We were getting ready for it to be a very slow summer ... Then all of a sudden we were saying, 'What recession?'"

— *Winnipeg Free Press*, December 2, 2009

While final results on the take-up of the HRTC are not yet available, all indicators to date clearly point to the timeliness and effectiveness of this measure in achieving its objective for the benefit of Canadian families and the economy as a whole. It has been a worthy complement to other government measures in support of homeownership, such as:

- Giving first-time home buyers greater access to their Registered Retirement Savings Plan savings to purchase or build a home, and up to $750 in tax relief from the First-Time Home Buyers' Tax Credit.

- Enhancing the ecoENERGY Retrofit – Homes program, which is encouraging the development and installation of next-generation energy products, as well as fostering improved techniques in home construction and renovation.

Homeowners have also benefited from the enhanced ecoENERGY Retrofit – Homes program to make energy efficiency improvements to their homes. The additional $300 million provided through the Economic Action Plan is expected to support an estimated 200,000 home retrofits.

The program has experienced unprecedented demand since the Economic Action Plan was announced and has met its targets. In response, the Government allocated $205 million from the Clean Energy Fund to finance up to an additional 120,000 retrofits for Canadian homeowners. A further $80 million is being provided to the program, bringing the total increase in funding for the program through the Economic Action Plan to $585 million.

Investments in Social Housing

Over the past year, historic investments in social housing have contributed significantly to supporting Canada's housing construction and renovation industries. Through Canada's Economic Action Plan, federal commitments of more than $1 billion in 2009–10 have helped Canadian families find suitable and affordable housing, while putting Canadians back to work.

A further $1 billion in funding is available in 2010–11, bringing the total federal investment in social housing to over $2 billion. Funding for 2009–10 and 2010–11 has been fully committed.

In 2009–10, $650 million of this investment is being matched by provincial and territorial governments, which are responsible for program design and delivery. As a result of this joint investment in social housing, in 2009–10 over 2,400 construction and renovation projects are underway across the country in support of some of the most vulnerable in our communities, including seniors, single-parent families, recent immigrants and Aboriginal Canadians living off reserve.

Canada's Economic Action Plan: Working for Canadians

Investments in Co-operative Housing in Nova Scotia

Through Canada's Economic Action Plan, the federal and provincial governments are contributing $3.1 million towards the renovation and retrofit of Nova Scotia's newest and largest housing co-op, the North End United Housing Co-operative. Work on this project includes replacing existing roofs, installing new windows and doors, and refurbishing older bathrooms.

The Government of Canada has also committed $75 million in 2009–10 to renovate and retrofit federally administered social housing. Over 700 projects are currently underway. In addition, in 2009–10, $300 million has already been committed through the Economic Action Plan in support of housing in over 400 First Nations communities and in the North.

In total, over 3,500 projects are underway across the country to improve housing conditions for some of the most vulnerable in our communities, including seniors, single-parent families, recent immigrants and Aboriginal households.

Canada's Economic Action Plan: Working for Canadians

Investments in First Nations Housing

Ontario First Nation Completes Canada's First Project Under the Economic Action Plan

The Whitesand First Nation celebrated the grand opening of its new $998,720, 8-plex housing unit geared towards single-parent families on December 1, 2009. Construction began on the housing project in August 2009 and was completed in November 2009. The building consists of eight two-bedroom, 624-square-foot units. The First Nation is the first nationally to complete a multi-unit housing project under Canada's Economic Action Plan.

In addition to direct funding for social housing, 93 low-cost loans have been approved in 2009–10, allowing municipalities to undertake housing-related infrastructure projects.

Canada's Economic Action Plan: Working for Canadians

Municipal Infrastructure: Low-Cost Loan Helps Growing City Meet Demand

The City of Saskatoon received approval for a $31-million direct low-cost loan through the Municipal Infrastructure Lending Program for a new water intake for the city's water treatment plant. This federal investment will help one of Canada's fastest-growing cities meet future demands while saving the city $1.2 million in interest payments.

Table 5.8

Building Infrastructure to Create Jobs

	2009–10		2010–11	
	Stimulus Value	Stimulus Committed	Stimulus Value	Stimulus Committed
	(millions of dollars)			
Building Infrastructure				
Investments in Provincial, Territorial and Municipal Infrastructure				
Accelerating payments under the Provincial/Territorial Base Funding Initiative	180	179	261	198
Infrastructure Stimulus Fund	1,209	1,209	2,791	2,791
Bonus for Community Projects	103	103	397	397
Green Infrastructure Fund (five-year program)	13	13	387	110
National recreational trails	25	25	–	–
Recreational Infrastructure Canada[1]	179	179	321	318
Investment in First Nations Infrastructure				
School construction	81	81	105	105
Water and wastewater projects	70	70	109	109
Critical community services (health facilities)	68	68	68	68
Critical community services (police facilities)	12	12	3	–
Investments in Federal Infrastructure Projects				
An improved rail system	140	140	199	199
Trans-Canada Highway	20	20	50	50
Federal bridges and Champlain Bridge	43	41	56	32
Alaska Highway (British Columbia)	13	13	–	–
Small craft harbours	117	117	100	100
Repair and restoration of federal buildings	175	173	158	32
Enhancing accessibility of federal buildings	20	18	20	1
Manège Militaire in the city of Québec	1	1	1	0
Accelerating action on federal contaminated sites	96	91	150	121
Border facilities	7	2	38	0
Aviation security	375	372	8	8

Table 5.8 *(cont'd)*

Building Infrastructure to Create Jobs

	2009–10		2010–11	
	Stimulus Value	Stimulus Committed	Stimulus Value	Stimulus Committed
	(millions of dollars)			
Stimulating Housing Construction				
Support for Home Ownership and the Housing Industry				
Home Renovation Tax Credit	3,000	3,000	–	–
Increasing withdrawal limits under the Home Buyers' Plan	15	15	15	15
First-Time Home Buyers' Tax Credit	175	175	180	180
Enhancing the energy efficiency of our homes	150	150	230	230
Investments in Social Housing for Canadians				
Renovation and retrofit of social housing (provincial/territorial)	425	425	425	425
Renovation and retrofit of social housing (federal)	75	75	75	75
First Nations housing	200	200	200	200
Northern housing	100	100	100	100
Housing for low-income seniors	200	200	200	200
Housing for persons with disabilities	25	25	50	50
Loans to municipalities	1,000	1,000	1,000	1,000
Total	**8,312**	**8,291**	**7,696**	**7,114**

[1] $35 million of funding under Recreational Infrastructure Canada that is allocated for projects in Quebec is being used for support to the forestry sector in Quebec.

Creating the Economy of Tomorrow

Canada's Economic Action Plan includes about $4 billion over two years for post-secondary education and research, technology and innovation, and environmental protection. These measures are helping to strengthen Canada's world-leading research and advanced training facilities and to prepare young Canadians for the jobs of tomorrow. The Economic Action Plan also includes measures to create business opportunities in all parts of Canada and to enable small and medium-sized companies to grow and create jobs.

Table 5.9

Creating the Economy of Tomorrow

	2009–10	2010–11	Total
	(millions of dollars)		
Action to Invest in Post-Secondary Education and Research			
Improving infrastructure at colleges and universities	1,000	1,000	2,000
Other	89	155	244
Subtotal—Action to Invest in Post-Secondary Education and Research	1,089	1,155	2,244
Investing in Science and Technology			
Renewing federal laboratories	93	157	250
Clean energy and the environment	366	336	702
Other	530	233	763
Subtotal—Investing in Science and Technology	990	726	1,715
Total—accrual value	2,079	1,881	3,959
Total—cash value	2,139	1,880	4,018
Total with provincial contribution—cash value	3,306	2,880	6,185

Notes: Totals may not add due to rounding. The accrual value may be somewhat smaller because some of these expenditures relate to construction and renovation costs of federal assets (for which only depreciation is recorded on a budgetary basis) and loans to third parties (where there is a budgetary impact only in the event that there is a risk of loss).

The Government is helping to build a strong, innovative economy through science, technology and research excellence, while training new generations of highly skilled individuals. Canada needs this new wave of highly qualified workers to prosper in a global economy that depends more and more on knowledge and innovation.

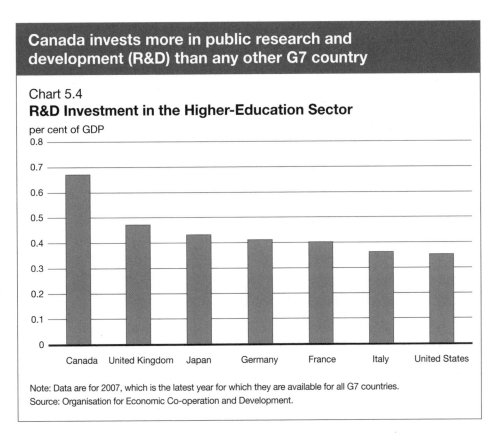

Canada invests more in public research and development (R&D) than any other G7 country

Chart 5.4
R&D Investment in the Higher-Education Sector
per cent of GDP

Note: Data are for 2007, which is the latest year for which they are available for all G7 countries.
Source: Organisation for Economic Co-operation and Development.

The Government is committed to maintaining Canada's global leadership position in post-secondary research. Funding has been provided to support research excellence at Canadian post-secondary institutions, help Canadian scientists focus on areas where we can be world leaders, and link our research strengths to the opportunities and challenges facing the private sector.

Canada's Economic Action Plan invests approximately $5 billion in multi-year science and technology initiatives, an unprecedented investment which underlines the Government's commitment to its science and technology strategy.

Post-Secondary Education and Research

The Knowledge Infrastructure Program is providing $2 billion over two years for university and college infrastructure projects (including repair, maintenance and construction). Federal funding covers up to half of eligible project costs incurred by March 31, 2011, with other partners providing the balance.

Twenty projects have already been completed, and planning, design, construction and renovation work has begun on a further 361 projects at colleges and universities across Canada. These projects represent over $1.8 billion in Knowledge Infrastructure Program funding, accounting for over 90 per cent of the total program budget.

**Canada's Economic Action Plan:
Working for Canadians**

Infrastructure Investments at Universities and Colleges: Creating Jobs for Canadians

- Vancouver Island University in Nanaimo, British Columbia, is building a new Deep Bay Field Station that is expected to create 99 direct jobs and 54 indirect jobs.

- Upgrades to infrastructure at the University of Prince Edward Island will create over 300 jobs and inject about $30 million into the economy.

- A new research laboratory at the Canadian Mennonite University in Winnipeg, Manitoba, will accommodate 24 students, and upgrades to existing laboratory space will support upper-level biology courses.

- The new energy programs building at New Brunswick Community College—Saint John Campus will add up to 400 training spaces to the campus' overall capacity.

- Renovating the auditorium at Collège Ahuntsic in Montréal, Quebec, will increase capacity by 200 spaces. The auditorium is used for conferences, classes, assemblies, performances and socio-cultural activities.

- Development of a new campus in Mississauga, Ontario, for the Sheridan College Institute of Technology and Advanced Learning will accommodate 1,760 students, including 1,200 business student spaces and 560 spaces for the training and retraining of new Canadians, foreign-trained professionals and unemployed workers.

Canada's Economic Action Plan: Working for Canadians

Infrastructure Investments at Universities and Colleges: Creating Jobs for Canadians *(cont'd)*

- Infrastructure and technology upgrades and research facility renovations at St. Peter's College in Muenster, Saskatchewan, are expected to result in a 300-per-cent increase in student enrolment and an increase from 34 to up to over 100 faculty after the project has been completed.

- The construction of the Dawson City Campus will increase the capacity of Yukon College to enroll more students while offering training in basic carpentry skills. This project will enable the college to continue to serve the almost 1,400 residents in Dawson City, including nearly 400 First Nations members.

- Completion of the Main Campus Renovation Project at Bow Valley College in Calgary, Alberta, will make room for an additional 960 practical nurse and health-care aid graduates, plus 300 additional graduates in Justice Studies, over a five-year period. This two-phase project will provide the capacity for 10,000 additional learners by 2020.

Through Budget 2009, the Government committed to provide the Canada Foundation for Innovation (CFI) with additional funding of $750 million to accelerate investment in state-of-the-art research facilities and equipment. This funding represents an investment in the economy of tomorrow, as the research infrastructure supported by the CFI will underpin the creation of new knowledge and provide invaluable learning experiences for our best and brightest students.

Of the funding announced in Budget 2009, the CFI has already committed $150 million to 28 exceptional projects through its 2009 competition.

The balance of $600 million will support the Foundation's future activities, including a new competition to be launched by December 2010. The CFI is finalizing its strategic plan, and remains committed to making strategic investments in current and new infrastructure that promotes leading-edge research; fostering partnerships among universities, colleges and business researchers that encourage innovation in the private sector; and ensuring that world-class research facilities in Canada maintain their global leadership.

The Minister of Industry will provide additional details on the allocation of the $600 million in the coming months.

 Chapter 5

Investing in Science and Technology

The Government has increased its direct support for science and technology through investments to modernize federal laboratories, improve broadband access, and spur research in clean energy and space technology.

Renewing Federal Laboratories: The Government has allocated almost $250 million to upgrade and modernize federal laboratories doing research in a wide array of fields, from health and food to natural resources, after several years in which maintenance had been delayed or deferred. Construction has begun or has been completed for over 95 per cent of projects at 14 federal departments and agencies. This work is providing employment in regions across Canada and will improve the federal government's science and technology capacity for years to come.

Canada's Economic Action Plan: Working for Canadians

Examples of Modernizing Federal Laboratories

- Natural Resources Canada is investing $47.8 million over two years to address deferred maintenance and modernize 12 facilities across Canada. For example, it is investing $13.4 million over two years on facilities at the Great Lakes Forestry Centre in Sault Ste. Marie, including $9 million over two years for the new Invasive Species Centre, which seeks to combat alien invasive species that threaten Canada's fragile ecosystems. Projects at Natural Resources Canada will create or maintain 477 jobs across the country.

- Work is well underway on projects at Health Canada facilities in Ottawa, Longueuil, Québec, Winnipeg and Scarborough. These projects—which will inject over $16 million over two years into the local economies—will support Health Canada's food safety and nutritional quality regulatory programs, and contribute to consumer protection services focusing on children and vulnerable populations.

- Library and Archives Canada is investing $3 million over two years to upgrade its preservation, digitization and archival processing laboratories in Gatineau, Quebec, to increase their efficiency, security, and flexibility in responding to technological advances. Construction on these projects is already employing 20 people directly, while spurring additional indirect employment among suppliers and manufacturers.

Clean Energy and the Environment: The Economic Action Plan established the $1-billion Clean Energy Fund, including up to $150 million for clean energy research and development and $850 million for clean energy demonstration projects. The projects to be supported by the fund are expected to assist in increasing the deployment of renewable and clean technologies.

Canada's Economic Action Plan: Working for Canadians

Examples of Projects Funded Under the Clean Energy Fund

To date, the Government has announced support for three large-scale carbon capture and storage (CCS) demonstrations under the Clean Energy Fund:

- $120 million for a Shell Quest CCS demonstration project.
- $315.8 million for the TransAlta Keephills Project to attach CCS to a coal-fired power plant near Edmonton.
- $30 million for the Alberta Carbon Trunk Line project.

This funding builds on substantial support provided for carbon capture and storage in previous years, including the ecoENERGY Technology Initiative and funding for other research, development and deployment projects. In total, the Government has announced over $800 million in support for carbon capture and storage.

The Government has also announced up to $146 million in support of 19 projects to demonstrate renewable and clean energy across Canada, including integrated community energy solutions, smart grid technology, and renewable applications with solar, wind, tidal and geothermal energy.

As announced in the Economic Action Plan, the Government conducted a consultation on the tax treatment of carbon capture and storage. The Government will continue to monitor the development of this important technology and assess the best policy approach. The current focus is on direct funding through initiatives like the Clean Energy Fund.

To date, federal funding totalling over $610 million has been announced for specific projects under the fund. In addition, in response to unprecedented demand under the ecoENERGY Retrofit – Homes program, $205 million under the Clean Energy Fund has been allocated to finance up to 120,000 additional retrofits for Canadian homeowners.

Broadband: Broadband Canada, an applications-based contribution program, will help to expand broadband coverage to as many unserved and underserved households in Canada as possible. This will help rural households, businesses and community institutions to make use of the Internet at levels similar to many of their urban counterparts.

A call for applications closed on October 23, 2009 and resulted in 570 proposals. Industry Canada is currently assessing the proposals with the goal of maximizing the reach of federal funds, and expects to identify successful applicants in 2010.

Canadian Space Agency: The Economic Action Plan also provided $110 million over three years to the Canadian Space Agency to support Canada's continued leadership in the design and construction of space robotics. Of this amount, approximately $36 million will be spent in 2010–11 on the development of the Next Generation Canadarm and Exploration Surface Mobility projects. This funding supports new opportunities for innovative Canadian companies and provides jobs for highly skilled employees. This new support will also help prepare Canadian astronauts to participate in future international space missions, similar to those in which astronauts Robert Thirsk and Julie Payette recently participated.

Canada Health Infoway: The Economic Action Plan provided $500 million to Canada Health Infoway to support the goal of having 50 per cent of Canadians with an electronic health record by 2010 and to speed up the implementation of electronic medical record systems for physicians. Canada Health Infoway has developed an action plan to strengthen accountability in response to the Auditor General of Canada's Report of November 3, 2009. The Government is moving forward with the transfer of the $500 million that was announced in Budget 2009 to Canada Health Infoway. This $500-million investment will both enhance the safety, quality and efficiency of the health care system, and create thousands of sustainable, knowledge-based jobs throughout Canada.

Table 5.10

Creating the Economy of Tomorrow

	2009–10		2010–11	
	Stimulus Value	Stimulus Committed	Stimulus Value	Stimulus Committed
	(millions of dollars)			
Action to Invest in Post-Secondary Education and Research				
Improving infrastructure at universities and colleges	1,000	1,000	1,000	1,000
Canada Foundation for Innovation	–	–	50	50
Institute for Quantum Computing	17	17	17	17
Arctic research infrastructure	35	35	52	52
Canadian Graduate Scholarships program	35	35	35	18
Industrial Research and Development Internship program	3	3	1	0
Investing in Science and Technology				
Modernizing federal laboratories	93	91	157	157
Clean Energy Fund[1]	65	65	335	272
Canadian Environmental Sustainability Indicators	10	10	0	0
Strengthening Canada's nuclear advantage	351	351	0	0
Canada's space industry	10	10	53	36
Canada Health Infoway	500	500		
Extending access to broadband in rural communities	20	20	180	0
Total	**2,139**	**2,136**	**1,880**	**1,602**

Note: Totals may not add due to rounding.

[1] $205 million in 2009–10 and 2010–11 funding (referred to in Budget 2009 under "Transformation to a Green Energy Economy") was allocated to the ecoENERGY Retrofit – Homes program to support an additional 120,000 home energy retrofits.

Supporting Industries and Communities

Canada's Economic Action Plan provides approximately $14 billion to
support adjustment and help create and protect jobs in regions, communities
and industries of the Canadian economy that have been most affected by the
severe downturn. This includes targeted support for traditional industries
such as forestry and agriculture, and manufacturing, which play important
roles in the economies of many communities. This support will help those
industries invest in their long-term success and create new opportunities
and jobs for Canadians in all areas of the country.

Table 5.11

Supporting Industries and Communities

	2008–09	2009–10	2010–11	Total
		(millions of dollars)		
Support for Industries				
Forestry		62	108	170
Agriculture		79	146	225
Mineral exploration		70	-15	55
Small businesses		170	195	365
Tourism		74	74	148
Shipbuilding		19	30	49
Culture		152	183	335
Tax and tariff relief				
Accelerated capital cost allowance for computers		340	355	695
Tariff relief for machinery and equipment	12	76	81	169
Subtotal—Support for Industries	12	1,042	1,157	2,211
Support for Communities				
Helping all regions prosper		770	750	1,520
Strengthening partnerships with Aboriginal Canadians		109	185	294
Subtotal—Support for Communities		879	935	1,813
Total—accrual value	12	1,921	2,092	4,024
Total—cash value		2,050	2,231	4,280
Federal support to auto sector		9,718		9,718
Total federal cash value		11,768	2,231	13,998
Ontario component of auto sector support		4,859		4,859
Total with provincial contributions—cash value		16,627	2,231	18,857

Notes: Totals may not add due to rounding. The accrual value may be somewhat smaller because some
of these expenditures relate to construction and renovation costs of federal assets (for which only depreciation
is recorded on a budgetary basis) and loans to third parties (where there is a budgetary impact only in the event
that there is a risk of loss).

Support for Communities: The Government is continuing to deliver support to vulnerable communities through initiatives such as the $1-billion Community Adjustment Fund. Approximately 80 per cent of the money available under the fund over two years has been committed and over 1,000 Community Adjustment Fund projects are now underway or completed.

Canada's Economic Action Plan: Working for Canadians

Examples of Community Adjustment Fund (CAF) projects

To date, about $800 million of CAF funding has been committed across the country. For example:

- The Morden Industrial Park in Manitoba has received $726,200 for the renovation of a building to house start-up businesses. Five businesses have been created, maintained or expanded as a result of this project, and the first business has relocated into the facility. Training has been provided to 10 people and 20 person-months of employment have been created.

- Miovision Technologies Inc. in Kitchener, Ontario, will receive a contribution of $50,000. The firm provides video and web-based technologies to help address automotive traffic management. The funding will be used to support the salaries of 10 skilled employees.

- St. Joseph's Health Centre in Sudbury, Ontario, will receive $1.9 million to help build a long-term care home in Chelmsford. It is estimated that this project will create 420 construction-related jobs throughout the entire building period—with approximately 160 employees to be hired to operate the facility by March 31, 2011.

- The Drummondville Economic Development Authority in Quebec has received $500,000 to build a second industrial incubator on the site of the Home of Industry in Drummondville. The incubator will host seven new manufacturing or technology firms. This project will create 15 temporary jobs.

- The West Point Development Corporation in Prince Edward Island has received $750,000 to renovate the historic West Point Lighthouse Inn and create a new welcome centre depicting the history of the area. The project is creating 37 short-term jobs in a rural area of the province with high unemployment. The longer-term impact will be the maintenance of 23 seasonal jobs.

Of the $206 million available to the Federal Economic Development Agency for Southern Ontario (FedDev Ontario) in 2009–10, $187 million has been committed to strategic investments to support job creation and economic growth in the region. For example, $28 million has been committed to the National Research Council's Industrial Research Assistance Program to support research and development–intensive small and medium-sized enterprises in the region. Also, the Government is investing $50 million in the Business Development Bank of Canada so businesses in southern Ontario will have greater access to venture capital. Through the Southern Ontario Development Program, FedDev Ontario has committed nearly $95 million to projects such as the Canadian Manufacturers & Exporters' SMART Program and commercialization in the field of diabetes research.

Canada's Economic Action Plan: Working for Canadians

Economic Development Initiatives in Southern Ontario

FedDev Ontario has recently committed funds to a number of initiatives, including:

- $400,000 to allow Melitron Corporation to increase productivity through the installation of new equipment and facility upgrades. Melitron will also be reconfiguring the layout of its plant in order to implement lean manufacturing process principles. This plant-wide upgrade will improve the company's competitiveness, providing immediate local economic stimulus and job creation.

- $362,500 to Springer's Meats Inc. to upgrade its meat processing plant. This investment will allow the family-run business to expand its plant with a shipping department fitted with a shipping office, refrigeration, and a racking system to optimize storage, warehousing and shipping to its clients. The company expects to create seven new jobs with these upgrades.

Automotive Sector: The automotive sector has faced significant challenges over the past year. The governments of Canada and Ontario, working closely with the government of the United States, have taken significant steps to help the automotive sector overcome these challenges, including jointly supporting the restructuring processes of Chrysler and General Motors through loans and debtor-in-possession financing.

Of the $3.7 billion committed to Chrysler by Canada and Ontario, $2.9 billion has been disbursed to date. Chrysler emerged from bankruptcy on June 10, 2009. The governments of Canada and Ontario received 2 per cent equity in the restructured firm. All of the $10.8 billion committed to General Motors by Canada and Ontario has been disbursed. General Motors emerged from bankruptcy on July 10, 2009. Canada and Ontario received a combined 11.7 per cent ownership stake in a restructured General Motors, as well as US$403 million of preferred shares.

These actions helped to save jobs in hard-hit communities.

Forestry: The global economic downturn and the collapse in the U.S. housing market have created challenges for the forestry sector. Under the Economic Action Plan, Natural Resources Canada has fully committed $170 million allocated over two years. This funding will support market diversification and innovation initiatives in the forestry sector, including research and demonstration projects on new forest products and initiatives to help forestry companies market innovative products internationally to protect and create jobs.

Since the release of the Economic Action Plan, the Government has announced the creation of a $1-billion program to support environmental improvements for the pulp and paper industry. The Pulp and Paper Green Transformation Program will allow pulp and paper mills in all regions, particularly focused in British Columbia, Quebec and Ontario, to reduce greenhouse gas emissions while helping them become leaders in the production of renewable energy from biomass.

This is helping mills located in many communities to improve their competitiveness and create and sustain jobs. These actions are in addition to the substantial financial support provided to the forestry sector by Export Development Canada.

Canada's Economic Action Plan: Working for Canadians

Examples of Support for Forestry

The forestry sector is an important contributor to the Canadian economy, forming the economic base in many regions. The forestry sector employed approximately 273,000 people across the country and contributed more than $28 billion to Canada's gross domestic product in 2008.

Canada's forest product companies have encountered intense competitive pressures in recent times, including greater competition from low-cost producers, higher input and energy costs, a variable Canadian dollar and low productivity. The Government has put in place significant support, including through the Economic Action Plan, to help the forestry sector address these challenges, become more competitive and create jobs. For example:

- Since 2008, Export Development Canada (EDC) has provided nearly $30 billion in financial services to Canadian-based forestry companies. This includes US$42.1 million provided by EDC as part of a US$270-million syndicated debtor-in-possession facility to support Abitibi Consolidated Inc.'s restructuring efforts. Over the same period, the Business Development Bank of Canada has provided nearly $300 million in loans to Canadian forestry firms.

- The $1-billion Pulp and Paper Green Transformation Program, announced in June 2009, will allow pulp and paper mills in all regions to invest in new technologies that improve energy efficiency or environmental performance, helping them become leaders in the production of renewable energy from biomass, while creating and sustaining jobs in their communities.

- The Canada-Quebec Forestry Task Team was established in April 2009 to address challenges facing the Quebec forestry industry. To date, the task team's work has led to a $200-million agreement announced in May 2009 to support silviculture in the province, and a further $30-million agreement announced in July 2009 for the restoration of bridges and culverts on Quebec public lands, which will enable greater natural resource and land development to take place. The federal government will contribute $115 million toward these two initiatives, sourced from the Community Adjustment Fund.

Tourism: The Government has provided support for 60 marquee festivals and events across Canada, such as the Royal Nova Scotia International Tattoo, the Montreal High Lights Festival, the Kitchener-Waterloo Oktoberfest, the Saskatoon Exhibition, and the Festival du Bois in Maillardville, Coquitlam, in order to attract visitors and create jobs in the tourism sector.

Our vast national parks help attract a large number of visitors from abroad each year, generating significant economic activity and bringing our natural heritage closer to Canadians. Canada's Economic Action Plan provides Parks Canada with $150 million over two years to upgrade facilities, including visitor centres and campgrounds, as well as roads at National Parks and National Historic Sites throughout the country. This funding is now fully committed to projects, including recently completed road improvement activities in Banff National Park, and a two-year, $3.5-million project to repair walls and arches at the Halifax Citadel National Historic Site of Canada.

Agriculture: Over the past year, the Government has worked closely with farmers, the agri-food industry and the provinces and territories to deliver on the agricultural measures announced in the Economic Action Plan.

- The Government continues to receive and evaluate new industry and provincial/territorial proposals to add to those already in place under the multi-year Agricultural Flexibility Fund. To date, $219 million has been committed to multi-year initiatives. A total of $10 million is expected to be spent in 2009–10, and to date $52 million has been committed to be spent in 2010–11.

- Investments in cattle processing plants to help improve their operations under the Slaughter Improvement Program have begun and will ramp up over the remaining two years of the program. To date, total funding of $41 million over three years has been committed to 13 projects. Some projects for 2009–10 will not be completed until 2010–11 due to the timing of contracts. A total of $9 million is expected to be spent in 2009–10, and to date $22 million has been committed to be spent in 2010–11.

- Since its launch in the summer of 2009, 1,683 loans totalling $84 million have been granted under the new Canadian Agricultural Loans Act. This represents an increase of 60 per cent in loans registered and an increase of 87 per cent in loan dollars registered last year.

- On January 1, 2010, the Government transferred the delivery of AgriStability to British Columbia and Saskatchewan to help streamline the administrative process for farmers.

Canada's Economic Action Plan: Working for Canadians

Examples of Support for Agriculture

- Projects funded under the five-year Agricultural Flexibility Fund include $7.8 million for a targeted market access strategy that will ensure Canadian canola producers have full and fair access to international markets, targeted Canada Brand initiatives in Mexico, Japan and South Korea to increase demand for Canadian products, and 8 projects for processors across the country totalling $6.6 million. In addition, $21 million has been committed over five years to projects in partnership with the governments of Alberta, Saskatchewan, Quebec, and Prince Edward Island.

- To date, total funding of $41 million over three years has been committed to 13 projects under the Slaughter Improvement Program. For example, the Government has committed $2.7 million for Écolait in Quebec to expand freezer capacity, upgrade product shipping and install new cutting equipment and $2.3 million for Conestoga Meat Packers in Ontario to add processing capacity for value-added bi-products.

Small Business: Canada's many innovative small and medium-sized companies are an important economic engine, introducing new goods and services, developing new technologies and creating jobs for highly skilled young graduates. The Economic Action Plan committed $200 million over two years to the Industrial Research Assistance Program to enable it to temporarily expand its initiatives for small and medium-sized enterprises. The National Research Council has committed the entire $100 million allocated in 2009–10 to help firms innovate and to hire new post-secondary graduates. In total, this funding has provided contributions to 1,200 small and medium-sized enterprises, helping maintain or create over 4,500 jobs, and has helped 460 post-secondary graduates find employment and gain invaluable experience.

Canada's Economic Action Plan: Working for Canadians

Examples of Support for Small Business

Through the Industrial Research Assistance Program (IRAP), the Government is helping small and medium-sized companies to invest in research and innovation and create high-value jobs. For example:

- Northern Radar Systems Limited, located in St. John's, Newfoundland and Labrador, manufactures computers and electronic products. This firm received contribution funding of $150,254 from the Economic Action Plan to fund the development of a new transmitter that will be able to achieve multi-kilowatt power levels.

- Mingus Software Inc., located in Montréal, Quebec, received IRAP funding of $195,000 to develop software to process Internet reservations and secure payments for hotel trade.

Shipbuilding: The Economic Action Plan has provided $175 million to the Canadian Coast Guard to purchase 98 new boats and to repair and refit 40 existing large vessels. Good progress is being achieved with contracts signed and in place with shipbuilding and repair companies in Canada. Some projects for 2009–10 will not be completed until 2010–11 due to the timing of contracts and the size and complexity of certain projects. As a result, in 2009–10, $82 million is scheduled to be spent. It is expected that a further $93 million will be spent in 2010–11.

Canada's Economic Action Plan: Working for Canadians

Examples of Support for Shipbuilding

- Contracts for 50 of the 60 new small craft, totalling $10.5 million, are in place. The first 10 boats, type 753 Rigid Hull Inflatable Boats, built by Zodiac Marine in Richmond, British Columbia, have been delivered to the Coast Guard in Victoria, B.C., Halifax, Nova Scotia, and St. John's, Newfoundland and Labrador. It is expected that the contracts will be awarded for the remaining 10 vessels over the next four months.

- 122 contracts across Canada totalling $20.8 million have been awarded for vessel refits of 33 Canadian Coast Guard vessels. The refit work consists of general repair, maintenance and updating of obsolete systems on board the large vessels to improve the reliability of the vessels to deliver Canadian Coast Guard services and programs and meet the on-water needs of other government departments.

- Five large vessels will undergo major repairs to extend their reliable service lives for a minimum of 10 additional years. A contract worth $15.5 million was awarded to Allied Shipbuilders in North Vancouver, B.C., for the major component of the CCGS Bartlett vessel life extension. This work has already begun. In addition, a contract worth $7 million was awarded to Heddle Marine Services Inc., of Burlington, Ontario, to carry out the vessel life extension of the CCGS Limnos and a contract worth $6.9 million was awarded to Verreault Navigation Inc., of Les Méchins, Quebec, to carry out the vessel life extension of the CCGS Tracy. Both of these vessels are in the shipyards and over 50 per cent of their work packages have been completed. The CCGS Tanu, CCGS Cape Roger and CCGS Griffon are undergoing preparatory work prior to their vessel life extensions scheduled for 2010–11.

Culture: The Government has delivered unprecedented levels of investment in Canada's cultural industries, creating jobs and supporting the creative economy. In the last year, the Government has charted a course that will allow our creative industries to navigate the changing technological and economic landscapes. The Economic Action Plan includes investments that go directly to our country's artists and cultural organizations. The Government has modernized several programs, such as the Canada Media Fund, to bring them into the digital age. Recent efforts have included stabilizing funding for programs that support Canadian music and books, as well as significantly increasing funding for solidifying the Canada Council for the Arts—funding for the Council is at its highest level in history.

Canada's Economic Action Plan included over $335 million in support for culture and the arts—recognizing the importance of Canada's artistic institutions, the role they play in Canadians' lives, and their contribution to the economy. The Government has made the following progress in implementing stimulus programs related to culture.

- In 2009–10, the Canada Cultural Spaces Fund committed $27 million of a total of $30 million in cultural infrastructure funding and committed $24 million of the 2010–11 allocation of $30 million, supporting 96 cultural infrastructure projects across Canada.

- As of March 2010, the Canada Arts Training Fund has funded nine projects worth $5 million to support the highest-calibre institutions in Canada to train the most talented emerging artists for professional careers.

- A $15-million investment in 2009–10 provided Canadians with continued access to more than 1,000 Canadian magazines and community newspapers.

- In 2009–10, a $100-million investment in the Canadian Television Fund is supporting projects, in partnership with the broadcasting industry, to produce high-quality, distinctively Canadian television programs.

Canada's Economic Action Plan: Working for Canadians

Examples of Support for Culture

- $490,000 towards the construction of a portable planetarium for the outreach program of Sudbury's Digital Dome Theatre at Science North. Taken together with other financial contributions, the completed $1.4-million project created 53 short-term jobs and one permanent position.

- $1.1-million investment for the renovation of the Laurel Packinghouse in Kelowna, a heritage landmark, which is the oldest and largest standing packinghouse in British Columbia and serves as home to the BC Orchard Industry Museum, BC Wine Museum and VQA Wine Shop. Taken together with other financial contributions, the $3.4-million project is creating 11 short-term and 12 long-term jobs.

> ## Canada's Economic Action Plan: Working for Canadians
>
> ### Examples of Support for Culture (cont'd)
>
> - A $1.8-million investment is contributing towards the construction of the Aanischaaukamikw Cultural Institute in the Cree territory of Oujé-Bougoumou in northwest Quebec. The facility aims to preserve and share the culture and heritage of nine Cree communities in James Bay by providing archival and storage facilities for archaeological assets, a resource centre, and an open area for a variety of artistic performances and workshops. Taken together with other financial contributions, the $14.7-million project is creating 115 short-term positions and 42 long-term positions.

Mining: Canada's rich mineral resources represent significant economic opportunities. Promoting the exploration and development of these resources offers important benefits in terms of employment, investment and infrastructure, especially for rural and remote communities. Canada's Economic Action Plan supports mineral exploration activity and jobs across Canada by extending the temporary 15-per-cent Mineral Exploration Tax Credit to flow-through share agreements entered into during the period from April 1, 2009 to March 31, 2010.

Tax and Tariff Relief: In addition to supporting key industries, the Economic Action Plan includes permanent and temporary measures which build on broad-based tax reductions that are lowering the federal general corporate income tax rate from 22.12 per cent (including the corporate surtax) in 2007 to 15 per cent in 2012. These reductions, in addition to other tax changes introduced since 2006, will give Canada the lowest overall tax rate on new business investment in the G7 this year.

The Economic Action Plan is helping Canadian firms create jobs, modernize their operations and better compete globally through the elimination of tariffs on a range of machinery and equipment, and through temporary measures to accelerate the capital cost allowance on manufacturing or processing machinery and equipment, and computers. Since the implementation of the tariff relief measure, businesses have benefited from over $2 billion worth of duty-free machinery and equipment imports on which they would have otherwise been required to pay duty.

Table 5.12
Supporting Industries and Communities

	2009–10		2010–11	
	Stimulus Value	Stimulus Committed	Stimulus Value	Stimulus Committed
	(millions of dollars)			
Support for Industries				
Autos				
Support for the auto sector	9,718	9,718		
Forestry				
Forestry marketing and innovation	62	62	108	108
Agriculture				
Agricultural flexibility program[1]	65	10	115	52
Strengthen slaughterhouse capacity	14	9	31	22
Mining				
Extending the Mineral Exploration Tax Credit	70	70	-15	-15
Small Business				
Reducing taxes for small businesses	45	45	80	80
Industrial Research Assistance Program	100	100	100	23
Canadian Youth Business Foundation	10	10		
Canada Business Networks	15	15	15	15
Tourism				
Canadian Tourism Commission	20	20	20	20
Marquee tourism events	50	48	50	1
Parks Canada	70	70	80	80
Shipbuilding				
Shipbuilding	82	82	93	93
Culture				
Cultural infrastructure	30	27	30	24
Canada Prizes for the Arts and Creativity			25	–
Canada Arts Training Fund	7	5	13	–
Community newspapers and magazines	15	15	15	–
Canadian Television Fund	100	100	100	–

Table 5.12 *(cont'd)*

Supporting Industries and Communities

	2009–10		2010–11	
	Stimulus Value	Stimulus Committed	Stimulus Value	Stimulus Committed
	(millions of dollars)			
Support for Industries *(cont'd)*				
Tax and Tariff Relief				
Temporary 100-per-cent capital cost allowance (CCA) rate for computers	340	340	355	355
Temporary accelerated CCA rate for manufacturing or processing machinery and equipment				
Tariff relief for machinery and equipment	76	76	81	81
Support for Communities				
Helping All Regions Prosper				
Community Adjustment Fund	496	477	504	329
Federal Economic Development Agency for Southern Ontario	206	187	206	28
Eastern Ontario Development Program	10	10	10	0
Strengthening economic development in the North	10	10	10	10
Strategic Investments in Northern Economic Development	10	9	20	3
Promoting energy development in Canada's North	38	38		
Strengthening Partnerships With Aboriginal Canadians				
First Nations and Inuit health programs	108	108	170	170
First Nations child and family services	2	2	15	15
Total	**11,768**	**11,663**	**2,231**	**1,494**

Note: Tolals may not add due to rounding.

[1] $10 million of 2010–11 funding available has been transferred to the Slaughter Improvement Program; remaining funding of $115 million includes $25 million that has been allocated to provide assistance to Canadian cattle processing plants that handle cattle over 30 months of age.

Improving Access to Financing and Strengthening Canada's Financial Sector

Canadians need access to affordable financing for their homes, cars and businesses. The level of interest rates and access to loans influence how Canadians invest and spend their money, which drives our economy and promotes job creation. Strong financial conditions are vital for a sustained recovery in Canada and elsewhere in the world.

The Canadian financial system withstood the global financial crisis better than most. The global crisis, however, made it difficult for Canadian banks and other lenders to obtain funds from international markets at reasonable costs. To soften the impact of this crisis, Canada's Economic Action Plan included measures to provide up to $200 billion to support lending to Canadian households and businesses through the Extraordinary Financing Framework.

The Extraordinary Financing Framework measures, most of which are ending as credit conditions improve, included: the Insured Mortgage Purchase Program; a new 10-year maturity in the ongoing Canada Mortgage Bond program; the Canadian Secured Credit Facility; support for the Bank of Canada's emergency liquidity measures; increased flexibilities and capacities for financial Crown corporations, including the introduction of the Business Credit Availability Program; and assurance facilities for banks and insurance companies. All of this support has been offered on a commercial basis to protect taxpayers.

The Government's actions under the Extraordinary Financing Framework have contributed significantly to improved credit conditions. In Canada, total credit growth has shown signs of stabilizing. Overall, total credit growth in Canada remained stronger than in the U.S. through the third quarter due to significantly stronger Canadian household growth (Chart 5.5). Improved financial market conditions have also led to a rebound in bond and equity issuances, following a retrenchment in these activities in late 2008 (Chart 5.6). Meanwhile, the difference between corporate and government bond rates has narrowed considerably.

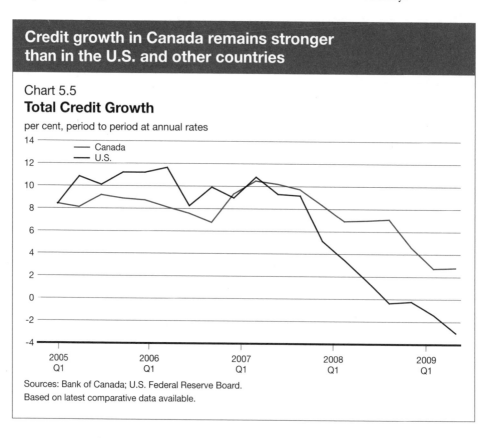

Credit growth in Canada remains stronger than in the U.S. and other countries

Chart 5.5
Total Credit Growth

per cent, period to period at annual rates

Sources: Bank of Canada; U.S. Federal Reserve Board.
Based on latest comparative data available.

Improvement in business lending conditions and financial market activity

Chart 5.6

Net Funds Raised by Canadian Non-Financial Businesses Through Equities, Bonds and Short-Term Paper

Long-Term Corporate Spreads

billions of dollars

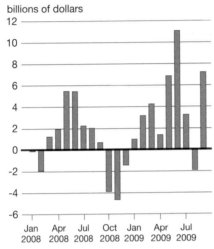

Source: Bank of Canada.

basis points

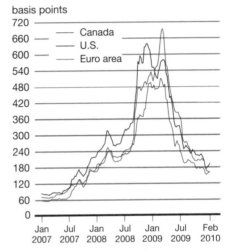

Notes: The spreads are the difference between corporate and government yield of bonds with a maturity between 7 and 10 years. Weekly data up to and including November 6, 2009.

Source: Merrill Lynch.

In Canada, credit growth has been combined with significantly lower interest rates for borrowers. In response to the global financial crisis, the Bank of Canada reduced its policy rate by 425 basis points between July 2007 and April 2009 to effectively zero and has held it there since (Chart 5.7). The Government's measures to support access to financing have helped to alleviate market uncertainty and supported a dramatic reduction in the interest rates faced by households and businesses. As a result, average effective interest rates for households and businesses, as estimated by the Bank of Canada, have fallen by over 200 basis points and about 260 basis points, respectively, since the fall of 2008.

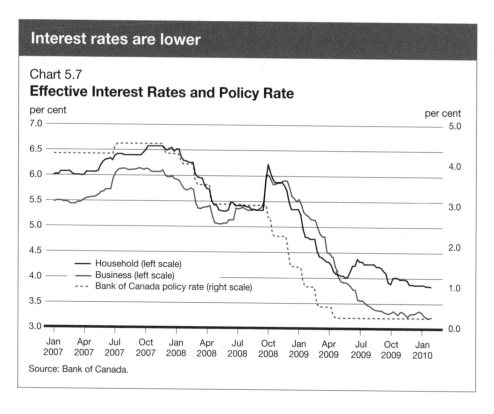

Interest rates are lower

Chart 5.7

Effective Interest Rates and Policy Rate

Source: Bank of Canada.

Direct Support for Small and Medium-Sized Business

The Business Credit Availability Program is continuing to help businesses find financing solutions to preserve jobs and fund growth. As of the end of January, Export Development Canada and the Business Development Bank of Canada reported total activity under the Business Credit Availability Program of about $5 billion, assisting almost 9,000 businesses. This achieves the target of at least $5 billion that was set out in Budget 2009. The financial Crown corporations have provided assistance in regions all across the country and in all sectors of the economy, with a particular focus on small businesses. A breakdown of activity by sector, region and size of borrower, as well as recent success stories can be found at www.fin.gc.ca/bcap.

The Business Credit Availability Program has successfully increased the collaboration of the financial Crown corporations and private sector lenders, which has benefited small and medium-sized businesses across Canada. This program will continue to assist the needs of creditworthy businesses as the economy recovers over the coming year.

Declining Need for Extraordinary Measures

As conditions have improved and the economic recovery continues to take shape, extraordinary support measures have achieved their goal. Ongoing need is declining and, as a result, most measures are ending.

The Canadian Lenders Assurance Facility and Canadian Life Insurers Assurance Facility expired at the end of December 2009. While these guarantee facilities were not used, they helped to support market confidence and contain borrowing spreads for Canadian financial institutions.

The Insured Mortgage Purchase Program will continue to make purchases of qualifying insured mortgages until the end of March 2010. This program has been successful in moderating the impact of the global financial crisis on credit conditions in Canada by providing funds to financial institutions that were then able to continue lending to businesses and consumers. To date, over $60 billion of term funding has been provided to banks and other lenders at a positive spread to the Government's funding costs. Recently, lenders have not participated as aggressively in the program, as access to funding through capital markets has improved and investor demand for issuance from financing institutions, particularly Canadian banks, has resurfaced.

The Canadian Secured Credit Facility, which is designed to support the financing of vehicles and equipment and to stimulate private lending to these sectors, will run to the end of March 2010. Under the facility, the Government has committed to purchase up to $12 billion of newly issued term asset-backed securities backed by loans and leases on vehicles and equipment and dealer floor plan (inventory financing) loans. Details of transactions completed to date can be found on the Business Development Bank of Canada's website at www.bdc.ca. A number of transactions are in process and are expected to be completed prior to the expiration of the facility. The facility continues to operate on a first-come, first-served basis for funds that have not been taken up by participants. At the same time, the facility is having a positive impact on the availability and cost of financing for vehicles and equipment with several market participants accessing securitization markets outside of the facility.

Reflecting improved credit conditions in funding markets, the Bank of Canada has taken steps to exit from its extraordinary liquidity facilities.[2] During the global financial crisis, the extraordinary liquidity provided by the Bank of Canada peaked at over $40 billion in December 2008.

---

[2] Further details on the changes to the extraordinary liquidity support provided by the Bank of Canada can be found on its website (www.bankofcanada.ca).

Summary and Next Steps

The Government has taken unprecedented steps to expedite implementation and ensure that Canada's Economic Action Plan is having an impact now— when it is most needed. Virtually all stimulus for year one of the Economic Action Plan has been committed. In every region of the country, Canadian communities, businesses, workers and families are receiving the support they need.

The Government's focus now is on delivering year two of the Economic Action Plan. Already, commitments are in place for more than 90 per cent of the available 2010–11 funding.

In the weeks and months ahead, the Government's priorities will be:

- Ensuring that the unemployed receive timely Employment Insurance benefits.
- Modernizing federal infrastructure to better serve Canadians.
- Lowering taxes for Canadians and Canadian businesses.
- Investing in higher education, science and technology and green infrastructure to create the economy of tomorrow.
- Providing assistance to sectors and communities affected by the economic downturn.
- Improving infrastructure in First Nations communities.
- Helping businesses access the financing they need to support the economic recovery.

The Government will also continue to work with provinces, territories and municipalities to ensure that:

- Workers have access to training when they need it.
- Infrastructure projects are proceeding in a timely manner.
- More social housing units are built and existing social housing is modernized.

Canadians are invited to monitor the progress of the Economic Action Plan on the Government's website, www.actionplan.gc.ca.

Annex 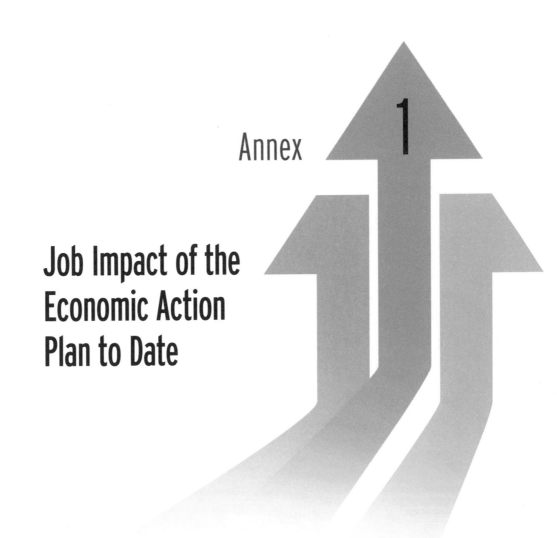 1

Job Impact of the
Economic Action
Plan to Date

Impact of the Economic Action Plan on Residential Investment

Canadian homeowners have received support from a variety of measures, including the introduction of the temporary Home Renovation Tax Credit and the First-Time Home Buyers' Tax Credit and enhancements to the Home Buyers' Plan. Combined with historically low interest rates, these initiatives have contributed to a strong recovery in housing activity.

After declines in the fourth quarter of 2008 and the first quarter of 2009, residential investment increased in each of the last three quarters of 2009. Renovation spending, which accounts for about 40 per cent of residential investment, has rebounded, averaging 15.8-per-cent growth in the last three quarters with support from the Home Renovation Tax Credit (Chart A1.5).

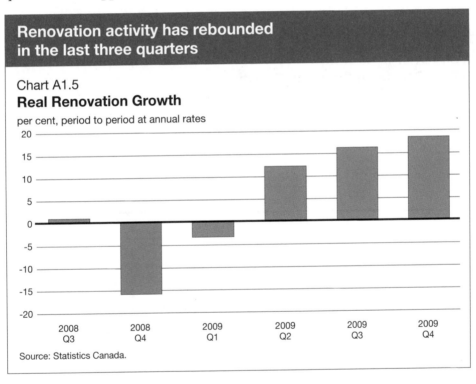

Renovation activity has rebounded in the last three quarters

Chart A1.5
Real Renovation Growth
per cent, period to period at annual rates

Source: Statistics Canada.

Impact of the Economic Action Plan on Infrastructure Investment

Building infrastructure is one of the cornerstones of the Economic Action Plan. Infrastructure measures in the Action Plan include the establishment of the Infrastructure Stimulus Fund and increased spending on railways, bridges, recreational facilities and federal buildings.

These measures have contributed to the economic recovery in Canada. Growth of government investment in infrastructure and capital goods averaged almost 20 per cent in the last three quarters of 2009, supported by infrastructure measures in the Economic Action Plan (Chart A1.6). This was more than twice the average growth rate observed in the previous three quarters.

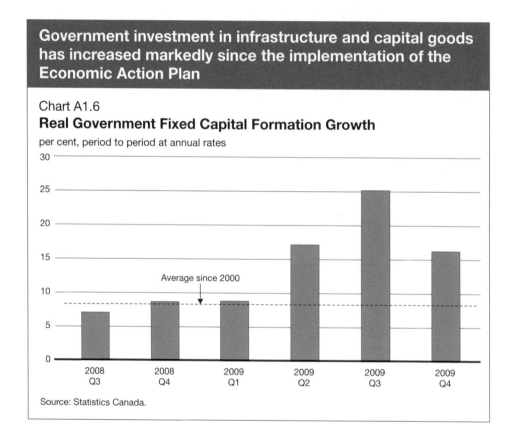

Government investment in infrastructure and capital goods has increased markedly since the implementation of the Economic Action Plan

Chart A1.6
Real Government Fixed Capital Formation Growth
per cent, period to period at annual rates

Source: Statistics Canada.

> ## The Job Impact of the International Partnership to Support the Automotive Industry *(cont'd)*
>
> In early 2009, General Motors and Chrysler assembly plants directly employed an estimated 14,000 workers. In addition, over 50,000 jobs in other industries were estimated to be tied to production at General Motors and Chrysler. Based on Statistics Canada's input-output model of the Canadian economy, the Department of Finance estimates that 52,000 jobs (all the assembly jobs and about three-quarters of the indirect jobs) are being protected by government action to support the automotive industry. This estimate does not take into account the induced effects arising from the maintenance of economic activity in the automotive and related industries.

The Job Impact of the Economic Action Plan to Date

Multipliers used in the 2009 budget analysis are used again in this analysis to assess the impact of the Economic Action Plan on jobs maintained or created to date, together with information on the proportion of Economic Action Plan measures actually flowing in the economy.

Determining the amount of stimulus flowing in the economy from tax reductions and measures to support the unemployed, industries and communities is fairly straightforward as flows correspond to amounts paid.

However, for infrastructure-related investment projects amounts paid to provinces, territories and third parties do not accurately reflect the full stimulus created. Amounts paid tend to lag the economic impact of fiscal stimulus as payments are typically made when the work is completed rather than as it is progressing. To account for this lag, infrastructure project start and end dates have been used to arrive at an estimate of funds flowing. Economic stimulus was assumed to flow in a linear fashion from project start to end. This approach has been used for approximately three-quarters of project-based infrastructure spending.

Table A1.2 shows the resulting estimated stimulus flowing in the economy as of January 31, 2010, the latest date for which amounts paid are available, to each area of the Economic Action Plan.

Table A1.2

Economic Action Plan Funds Flowing in the Economy

	Dollars Flowing as of January 2010
	(millions of dollars)
Reducing the Tax Burden for Canadians	2,571
Helping the Unemployed	1,978
Building Infrastructure to Create Jobs[1]	7,850
Creating the Economy of Tomorrow[1]	1,807
Supporting Industries and Communities[1]	15,157
Total	**29,362**

Note: Totals may not add due to rounding.

[1] Includes provincial, territorial and municipal leverage assumed in Budget 2009.

It is estimated that over $4 billion has been devoted to reducing the tax burden and helping the unemployed. Almost $8 billion has been invested in new public and housing infrastructure. Almost $2 billion has been invested in knowledge infrastructure and science and technology to help create the economy of tomorrow. Finally, more than $15 billion has been disbursed to support industries and communities.

The results suggest that the implementation of the Economic Action Plan has had a substantial beneficial impact on production and employment (Table A1.3). The funds disbursed are estimated to have reduced the decline in real GDP in the second quarter, avoided another contraction in the third quarter and increased growth by 2.2 percentage points in the fourth quarter of 2009.

Improved economic growth translates into a higher level of employment. Indeed, the Economic Action Plan reduced the size of the contraction in employment in both the second and third quarters of 2009, and led to a larger increase in employment in the fourth quarter. As of January 2010, it is estimated that the Economic Action Plan has created or maintained 130,000 jobs.

Table A1.3

Impact of Economic Action Plan Measures Implemented to Date on Real GDP and Employment

	2009Q2	2009Q3	2009Q4	January 2010
	(per cent, unless otherwise indicated)			
Real GDP Growth				
Actual	-3.5	0.9	5.0	–
Without Economic Action Plan (EAP) measures	-5.1	-0.8	2.8	–
Impact of the EAP (percentage points)	1.6	1.7	2.2	–
Employment Growth				
Actual	-1.1	-0.1	1.3	–
Without EAP measures	-1.7	-0.8	0.3	–
Impact of the EAP (percentage points)	0.6	0.7	1.0	–
Employment level (thousands)	29	57	100	130

Since October 2008, cumulative net job losses in the Canadian economy have amounted to about 280,000. Most of these occurred from October 2008 to March 2009, with the labour market improving thereafter. Had the Economic Action Plan not been implemented, the cumulative number of job losses would have been close to 410,000.

Table A1.4 breaks down the jobs estimated to have been created or maintained according to the five elements of the Economic Action Plan. To date, most of the jobs created or maintained have been the result of infrastructure investment and support to industries and communities.

Table A1.4

Jobs Estimated to Have Been Created or Maintained According to Each Element of the Economic Action Plan

	January 2010	End of 2010
Reducing the Tax Burden for Canadians	8,000	19,000
Helping the Unemployed	10,000	24,000
Building Infrastructure to Create Jobs	42,000	84,000
Creating the Economy of Tomorrow	13,000	27,000
Supporting Industries and Communities	58,000	66,000
Total	**130,000**	**220,000**

Note: Totals may not add due to rounding.

Sectoral Impact of the Economic Action Plan on Jobs

The manufacturing and construction sectors were particularly hard hit by the economic slowdown. The Economic Action Plan responded with several measures to support these sectors directly, particularly through infrastructure investment and funding to support housing as well as industries and communities.

From October 2008 to March 2009, the economy shed over 385,000 jobs. More than 250,000 of the job losses, or about two-thirds of the total, occurred in the manufacturing and construction sectors. These two sectors, however, account for less than 20 per cent of Canada's employment.

Since March 2009, the labour market has shown some stability, with notable improvements occurring in the manufacturing, construction and service sectors. Employment in construction has risen by about 40,000 while job losses in manufacturing have slowed considerably. Continued job losses in the manufacturing sector reflect weak U.S. demand and the appreciation of the Canadian dollar. Employment in the service sector has increased significantly since March 2009, returning above pre-recession levels.

Table A1.5 provides a sectoral breakdown of the jobs estimated to have been created or maintained by the Economic Action Plan.[5] It is estimated that about 45 per cent of the jobs created or maintained by January 2010 have been in the manufacturing and construction industries.

The actual timing of improvements in the labour market and developments at the industry level are consistent with the roll-out of the Economic Action Plan, suggesting it played an important role in improving the labour market situation.

Table A1.5

Sectoral Breakdown of the Number of Jobs Estimated to Have Been Created or Maintained by the Economic Action Plan

	January 2010	End of 2010
Primary and utilities	3,000	5,000
Construction	29,000	50,000
Manufacturing	32,000	37,000
Services	67,000	129,000
Total	**130,000**	**220,000**

Note: Totals may not add due to rounding.

[5] The results are based on estimates from the CEFM and simulations from an input-output model of the Canadian economy.

Conclusion

The evidence presented in this analysis indicates that the Economic Action Plan has played an important role in stabilizing the economy and fostering a recovery in Canada. It has helped get the economy growing again and supported employment, particularly in the industries most affected by the global recession.

Overall, indications are that the implementation of the Economic Action Plan has created or maintained about 130,000 jobs to date.

Because of the inherent uncertainty in estimating the impact of fiscal stimulus, the approach taken has been prudent.

- The fiscal multipliers used to generate the model-based estimates, a key input to the model, are similar to or lower than those used by the U.S. Council of Economic Advisors and those found in models of recognized Canadian private sector forecasters.

- Multipliers have not been adjusted upward to take into account the notion that they are larger when the policy interest rate is at its effective lower bound.

- The estimated impacts on employment do not fully include the impact of the work-sharing program on preserving jobs. Over 160,000 Canadians are benefiting from this program.

- The estimated impacts on employment do not take into account actions taken by the Government to improve access to financing for consumers and businesses through the Extraordinary Financing Framework.

External Assessment

The Department of Finance's analysis of the job impact of the Economic Action Plan to date was reviewed by well-respected economic experts from the private sector and academia:

- Peter Dungan, Director, and Steve Murphy, Research Associate, Policy and Economic Analysis Program, Rotman School of Management, University of Toronto.

- Glen Hodgson, Senior Vice-President and Chief Economist, and Pedro Antunes, Director of the National and Provincial Forecast, Conference Board of Canada.

- Stéfane Marion, Chief Economist and Strategist, National Bank Financial Group.

The reviewers believe that the Department of Finance's analysis presents a reasonable representation of the economic impact of the Economic Action Plan to date.

Canada Border Services Agency

The Canada Border Services Agency contributes to the security and prosperity of Canada by providing integrated border services that protect Canadians while facilitating the flow of people and goods across the border.

Through its strategic review, the Canada Border Services Agency streamlined operations and business processes through automation and consolidated service delivery to optimize resources.

As a result, the Canada Border Services Agency has strengthened its approach to managing the border, allowing it to better focus its resources on higher-risk travellers and cargo, to protect Canadians and support the effective flow of goods.

As discussed in Chapter 3, this budget is reinvesting funds in the Canada Border Services Agency to ensure that it continues to deliver efficient and secure border services.

Table A2.2
Strategic Review Savings

	2010–11	2011–12	2012–13
	(millions of dollars)		
Increasing Efficiency and Effectiveness			
Reduce the burden on clients through streamlining of operations and use of innovative technology	5.5	26.1	29.1
Eliminate subsidies to other federal organizations or modify partnership agreement		22.8	22.8
Reduce programs where funding is in excess of needs	1.0	1.2	1.1
Focusing on Core Role			
Reduce or eliminate activities that are not part of the department's core role		4.0	5.3
	6.5	54.1	58.4

Note: Totals may not add due to rounding.

Canada Mortgage and Housing Corporation

As the Government's national housing agency, Canada Mortgage and Housing Corporation helps Canadians access affordable, quality housing and contributes to the development of a strong Canadian housing system.

Through its strategic review, Canada Mortgage and Housing Corporation identified ways to be more efficient in managing market housing programs and in administering its social housing portfolio, while ensuring there are no impacts on low-income Canadians who receive housing assistance.

These changes will ensure continued value for money while helping low-income families, Aboriginal Canadians, seniors, persons with disabilities, and those seeking to break free from the cycles of homelessness and poverty.

Table A2.3

Strategic Review Savings

	2010–11	2011–12	2012–13
	(millions of dollars)		
Increasing Efficiency and Effectiveness			
Efficiencies from lower-than-expected interest and inflation rates and decreasing loan defaults	95.4	95.4	95.4
Focusing on Core Role			
Adjust approach to research and service delivery to better align with core mandate	1.6	4.5	6.8
	97.0	**99.9**	**102.2**

Note: Totals may not add due to rounding.

Environment Canada

Environment Canada is responsible for preserving and enhancing the quality of the natural environment, providing weather forecasts and warnings and protecting Canadians from environmental threats through its scientific expertise, legislation and regulatory tools.

Through its strategic review, Environment Canada identified opportunities to focus on priorities and deliver its suite of programs and services more efficiently, while ensuring the right balance between environmental stewardship and economic interests.

As a result, Environment Canada is strengthening its capacity to preserve and enhance the environment through improved scientific capacity and an efficient approach to regulation.

As discussed in Chapter 3, this budget is reinvesting funds in Environment Canada to sustain the Government's annual reporting on environmental indicators, deliver meteorological services in the Arctic and clean up the Great Lakes.

Table A2.8

Strategic Review Savings

	2010–11	2011–12	2012–13
	(millions of dollars)		
Increasing Efficiency and Effectiveness			
Find efficiencies in the delivery of programs, services and research	6.5	10.0	10.0
Consolidate activities and eliminate reporting that is not required by legislation	1.9	1.9	1.9
Focusing on Core Role			
Reduce or eliminate activities that are not part of the department's core role or fall within the core mandate of other organizations	5.2	7.7	7.7
	13.7	**19.7**	**19.7**

Note: Totals may not add due to rounding.

Labour Program

The Labour Program helps build safe, fair and productive workplaces and fosters cooperative employer-worker relations.

Through its strategic review, the Labour Program identified ways to better align services and resources with actual needs and reduce red tape.

These changes will improve value for money while ensuring the Labour Program continues to help build safe, fair and productive workplaces and cooperative employer-worker relations for Canadians.

Table A2.9
Strategic Review Savings

	2010–11	2011–12	2012–13
	(millions of dollars)		
Increasing Efficiency and Effectiveness			
Eliminate red tape and streamline service delivery	0.6	0.9	2.2
Better align program funding with actual needs		0.1	3.2
Focus programs on core mandate and high priority areas	1.5	1.5	1.9
	2.1	**2.5**	**7.3**

Note: Totals may not add due to rounding.

National Capital Commission

The National Capital Commission is creating a better National Capital for all Canadians that is a source of pride and national significance.

By applying sound environmental stewardship of its lands and by further aligning its programs with its core mandate, the National Capital Commission will ensure its activities provide more benefits to the entire nation and provide more value for money.

The National Capital Commission is committed to instilling pride in Canadians for their National Capital while meeting the Government's priorities and those of Canadians.

Table A2.10
Strategic Review Savings

	2010–11	2011–12	2012–13
	(millions of dollars)		
Focusing on Core Role			
Align operations with core mandate	0.2	1.4	2.5
Meeting the Priorities of Canadians			
Refocus programming to benefit all Canadians	0.4	1.7	1.7
	0.7	**3.0**	**4.2**

Note: Totals may not add due to rounding.

National Energy Board

The National Energy Board is key to the responsible development of Canada's energy sector.

Through its strategic review, the National Energy Board identified ways to improve and streamline programs and processes by eliminating inefficiencies and reducing costs, with a balanced approach to environmental, social and economic considerations.

As a result, the National Energy Board is better positioned to support and promote social and economic development, as well as positive environmental outcomes for the benefit of all Canadians.

Table A2.11
Strategic Review Savings

	2010–11	2011–12	2012–13
	(millions of dollars)		
Increasing Efficiency and Effectiveness			
Streamline processes for environmental assessment applications received under the Canada Oil and Gas Operations Act	0.1	0.2	0.3
	0.1	**0.2**	**0.3**

Annex

3

Debt Management
Strategy 2010-2011

Purpose

The *Debt Management Strategy* sets out the Government of Canada's objectives, strategy and plans for the management of its domestic debt and foreign currency liabilities. Borrowing activities support the ongoing refinancing of government debt coming to maturity, the execution of the budget plan, and other financial operations of the Government, including borrowing on behalf of some Crown corporations.

The Financial Administration Act requires that the Government table the *Debt Management Strategy* in Parliament prior to the start of the fiscal year. Further information on the management of the Government's debt and liquid financial assets, including a description of the governance framework and details on program activities and outcomes, can be found in two annual reports that are tabled in Parliament following the tabling of the *Public Accounts of Canada*: the *Debt Management Report* and the *Report on the Management of Canada's Official International Reserves*, both of which can be found on the Department of Finance website.

Highlights of the Federal Debt Management Strategy

✓ Borrowing requirements in 2010–11 are expected to be lower than in 2009–10 as financing for various initiatives under the Extraordinary Financing Framework winds down.

✓ In 2010–11, the Government of Canada will continue to issue bonds across all maturity sectors, but at slightly lower levels than in 2009–10.

✓ Gross issuance of domestic marketable bonds is planned to be about $95 billion in 2010–11, $7 billion lower than the projected $102 billion for 2009–10. The total bond stock is planned to increase by $60 billion to $428 billion.

✓ To help smooth the cash flow profile of upcoming maturities, the Government is considering adjusting the maturity dates of certain benchmarks. Market participants will be consulted and any changes will be published well in advance.

✓ The size of the regular bond buyback program is planned to be $5 billion in 2010–11, about $3 billion higher than the projected amount for 2009–10, and buyback operations will continue to be conducted on a switch basis only.

✓ The average size of bi-weekly treasury bill auctions will decrease for 3-month, 6-month and 1-year terms. By the end of 2010–11, the treasury bill stock is projected to be $150 billion, about $28 billion lower than the level projected for the end of 2009–10.

Planned Borrowing Activities for 2010–11

Sources of Borrowing

The aggregate principal amount of money required to be borrowed by the Government from financial markets in 2010–11 to finance Budget 2010 stimulus measures, meet refinancing needs and meet other financial requirements is projected to be $251 billion.

Uses of Borrowing

Refinancing Needs

In 2010–11, refinancing needs are projected to be approximately $220 billion. The main source of refinancing needs during the year stems from the turnover of treasury bills, which have a term to maturity of one year or less, and bonds that will mature in 2010–11. Other lesser amounts include retail debt (Canada Savings Bonds and Canada Premium Bonds) and foreign currency obligations that mature in 2010–11.

Financial Source/Requirement

The other main determinant of borrowing needs is the Government's financial source or requirement. If the Government has a financial source, it can use the source for some of its refinancing needs. If it has a financial requirement, then it must meet that requirement along with its refinancing needs.

The financial source/requirement measures the difference between cash coming into the Government and cash going out. This measure is affected not only by the budgetary balance but also by the Government's non-budgetary transactions.

The budgetary balance is presented on a full accrual basis of accounting, recording government liabilities and assets when they are incurred or acquired, regardless of when the cash is paid or received.

Non-budgetary transactions include changes in federal employee pension accounts; changes in non-financial assets; investing activities through loans, investments and advances (including loans to three Crown corporations—BDC, CMHC and FCC); and other transactions (e.g. changes in other financial assets and liabilities and foreign exchange activities).

For 2010–11, a budgetary deficit of $49 billion and a financial requirement of $45 billion are projected. As the planned amount to be borrowed is lower than the planned uses of borrowing, the year-end cash position is projected to decrease by $15 billion.

Actual borrowing for the year may differ from the forecast due to uncertainty associated with economic and fiscal projections, the timing of cash transactions, and other factors such as changes in foreign reserve needs and Crown borrowings. A full account of actual borrowing against the plan presented here will be provided in the 2010–11 *Debt Management Report*, which will be tabled in Parliament in the fall of 2011.

Table A3.1

Planned Sources and Uses of Borrowing for 2010–11

	($ billions)
Sources of Borrowings	
Payable in Canadian currency	
Treasury bills[1]	150
Bonds	95
Retail debt	2
Total payable in Canadian currency	247
Payable in foreign currencies	4
Total cash raised through borrowing activities	251
Uses of Borrowings	
Payable in Canadian currency	
Treasury bills	178
Bonds	35
Of which:	
Regular bond buybacks	5
Cash management bond buybacks	10
Retail debt	3
Canada Pension Plan bonds and notes	–
Total payable in Canadian currency	216
Payable in foreign currencies	4
Total refinancing needs	220
Financial source/requirement	
Budgetary balance	49
Non-budgetary transactions	
Pension and other accounts	-6
Non-financial assets	4
Loans, investments and advances	
Enterprise Crown corporations	6
Other	-3
Total Loans, investments and advances	3
Other transactions[2]	-5
Total non-budgetary transactions	-5
Total financial source/requirement	45
Total uses of borrowings	265
Other unmatured debt transactions[3]	–
Net Increase or Decrease (-) in Cash	**-15**

Notes: Numbers may not add due to rounding. A negative sign denotes a financial source.

[1] These securities are rolled over, or refinanced, a number of times during the year. This results in a larger number of new issues per year than the stock outstanding at the end of the fiscal year, which is presented in the table.

[2] Other transactions primarily comprise the conversion of accrual adjustments into cash, such as tax and other account receivables, provincial and territorial tax collection agreements, and tax payables and other liabilities.

[3] These transactions comprise cross-currency swap revaluation, unamortized discounts on debt issues and obligation related to capital leases.

2010–11 Debt Strategy

Objectives

The fundamental objective of debt management is to raise stable and low-cost funding to meet the needs of the Government of Canada.

An associated objective is to maintain a well-functioning market in Government of Canada securities, which helps to keep debt costs low and stable and is generally to the benefit of a wide array of domestic market participants.

Debt Structure

In general, achieving stable, low-cost funding involves striking a balance between cost and risk in the debt structure, which is achieved through the selection of debt instruments.

The main operational measure used to describe the debt structure is the fixed-rate share, which is the proportion of all interest-bearing debt that does not mature or need to be repriced within one year relative to the total amount of Government of Canada interest-bearing debt. The fixed-rate measure is used in combination with other measures to assess the Government's exposure to changes in interest rates over time. The fixed-rate share of the debt was 61 per cent at the end of 2008–09. It is projected to rise to almost 63 per cent by the end of 2009–10, and rise slightly further in 2010–11. This increase in the fixed-rate share largely reflects an increase in the size of the bond stock relative to the stock of treasury bills.[2]

Maintaining a Well-Functioning Government Securities Market

Maintaining a well-functioning government securities market ensures that large volumes of funding can be raised efficiently to meet the Government's increased operational needs in difficult economic times. To support a liquid and well-functioning market for its securities, the Government has strived to maintain transparent, regular and diversified borrowing programs.

---

[2] More precisely, the fixed-rate share is calculated on a net basis by excluding components of the debt that are matched with financial assets of the same term and therefore do not represent an exposure to interest rate risk. The federal liabilities netted out from the fixed-rate share calculation include liabilities funding the assets in the Exchange Fund Account; debt securities matched with corresponding loans to Crown corporations; Government of Canada debt securities held by the Bank of Canada; matched assets related to the Insured Mortgage Purchase Program; and the debt offset by Receiver General cash and deposit balances.

Treasury Bill Program

The average size of bi-weekly treasury bill auctions will decrease for 3-month, 6-month and 1-year terms. By the end of 2010–11, the treasury bill stock is projected to be $150 billion, about $28 billion lower than the end-of-year level projected for 2009–10.

Cash management bills (i.e. short-dated treasury bills) help the Government manage its cash requirements in an efficient manner. The Government intends to continue to actively use cash management bills in 2010–11.

Retail Debt Program

The objective of the retail debt program for 2010–11 is to provide Canadians with access to Government of Canada retail savings products (Canada Savings Bonds and Canada Premium Bonds) in a cost-effective manner.

In 2010–11, the retail debt stock is expected to decline as redemptions continue to exceed sales in an environment of continued competition from other retail savings instruments in the marketplace. Over the coming year, the Government will continue to look for opportunities to reduce overall program delivery costs in order to support the sustainability of the program.

Further information on the retail debt program is available at www.csb.gc.ca.

Foreign Currency Funding

The Government's foreign currency reserves are financed through foreign currency liabilities to minimize exposure to currency risk. The purpose of the Exchange Fund Account (EFA) is to aid in the control and protection of the external value of the Canadian dollar. Assets held in the EFA are managed to provide foreign currency liquidity to the Government and to promote orderly conditions for the Canadian dollar in the foreign exchange markets, if required.

The Government has access to a range of direct sources of funding for its foreign currency assets. These include a short-term US-dollar paper program, medium-term note issuance in various markets, international bond issues, short-term purchases and sales of US dollars in foreign exchange markets, and cross-currency swaps involving the exchange of domestic liabilities for US-dollar and euro-denominated liabilities.

The mix of funding sources used in 2010–11 will depend on a number of considerations, including relative cost, market conditions, and the objective of maintaining a prudent foreign-currency-denominated debt maturity structure.

Further information on the management of foreign currency reserves and funding objectives is provided in the *Report on the Management of Canada's Official International Reserves*, which is available on the Department of Finance website.

Annex **4**

Promoting Strong, Sustained and Balanced Growth Through G20 Cooperation

The global recession of 2008 and 2009 was the most severe global downturn since the Second World War. The timely, substantial and coordinated policy actions of the Group of Twenty (G20) countries helped to prevent a collapse in the global financial system and mitigated the disruption to global economic activity. The unprecedented cooperation of G20 countries was possible because members recognized the severity of the risks confronting them and the need to protect their citizens.

G20 countries must sustain this cooperation in order to complete the reform of financial sector regulations that has begun under the auspices of the G20. Moreover, while there are encouraging signs that the global economy has stabilized, the economic recovery is proceeding unevenly. The G20 will need to continue delivering stimulus measures until a self-sustaining recovery is assured.

To push forward and coordinate key elements of the ambitious global reform agenda, the Prime Minister of Canada joined G20 Leaders in launching the Framework for Strong, Sustainable and Balanced Growth at the Pittsburgh G20 Summit in April 2009. The Framework commits the G20 to:

• Work together to assess how individual country policies interact.

• Evaluate whether individual country policies are collectively consistent with more sustainable and balanced growth.

• Act as necessary to meet the G20's common objectives.

At their meeting in St. Andrews following the Pittsburgh Summit, G20 Finance Ministers and Central Bank Governors formally initiated a cooperative process of mutual assessment of G20 economic policy frameworks, in accordance with their Leaders' commitment. The St. Andrews agreement called on each G20 country to submit its medium-term policy framework to the G20, International Monetary Fund (IMF) and World Bank. In line with the Pittsburgh agreement, the IMF and World Bank were asked to collect this information to help the G20 with its analysis of how respective national or regional policy frameworks fit together and to advise the G20 on progress in promoting development and poverty reduction as part of the rebalancing of global growth.

As host of the upcoming June G20 Summit in Toronto, Canada is working with its G20 partners to deliver on these commitments. Rebalancing global growth is critically important to reducing the risk of future crises and could raise potential growth globally. As a result, the Government has provided a detailed medium-term forecast to the G20, IMF and World Bank (Table A4.1).

Table A4.1
G20 Mutual Assessment: Macrofinancial Framework

	2009	2010	2011	2012	2013	2014
	(per cent, unless otherwise indicated)					
National accounts						
Real GDP growth	-2.5	2.6	3.2	3.0	2.8	2.6
Nominal GDP growth	-4.6	4.9	5.4	5.3	4.9	4.7
Private consumption growth	0.1	3.0	2.7	2.7	2.9	2.6
Government spending growth	2.9	3.3	2.1	2.2	2.3	2.2
Gross fixed investment growth	-8.2	6.4	3.0	4.3	4.1	3.3
Growth in imports of goods and services	-13.4	8.5	3.3	3.7	4.1	4.3
Growth in exports of goods and services	-13.9	4.1	4.3	3.8	3.6	3.6
Monetary and financial policy						
Consumer Price Index (CPI) inflation	0.5	1.8	2.0	2.0	2.0	2.0
House Price Index inflation	4.2	9.2	1.6	2.6	2.2	2.2
Key interest rate assumptions, including on the long-term rate						
3-month treasury bill rate	0.3	0.7	2.4	3.8	4.3	4.4
10-year government bond rate	3.3	3.7	4.3	4.9	5.2	5.3
Labour markets						
Population growth	1.2	1.0	0.8	0.9	0.8	0.8
Unemployment rate	8.3	8.5	7.9	7.4	6.9	6.6

Table A4.1 *(cont'd)*

G20 Mutual Assessment: Macrofinancial Framework

	2009	2010	2011	2012	2013	2014
External variables						
Current account balance (per cent of GDP)	-2.8	-2.6	-1.6	-1.6	-1.2	-1.2
Nominal and real exchange rate assumptions (US cents/C$)						
Nominal	87.9	95.5	98.3	97.7	99.3	98.5
Real (index, real = nominal in 2002)	87.4	96.0	99.2	98.9	100.5	99.7
Oil and other relevant commodity price assumptions						
Price of natural gas (US$ per MMBtu)	4.0	5.4	6.3	6.3	6.8	7.2
Price of West Texas Intermediate crude oil at Cushing (US$ per barrel)	61.7	76.0	84.7	93.3	100.0	104.2
Potential GDP growth	1.8	1.4	1.5	1.7	1.9	2.0

	2009–10	2010–11	2011–12	2012–13	2013–14	2014–15
			(per cent of GDP)			
Fiscal policy						
Federal government revenue	14.0	14.4	14.8	15.0	15.2	15.2
Of which: tax revenue	11.4	11.8	12.0	12.0	12.2	12.2
Federal government expenditure	17.5	17.5	16.4	16.0	15.6	15.3
Of which: interest payments	2.0	2.0	2.1	2.2	2.1	2.1
Net federal government debt	33.9	35.4	35.2	34.4	33.3	31.9

Note: Consistent with Canada's established approach to fiscal planning, this forecast reflects the average of the December 2009 survey of private sector forecasters. The only exception is for the CPI inflation forecast, which is based on the Bank of Canada's projection, consistent with the January 2010 *Monetary Policy Report*. Fiscal policy forecasts are on a Public Accounts basis. Figures for 2009 are from the December 2009 survey of private sector forecasters and have not been adjusted to include data released since December 18, 2009.

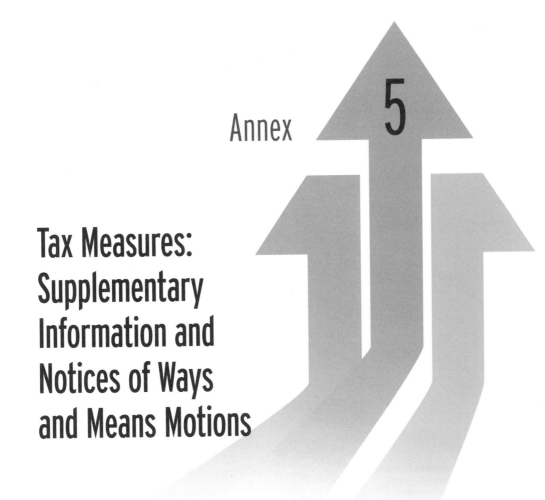

Annex 5

Tax Measures: Supplementary Information and Notices of Ways and Means Motions

Overview

This annex provides detailed information on each of the tax measures proposed in the Budget.

Table A5.1 lists these measures and provides estimates of their budgetary impact.

The annex also provides Notices of Ways and Means Motions to amend the *Income Tax Act*, and the regulations thereunder, the *Excise Tax Act*, the *Customs Tariff,* the *Universal Child Care Benefit Act*, the *Excise Act, 2001*, the *Air Travellers Security Charge Act*, the *Canada Pension Plan* and the *Employment Insurance Act*.

Table A5.1

Cost of Proposed Tax and Tariff Measures[1]

	2009–2010	2010–2011	2011–2012	2012–2013	2013–2014	2014–2015	Total
	Fiscal Costs (millions of dollars)						
Personal Income Tax Measures							
Benefits Entitlement – Shared Custody	–	–	–	–	–	–	–
Universal Child Care Benefit for Single Parents	–	5	5	5	5	5	25
Medical Expense Tax Credit – Purely Cosmetic Procedures	–	-40	-40	-40	-40	-40	-200
Rollover of RRSP Proceeds to an RDSP	–	–	5	5	5	5	20
Carry Forward of RDSP Grants and Bonds[2]	–	20	70	45	30	10	175
Provincial Payments into RESPs and RDSPs	–	–	–	–	–	–	–
Scholarship Exemption and Education Tax Credit	–	–	–	–	–	–	–
Charities: Disbursement Quota Reform	–	–	–	–	–	–	–
Employee Stock Options	-20	-270	-300	-320	-355	-395	-1,660
U.S. Social Security Benefits	–	5	5	5	5	5	25
Mineral Exploration Tax Credit	–	85	-20	–	–	–	65
Business Income Tax Measures							
Accelerated Capital Cost Allowance for Clean Energy Generation	–	–	–	5	5	10	20
Television Set-top Boxes – Capital Cost Allowance	–	5	5	5	5	5	25
Interest on Overpaid Taxes	–	-45	-100	-140	-170	-190	-645
Federal Credit Unions	–	–	–	–	–	–	–
SIFT Conversions and Loss Trading	–	–	–	–	–	–	–

[1] A "-" indicates a nil amount, a small amount (less than $5 million) or an amount that cannot be determined in respect of a measure that is intended to protect the tax base.

[2] The cost of this measure is attributable to program expenditures.

Table A5.1 *(cont'd)*
Cost of Proposed Tax and Tariff Measures

	2009–2010	2010–2011	2011–2012	2012–2013	2013–2014	2014–2015	Total
	Fiscal Costs (millions of dollars)						
International Taxation							
Section 116 and Taxable Canadian Property	–	30	25	25	25	25	130
Refunds under Regulation 105 and Section 116	–	–	–	5	5	5	15
Foreign Tax Credit Generators	–	–	–	–	–	–	–
Foreign Investment Entities and Non-Resident Trusts	–	–	–	–	–	–	–
Sales Tax Measures							
GST/HST and Purely Cosmetic Procedures	–	–	–	–	–	–	–
Simplification of the GST/HST for the Direct Selling Industry	–	–	–	–	–	–	–
Other Tax Measures							
Specified Leasing Property Rules	–	–	–	–	–	–	–
Information Reporting of Tax Avoidance Transactions – Public Consultation	–	–	–	–	–	–	–
Online Notices	–	–	–	–	–	–	–
Tax Evasion and the Proceeds of Crime and Money Laundering Regime	–	–	–	–	–	–	–
Taxation of Corporate Groups	–	–	–	–	–	–	–
Aboriginal Tax Policy	–	–	–	–	–	–	–
Customs Tariff Measures							
Tariff Reductions on Manufacturing Inputs and Machinery and Equipment	17	210	230	252	275	292	1,276

Personal Income Tax Measures

Benefits Entitlement – Shared Custody

Under existing rules, only one eligible individual can receive the Canada Child Tax Benefit and Universal Child Care Benefit in respect of a qualified dependant each month. Similarly, the child component of the Goods and Services Tax/Harmonized Sales Tax Credit (GST/HST credit) is payable in respect of a qualified dependant to only one eligible individual each quarter.

To improve the allocation of child benefits between parents who share custody of a child, Budget 2010 proposes to allow two eligible individuals to receive Canada Child Tax Benefit and Universal Child Care Benefit amounts in a particular month, and two eligible individuals to receive GST/HST credit amounts in respect of a particular quarter, in respect of a child if the recipients would be eligible to receive amounts under the Canada Revenue Agency's existing shared eligibility policy. This policy applies when a child lives more or less equally with two individuals who live separately. The Canada Child Tax Benefit and Universal Child Care Benefit payments will be equivalent to each eligible individual receiving one-half of the annual entitlement that they would receive if they were the sole eligible individual, paid in monthly instalments over the year. The child component of the GST/HST credit will similarly be equivalent to each eligible individual receiving one-half of the annual entitlement that they would receive if they were the sole eligible individual, paid in quarterly instalments over the year.

Corresponding amendments will be made to the *Universal Child Care Benefit Act*.

This measure will apply to benefits payable commencing July 2011.

Universal Child Care Benefit for Single Parents

The Universal Child Care Benefit provides families with $100 a month for each child under the age of six years. In two-parent families, the Universal Child Care Benefit is included in the income of the lower-income spouse or common-law partner. In the case of a single-parent family, the Universal Child Care Benefit is generally included in the single parent's income and taxed at his or her marginal tax rate. As a result, a single parent can pay more tax on Universal Child Care Benefit amounts than a single-earner couple, with the same income, receiving the same Universal Child Care Benefit.

Annual RDSP contributions attract CDSGs of up to $3,500, depending on the beneficiary's family income and the amount contributed, up to a lifetime limit of $70,000. The family income ranges and the corresponding maximum annual CDSGs are set out in Table A5.2.[1]

In addition, CDSBs of up to $1,000 annually are provided to RDSPs established by low- and modest-income families, based on a beneficiary's family income, up to a lifetime limit of $20,000. The amount of the CDSB begins to be phased out for incomes above $23,855 and is fully phased-out at $40,970 (for 2010). Beneficiaries are currently unable to carry forward unused CDSG and CDSB entitlements to future years.

Table A5.2
Maximum Annual Canada Disability Savings Grants

Family Income[1] ($)	
Up to 81,941	Over 81,941
300% on the first $500	100% on the first $1,000
200% on the next $1,000	

[1] Family net income thresholds are in 2010 dollars. These income thresholds are indexed to inflation.

In recognition of the fact that families of children with disabilities may not be able to contribute regularly to their plans, Budget 2010 proposes to amend the *Canada Disability Savings Act* to allow a 10-year carry forward of CDSG and CDSB entitlements.

Upon opening an RDSP, CDSB entitlements will be determined and paid into the plan for the preceding 10 years (not before 2008, the year RDSPs became available), based on the beneficiary's family income in those years. Balances of unused CDSG entitlements will also be determined and maintained for the same period. CDSGs will be paid on unused entitlements, up to an annual maximum of $10,500.

---

[1] Budget 2009 increased the two lowest personal income tax brackets above their indexed values. Consequential changes will be made to the family income thresholds used to determine eligibility for Canada Education Savings Grants, Canada Disability Savings Grants, and Canada Disability Savings Bonds to ensure that these thresholds correspond to the income tax brackets. These changes will apply to the 2009 and subsequent contribution years.

The matching rate on unused CDSG entitlements will be the same as that which would have applied had the contribution been made in the year in which the entitlement was earned. Matching rates on RDSP contributions will be paid in descending order, with contributions using up any grant entitlements at the highest available matching rate first, followed by any grant entitlements at lower rates. Plan holders will receive annual statements of CDSG entitlements.

The carry forward will be available starting in 2011.

Tax Measures
Supplementary Information

Benefits of the RDSP Carry Forward: An Example

Roger, who is a low-income adult who has been eligible for the Disability Tax Credit his whole life, opens an RDSP in 2011.

In each of 2008 (the year RDSPs became available), 2009, 2010 and 2011, Roger will have accumulated $500 in grant entitlements at a 300-per-cent matching rate, $1,000 in grant entitlements at a 200-per-cent matching rate, and $1,000 in CDSB entitlements based on his family income.

When Roger opens an RDSP in 2011, his RDSP will automatically receive $4,000 in CDSBs.

After the RDSP is opened, Roger's family contributes $400 to his plan in 2011, for which his RDSP receives $1,200 in CDSGs. Roger carries forward $1,600 in unused grant entitlements at the 300-per-cent rate and $4,000 in unused grant entitlements at the 200 per-cent-rate. When these unused entitlements are added to his grant entitlements for 2012, Roger has $2,100 in grant entitlements at the 300-per-cent matching rate and $5,000 in grant entitlements at the 200-per-cent matching rate.

In 2012, Roger's family contributes $3,000 to his RDSP. The first $2,100 of this contribution uses up Roger's grant entitlements at the 300-per-cent matching rate. The next $900 is matched at the 200-per-cent matching rate. In total, Roger's RDSP receives $8,100 in CDSGs in 2012. In addition, his RDSP receives a CDSB of $1,000 based on his bond entitlements for 2012.

Grant and Bond Entitlements Example

Year	Contributions	Accumulated grant entitlements			CDSGs paid	Accumulated bond entitlements	CDSBs paid
		300%	200%	100%			
		($)					
2008	–	500	1,000	0	–	1,000	–
2009	–	1,000	2,000	0	–	2,000	–
2010	–	1,500	3,000	0	–	3,000	–
		RDSP opened					
2011	400	1,600	4,000	0	1,200	0	4,000
2012	3,000	0	4,100	0	8,100	0	1,000
Total	**3,400**				**9,300**		**5,000**

347

Provincial Payments into RESPs and RDSPs

The Government of Canada provides financial assistance to Canadian families saving for their children's education through Registered Education Savings Plans and the associated Canada Education Savings Grants and Canada Learning Bond. It also helps families with severely disabled children save for their children's long-term financial security through Registered Disability Savings Plans and the associated Canada Disability Savings Grants and Canada Disability Savings Bonds.

Provincial and territorial governments may also support the efforts of parents to save by making payments into Registered Education Savings Plans and Registered Disability Savings Plans. These provincial programs receive the same treatment as federal grants and bonds paid into these plans – they do not use up a beneficiary's Registered Education Savings Plan or Registered Disability Savings Plan contribution room and they do not attract federal grants. Under the current rules, provincial initiatives that are not administered by the federal government have to be prescribed in order to be treated as provincial programs, which can create uncertainty about the status of payments from these programs.

Budget 2010 proposes to clarify that all payments made to a Registered Education Savings Plan or a Registered Disability Savings Plan through a program funded, directly or indirectly, by a province or administered by a province will be treated the same way as federal grants and bonds and will therefore not themselves attract or reduce federal grants and bonds.

In the case of programs that are administered by a province, this measure will apply to payments made after 2006. In the case of programs that are not administered by a province, this measure will apply to payments made after 2008.

Scholarship Exemption and Education Tax Credit

Budget 2006 introduced a full tax exemption for post-secondary scholarships, fellowships and bursaries to help foster academic excellence by providing tax relief to post-secondary students. The scholarship exemption applies to amounts received in connection with the student's enrolment in an educational program that entitles the student to the Education Tax Credit. The Education Tax Credit is generally available in respect of programs at the post-secondary level, and programs at educational institutions that are certified by the Minister of Human Resources and Skills Development as providing skills in an occupation.

Budget 2010 proposes to clarify that a post-secondary program that consists principally of research will be eligible for the Education Tax Credit, and the scholarship exemption, only if it leads to a college or CEGEP diploma, or a bachelor, masters or doctoral degree (or an equivalent degree). Accordingly, post-doctoral fellowships will be taxable.

Occupational training programs certified by the Minister of Human Resources and Skills Development will continue to qualify for the Education Tax Credit.

Budget 2010 also proposes that an amount will be eligible for the scholarship exemption only to the extent it can reasonably be considered to be received in connection with enrolment in an eligible educational program for the duration of the period of study related to the scholarship.

If a scholarship, fellowship or bursary amount is provided in connection with a part-time program, it is proposed that the scholarship exemption be limited to the amount of tuition paid for the program plus the costs of program-related materials, except if the part-time program is undertaken by a student entitled to the Disability Tax Credit or a student who cannot be enrolled on a full-time basis because of a mental or physical impairment.

The proposed measures will help ensure that the scholarship exemption for post-secondary scholarships, fellowships and bursaries remains targeted to its original purpose. The measures will apply to the 2010 and subsequent taxation years.

Charities: Disbursement Quota Reform

Background

It is estimated that Canadian individuals will receive $2.4 billion in federal tax relief on charitable donations of $8.8 billion in 2009. In addition, corporations benefit from a deduction with respect to charitable donations.

Charitable activities are not defined in the *Income Tax Act*; instead, the meaning of charitable purposes and charitable activities in Canada is largely determined by jurisprudence. Charities must devote their resources to charitable purposes. The *Income Tax Act* specifies requirements for registration as a charity as well as grounds for revocation of that status. The Canada Revenue Agency determines the eligibility of an organization to be a registered charity for federal income tax purposes, based on an examination of the organization's purposes and activities. In addition, charities are subject to corporate and trust law.

The disbursement quota was introduced in 1976 to help curtail fundraising costs and limit capital accumulation. The disbursement quota is intended to ensure that a significant portion of a registered charity's resources are devoted to charitable purposes.

In general terms, the disbursement quota requires that the amount a charity spends each year on charitable activities (including gifts to qualified donees) be at least the sum of:

- 80 per cent of the previous year's tax-receipted donations plus other amounts relating to enduring property and transfers between charities (in other words, a "charitable expenditure rule"); and

- 3.5 per cent of all assets not currently used in charitable programs or administration, if these assets exceed $25,000 (in other words, a "capital accumulation rule").

Some have observed that the impact of the charitable expenditure rule can vary considerably, for reasons unrelated to the manner in which a charity conducts its charitable activities. For example, some charities have a wide range of revenue sources from which to fund their charitable activities, such as grants received from governments and revenues from related business activities. Since all charitable expenditures count toward meeting the disbursement quota, these charities have little difficulty satisfying it even if they do not spend their tax-receipted donations on charitable activities. In contrast, the rule is much more constraining on many small and rural charities that rely mainly on tax-receipted donations.

Stakeholders such as Imagine Canada have called for the elimination of the disbursement quota because it imposes "an unduly complex and costly administrative burden on charities - particularly small and rural charities" and it constrains the flexibility of charities, without achieving its core purpose of limiting spending on fundraising and non-charitable activities.

Recent legislative and administrative initiatives have strengthened the Canada Revenue Agency's ability to ensure that a charity's fundraising and other practices are appropriate. For example, the Canada Revenue Agency publication "Fundraising by Registered Charities" provides guidance for charities on acceptable fundraising practices.

The Canada Revenue Agency may impose sanctions or revoke the registration of a charity in situations where charities use their funds inappropriately, such as in cases where there is undue private benefit. These tools provide a more effective and direct means to fulfill the objectives of the charitable expenditure rule of the disbursement quota.

Budget 2010 proposes to reform the disbursement quota for fiscal years that end on or after March 4, 2010. Specifically, Budget 2010 proposes to:

- repeal the charitable expenditure rule;

- modify the capital accumulation rule; and

- strengthen related anti-avoidance rules for charities.

The Government will monitor the effectiveness of the Canada Revenue Agency's guidance on "Fundraising by Registered Charities", and take action if needed to ensure its stated objectives are achieved.

Repeal of Charitable Expenditure Rule

Budget 2010 proposes to repeal the charitable expenditure rule. Consequently, provisions relating to a number of concepts will no longer be required to calculate the disbursement quota:

- enduring property (gifts to a charity for endowments or multi-year charitable projects which are not subject to the charitable expenditure rule);

- the capital gains reduction and the capital gains pool (provisions that ensure that capital gains realized from the disposition of enduring property are not subject to the charitable expenditure rule and the capital accumulation rule);

- specified gifts (a provision that allows charities with disbursement excesses to help charities with disbursement shortfalls to meet their disbursement quota requirements); and

- exclusions from the calculation of the base to which the 3.5-per-cent disbursement rate is applied (provisions that ensure that funds subject to the charitable expenditure rule are not also subject to the capital accumulation rule).

Budget 2010 also proposes to amend the existing rule that provides the Canada Revenue Agency with the discretion to allow charities to accumulate property for a particular purpose, such as a building project. The existing provision states that property accumulated after approval from the Canada Revenue Agency and any income earned in respect of that property is deemed to have been spent on charitable activities. This rule will require amendment in the absence of the charitable expenditure rule. In order to allow a charity to accumulate property for a particular project, the Canada Revenue Agency will be given the discretion to exclude the accumulated property from the capital accumulation rule calculation.

Modify the capital accumulation component

There is currently an exemption from the capital accumulation rule for charities having $25,000 or less in assets not used in charitable programs or administration. Budget 2010 proposes to increase this threshold to $100,000 for charitable organizations. This increase will reduce the compliance burden on small charitable organizations and provide them with greater ability to maintain reserves to deal with contingencies. The threshold for charitable foundations will remain at $25,000.

The amount of all assets not currently used in charitable programs or administration, for the purpose of the capital accumulation rule in the disbursement quota, is subject to a calculation provided for in the *Income Tax Regulations*. This calculation requires a technical amendment to clarify that it applies both to charitable foundations and charitable organizations.

Strengthen anti-avoidance rules

Budget 2010 proposes to extend existing anti-avoidance rules to situations where it can reasonably be considered that a purpose of a transaction was to delay unduly or avoid the application of the disbursement quota.

Budget 2010 proposes provisions to ensure that amounts transferred between non-arm's length charities will be used to satisfy the disbursement quota of only one charity. It is proposed that a recipient charity, in such circumstances, be required to spend the full amount transferred on its own charitable activities, or to transfer the amount to a qualified donee with which it deals at arm's length, in the current or subsequent taxation year. Alternatively, the transferring charity will be able to elect that the amount transferred will not count towards satisfying its disbursement quota, in which case the recipient charity would not be subject to the immediate disbursement requirement under the anti-avoidance rules.

Employee Stock Options

Budget 2010 proposes the following measures associated with the tax treatment of employee stock options.

Stock Option Cash Outs

If an employee acquires a security of his or her employer under a stock option agreement in the course of his or her employment, the difference between the fair market value of the security at the time the option is exercised and the amount paid by the employee to acquire the security is treated as a taxable employment benefit. If certain conditions are met, the employee is entitled to a deduction equal to one-half of the employment benefit (the stock option deduction).

The stock option deduction results in the taxation of stock option benefits at capital gains tax rates, and as such provides Canadian businesses with a valuable tool to attract and retain highly-skilled workers. In 2007, about 78,000 employees took advantage of the deduction, claiming an average amount of $53,000; three-quarters of the aggregate value of the deduction was claimed by individuals earning more than $500,000.

Table A5.3

Distribution of stock option deduction by income (2007)

Individual's total income[1] ($)	Number of individuals claiming a stock option deduction	Stock option deduction claimed		
		Average amount ($)	Aggregate amount ($ millions)	% of total
Under 100,000	32,483	3,000	100	2%
100,000 to 500,000	38,034	23,000	890	22%
Over 500,000	7,985	393,000	3,140	75%
Total	78,502	53,000	4,130	100%

[1] Including stock option benefits
Source: Tax filer data for the 2007 taxation year.
Numbers may not add due to rounding.

Given the considerable tax benefits provided by the stock option deduction, particularly to high-income individuals, it is important to ensure that it is used in a manner consistent with its intended policy objectives.

The tax rules currently ensure that, when an employee acquires securities under a stock option agreement, only one deduction (at the employee level) is provided. This is because employers are, in this context, prevented from claiming a tax deduction for the issuance of a security.

It is possible, however, to structure employee stock option agreements so that, if employees dispose of ("cash out") their stock option rights for a cash payment from the employer (or other in-kind benefit), the employment benefit is eligible for the stock option deduction while the cash payment is fully deductible by the employer.

Budget 2010 proposes to prevent both the stock option deduction and a deduction by the employer from being claimed for the same employment benefit. To this effect, the stock option deduction will generally be available to employees only in situations where they exercise their options by acquiring securities of their employer. An employer may continue to allow employees to cash out their stock option rights to the corporation without affecting their eligibility for the stock option deduction provided the employer makes an election to forgo the deduction for the cash payment. This will ensure a comparable tax rate with that available on other compensation, when considered on a total employer-employee basis.

Table A5.4

Federal tax collected on $100 of employment benefit ($)

			Type of benefit		
				Stock option cash out	
			Current	Proposed	
	Bonus/ Salary	Stock option exercise		With election	Without election
Employee[1]	29	14.5	14.5	14.5	29
Employer[2]	0	18	0	18	0
Total	29	32.5	14.5	32.5	29

[1] Assumed to be taxed at 29 per cent (the highest federal personal income tax rate).

[2] Assumed to be taxed at 18 per cent (the general federal corporate income tax rate for 2010).

The proposed measure will also help preserve symmetry in the tax treatment of stock-based compensation: that is, where preferential tax treatment is provided to the employee on stock-based benefits, the employer is generally not allowed a tax deduction for the cost of such benefits.

The proposed tax remittance measure will not apply in respect of options granted before 2011 pursuant to an agreement in writing entered into before 4:00 p.m. Eastern Standard Time on March 4, 2010 where the agreement included, at that time, restrictions on the disposition of the optioned securities.

Special Relief for Tax Deferral Elections

Some taxpayers who took advantage of the tax deferral election on stock options introduced in Budget 2000 have experienced financial difficulties as a result of a decline in the value of the optioned securities to the point that the value of the securities is less than the deferred tax liability on the underlying stock option benefit.

To provide relief for taxpayers in these situations, Budget 2010 proposes to introduce a special elective tax treatment for affected taxpayers who elected under the current rules to defer taxation of their stock option benefits until the disposition of the optioned securities. In effect, the special elective treatment will ensure that the tax liability on a deferred stock option benefit does not exceed the proceeds of disposition of the optioned securities, taking into account tax relief resulting from the use of capital losses on the optioned securities against capital gains from other sources.

In any year in which a taxpayer is required to include in income a qualifying deferred stock option benefit, the taxpayer may elect to pay a special tax for the year equal to the taxpayer's proceeds of disposition[2], if any, from the sale or other disposition of the optioned securities. Where such an election is made:

- the taxpayer will be able to claim an offsetting deduction equal to the amount of the stock option benefit; and

- an amount equal to half of the lesser of the stock option benefit and the capital loss on the optioned securities will be included in the taxpayer's income as a taxable capital gain. That gain may be offset by the allowable capital loss on the optioned securities, provided this loss has not been otherwise used.

---

[2]   The special tax will be equal to two-thirds of such proceeds for residents of Québec.

Only stock option benefits for which an election to defer taxation has been made will qualify for this special elective tax treatment. In addition:

- individuals who disposed of their optioned securities before 2010 will have to make an election for this special treatment on or before their filing-due date for the 2010 taxation year (generally April 30, 2011); and

- individuals who have not disposed of their optioned securities before 2010 must do so before 2015. They will then have until their filing-due date for the taxation year of disposition to make an election for this special treatment.

This special tax treatment will provide relief for federal income tax liabilities on qualifying deferred stock option benefits, and provincial and territorial income tax on those benefits for residents of provinces and territories participating in a Tax Collection Agreement. Amendments will be made to allow for the sharing of the special tax with provinces and territories.

U.S. Social Security Benefits

Prior to 1996, pursuant to the Canada-United States Tax Convention (1980), Canadian residents receiving benefits under the social security legislation in the United States, including tier 1 railroad retirement benefits but not including unemployment benefits ("U.S. Social Security benefits"), were required to include only 50 per cent of those benefits in computing income. Changes made to the Canada-U.S. Tax Convention effective beginning in 1996 increased the inclusion rate for U.S. Social Security benefits to 85 per cent from 50 per cent.

Budget 2010 proposes to reinstate the 50-per-cent inclusion rate for Canadian residents who have been in receipt of U.S. Social Security benefits since before January 1, 1996 and for their spouses and common-law partners who are eligible to receive survivor benefits.

This measure will apply to U.S. Social Security benefits received on or after January 1, 2010.

Mineral Exploration Tax Credit

Flow-through shares allow companies to renounce or "flow through" tax expenses associated with their Canadian exploration activities to investors, who can deduct the expenses in calculating their own taxable income. This facilitates the raising of equity to fund exploration by enabling companies to sell their shares at a premium. The mineral exploration tax credit is an additional benefit, available to individuals who invest in flow-through shares, equal to 15 per cent of specified mineral exploration expenses incurred in Canada and renounced to flow-through share investors.

Budget 2010 proposes to extend eligibility for the mineral exploration tax credit for one year, to flow-through share agreements entered into on or before March 31, 2011. Under the existing "look-back" rule, funds raised in one calendar year with the benefit of the credit can be spent on eligible exploration up to the end of the following calendar year. Therefore, for example, funds raised with the credit during the first three months of 2011 can support eligible exploration until the end of 2012.

Mineral exploration, as well as new mining and related processing activity that could follow from successful exploration efforts, can be associated with a variety of environmental impacts to soil, water and air. All such activity, however, is subject to applicable federal and provincial environmental regulations, including project-specific environmental assessments where required.

Business Income Tax Measures

Accelerated Capital Cost Allowance for Clean Energy Generation

Under the capital cost allowance (CCA) regime in the income tax system, Class 43.2 of Schedule II to the *Income Tax Regulations* provides accelerated CCA (50 per cent per year on a declining balance basis) for specified clean energy generation and conservation equipment. The class incorporates by reference a detailed list of eligible equipment that generates or conserves energy by:

- using a renewable energy source (for example, wind, solar, small hydro);

- using fuels from waste (for example, landfill gas, wood waste, manure); or

- making efficient use of fossil fuels (for example, high efficiency cogeneration systems, which simultaneously produce electricity and useful heat).

Providing accelerated CCA in this context is an explicit exception to the general practice of setting CCA rates based on the useful life of assets. Accelerated CCA provides a financial benefit by deferring taxation. This incentive for investment is premised on the environmental benefits of low-emission or no-emission energy generation equipment.

Accelerated CCA for Clean Energy Generation

Class 43.2 was introduced in 2005 and is currently available for assets acquired on or after February 23, 2005 and before 2020. For assets acquired before February 23, 2005, accelerated CCA is provided under Class 43.1 (30 per cent). The eligibility criteria for these two classes are generally the same, except that cogeneration systems that use fossil fuels must meet a higher efficiency standard for Class 43.2 than for Class 43.1. Systems that only meet the lower efficiency standard are eligible for Class 43.1.

Class 43.2 includes a variety of stationary clean energy generation or conservation equipment that is used to produce electricity or thermal energy, or used to produce certain fuels from waste that are in turn used to produce electricity or thermal energy. Subject to detailed rules in the regulations, eligible equipment includes:

Electricity

- High efficiency cogeneration equipment;
- Wind turbines;
- Small hydroelectric facilities;
- Fuel cells;
- Photovoltaic equipment;
- Wave and tidal power equipment;
- Equipment that generates electricity using geothermal energy; and
- Equipment that generates electricity using an eligible waste fuel.

The Auditor General raised concerns in her Spring 2009 report about interest paid on tax overpayments by corporations:

> If the [Canada Revenue] Agency unnecessarily holds large amounts on deposit, with an obligation to pay interest when making a refund, the federal government effectively is borrowing those funds at a higher interest rate than necessary. Instead of borrowing at Treasury bill rates, it will pay a rate that is at least two percentage points higher.

Budget 2010 proposes that, effective July 1, 2010, the interest rate payable by the Minister of National Revenue to corporations will be set at the average yield of three-month Government of Canada Treasury Bills sold in the first month of the preceding quarter, rounded up to the nearest percentage point. This new rate for corporations will apply in respect of income tax, Goods and Services Tax / Harmonized Sales Tax (GST/HST), employment insurance premiums, Canada Pension Plan contributions, excise tax and duty (except in respect of excise duty on beer), the Air Travellers Security Charge and the softwood lumber products export charge. The interest rate calculations in respect of non-corporate taxpayers will not change.

Federal Credit Unions

Consequential to the Budget 2010 proposal to allow for the establishment of federal credit unions, certain amendments may be required to the *Income Tax Act* to provide that federal credit unions that satisfy the existing definition "credit union" in the *Income Tax Act* will be subject to the same income tax rules as other credit unions.

SIFT Conversions and Loss Trading

The *Income Tax Act* includes provisions intended to allow specified investment flow-through (SIFT) trusts and partnerships – commonly referred to as income trusts and partnerships – to convert their structures into corporate form on a tax-deferred basis. Aggressive schemes have been designed to use these provisions to achieve inappropriate tax loss trading that would not be allowed as between two corporations.

In particular, the ability of a corporation to utilize its tax losses is constrained where control of the corporation has been acquired. In the case of a "reverse takeover" of a public corporation, an existing rule in the *Income Tax Act* generally deems there to be an acquisition of control of the public corporation in situations where shares of the public corporation are exchanged for shares of another corporation. Budget 2010 proposes to extend this rule to ensure that it also applies to impose restrictions on the use of losses in situations where units of a SIFT trust or SIFT partnership are exchanged for shares of a corporation.

Budget 2010 also proposes to amend the acquisition-of-control rules in the *Income Tax Act* to ensure that they do not inappropriately restrict the use of losses where a SIFT trust is wound up and distributes the shares of a corporation it holds. The rules will be amended to provide that where a SIFT trust, the sole beneficiary of which is a corporation, owns shares of another corporation, the wind-up of the trust will not cause an acquisition of control of the other corporation and restrict the subsequent use of that corporation's losses.

It is proposed that these amendments apply to transactions undertaken after 4:00 p.m. Eastern Standard Time on March 4, 2010, other than transactions that the parties are obligated to complete pursuant to the terms of an agreement in writing between the parties entered into before that time. A party shall be considered not to be obligated to complete a transaction if the party may be excused from completing the transaction as a result of changes to the *Income Tax Act*. These amendments will also apply to other SIFT conversion transactions if the parties to the transaction make the appropriate election.

International Taxation

Section 116 and Taxable Canadian Property

Canada taxes non-residents on their income and gains from the disposition of "taxable Canadian property". Where such property is disposed of by a non-resident, generally the purchaser must withhold a portion of the amount paid, and remit it to the Government on account of the non-resident vendor's potential Canadian tax liability. However, the purchaser's obligation to withhold does not apply if the non-resident vendor obtains a "clearance certificate" from the Canada Revenue Agency. To obtain a clearance certificate, the non-resident vendor needs to remit an amount, post security, or satisfy the Canada Revenue Agency that no tax will be owing. These rules are contained in section 116 of the *Income Tax Act*.

Taxable Canadian property includes shares of corporations resident in Canada, as well as real or immovable property (including Canadian resource property and timber resource property) that is situated in Canada. It also includes certain shares and other interests the value of which is, or was within the previous 60 months, derived principally from such real or immovable property. Gains from dispositions of taxable Canadian property by non-residents, other than of taxable Canadian property that is real or immovable property or shares that derive their value principally from real or immovable property, are generally exempt under many of Canada's tax treaties.

Dispositions of shares of corporations resident in Canada that do not derive their value principally from real or immovable property are still subject to the withholding process contained in section 116 of the *Income Tax Act*, regardless of the possibility of a treaty exemption. It was with this in mind that Budget 2008 implemented certain changes to streamline and simplify the section 116 compliance process.

Building upon the measures introduced in Budget 2008, Budget 2010 proposes that the definition of taxable Canadian property in the *Income Tax Act* be amended to exclude shares of corporations, and certain other interests, that do not derive their value principally from real or immovable property situated in Canada, Canadian resource property, or timber resource property (subject to the 60 month rule mentioned above). This measure will eliminate section 116 compliance obligations for these types of properties and will also bring Canada's domestic tax rules more in line with our tax treaties and the tax laws of our major trading partners.

Narrowing the definition of taxable Canadian property will eliminate the need for tax reporting under section 116 of the *Income Tax Act* for many investments, enhancing the ability of Canadian businesses, including innovative high-growth companies that contribute to job creation and economic growth, to attract foreign venture capital.

This measure will apply in determining after March 4, 2010 whether a property is taxable Canadian property of a taxpayer.

Refunds under Regulation 105 and Section 116

Section 105 of the *Income Tax Regulations* and section 116 of the *Income Tax Act* impose requirements on payors of funds to non-resident service providers and purchasers of taxable Canadian property from non-residents, respectively, to withhold and remit to the Canada Revenue Agency a portion of the amount paid to the non-resident in certain circumstances. The amounts are to be withheld and remitted on account of the non-resident's potential Canadian tax liability. The obligation to withhold and remit can arise even where the non-resident is not liable for Canadian tax, for example because of protection under an applicable tax treaty.

Section 164 of the *Income Tax Act* permits a taxpayer to receive a refund of tax overpaid for a taxation year provided that the taxpayer has filed its income tax return for the year in question within the period prescribed in the *Income Tax Act*. A unique problem affecting non-residents has been noted in the interaction of the prescribed time limits to obtain a refund and the lack of a deadline for the Canada Revenue Agency to assess a payor who fails to withhold taxes. In some circumstances, this interaction could result in the non-resident being unable to recoup any overpayment of tax.

Budget 2010 proposes an amendment to section 164 of the *Income Tax Act* to also permit the issuance of a refund of an overpayment of tax under Part I of the *Income Tax Act* if the overpayment is related to an assessment of the payor or purchaser in respect of a required withholding under section 105 of the *Income Tax Regulations* or section 116 of the *Income Tax Act* and the taxpayer files a return no more than two years after the date of that assessment.

This measure will be effective for applications for refunds claimed in returns filed after March 4, 2010.

Foreign Tax Credit Generators

The Canadian income tax system generally taxes Canadian residents on their worldwide income. However, in recognition of the fact that foreign countries may also assert the right to tax income earned in their territory by a Canadian resident, Canada generally provides a credit for foreign income taxes paid in respect of such income. This foreign tax credit (FTC) is aimed at relieving Canadian residents from double taxation.

Similar relief is provided in the computation of the income of a foreign affiliate that is subject to tax in the hands of its Canadian shareholder. This relief is provided either through the foreign accrual tax (FAT) mechanism, in the case of the foreign accrual property income (FAPI) of a controlled foreign affiliate, or through the underlying foreign tax (UFT) mechanism, in the case of dividend distributions out of taxable surplus.

Some Canadian corporations have recently been engaging in schemes, often referred to as "foreign tax credit generators", that are designed to shelter tax otherwise payable in respect of interest income on loans made, indirectly, to foreign corporations. These schemes artificially create foreign taxes that are claimed by the Canadian corporation as a FTC, or a FAT or UFT deduction, in order to offset Canadian tax otherwise payable.

There are two main categories of these schemes, and many variations within these categories. The first category involves the use of a foreign partnership, the second involves the use of a foreign corporation that is intended to qualify as a foreign affiliate. The main thrust of all of these schemes is to exploit asymmetry, as between the tax laws of Canada and those of a foreign country, in the characterization of the Canadian corporation's direct or indirect investment in a foreign entity earning the income that is subject to the foreign tax.

369

These foreign tax credit generator schemes generally involve a complex series of transactions which, in substance, amount to a Canadian corporation making a loan to a corporation resident in a foreign jurisdiction that taxes on the basis of the substantive effect of the transaction, while relying on Canadian tax law looking only to the form of the transaction. The form is that of an investment by the Canadian corporation in a foreign special purpose entity which pays full foreign tax on an amount of income that is, in part, the return derived on the Canadian taxpayer's investment. However, an offsetting tax reduction is generated in respect of that return within the foreign corporation's group. If the Canadian corporation had instead made a simple loan to the foreign corporation, the interest income on that loan would generally not be subject to any foreign tax. As such, no FTC, nor any UFT or FAT deduction, would be available in Canada and full Canadian tax would be levied on the interest income in respect of that loan. By using these foreign tax credit generator schemes, the foreign corporation receives the same substantive foreign tax treatment as it would for a simple borrowing but the Canadian corporation is able to claim an FTC, or a UFT or FAT deduction, in order to partly or fully offset its Canadian tax otherwise payable in respect of its interest income. The Canadian tax savings are generally shared between the Canadian lender and the foreign borrower in determining the terms of the loan and related matters.

Although the Government believes that these foreign tax credit schemes can be successfully challenged under existing rules in the *Income Tax Act*, the magnitude of this problem warrants greater assurance through specific and immediate legislative action. Consequently, Budget 2010 proposes measures that will deny claims for FTCs, and FAT and UFT deductions, in circumstances in which the income tax law of the jurisdiction levying the foreign income tax, or another relevant jurisdiction, considers the Canadian corporation to have a lesser direct or indirect interest in the foreign special purpose entity than the Canadian corporation is considered to have for the purposes of the *Income Tax Act*. This measure should generally put the Canadian corporation in the same tax position as if it had made a simple loan to the foreign corporation.

This measure is proposed to be effective for foreign taxes incurred in respect of taxation years that end after March 4, 2010. The Government will be accepting comments in the finalization of the legislation to implement this measure and encourages stakeholders to submit any such comments before May 4, 2010.

Foreign Investment Entities and Non-Resident Trusts

The *Income Tax Act* includes rules designed to prevent Canadians from using foreign intermediaries to avoid paying their fair share of tax. However, the rules are not fully effective in certain circumstances where aggressive offshore tax-planning schemes are used to circumvent their application.

The Government continues to make efforts to ensure that appropriate rules exist to counter these schemes. Most recently, proposals for amendments were tabled during the second session of the 39th Parliament. Those proposals were not enacted before Parliament was dissolved in September 2008. Budget 2009 stated that the Government would review the outstanding proposals before proceeding with measures in this area. As a result of this review, the Government has developed the following revised proposals to replace the outstanding proposals for public consultation with a view to developing revised legislation, which will then also be released for comment.

Foreign Investment Entities

The revised proposals replace the outstanding proposals with respect to foreign investment entities with the following limited enhancements to the existing rules in the *Income Tax Act*:

- Section 94.1 of the *Income Tax Act* currently requires an income inclusion with respect to interests in an "offshore investment fund property" in certain circumstances. It is proposed that the prescribed rate applicable in computing the income inclusion for an interest in an offshore investment fund property be increased to the three-month-average Treasury Bill rate plus two percentage points. This increase in the prescribed rate is intended to better reflect actual long-term investment returns.

- Section 94 of the *Income Tax Act* currently requires certain beneficiaries of a non-resident trust that is not otherwise deemed resident in Canada to report income on a modified foreign accrual property income basis where the fair market value of the beneficiary's interest in the trust exceeds 10 per cent of the value of all interests in the trust. It is proposed that these rules be broadened to apply to any resident beneficiary who, together with any person not dealing at arm's length with the beneficiary, holds 10 per cent or more of any class of interests in a non-resident trust determined by fair market value. They will also apply to any resident who has contributed "restricted property" (as proposed to be defined, which is described below) to a non-resident trust. These changes will be relevant for beneficiaries of non-resident trusts that are not deemed resident in Canada by the revised proposals discussed below.

- It is proposed that the relevant reassessment period in respect of interests in offshore investment fund property and interests in trusts described in the previous paragraph be extended by three years. It is also proposed that the existing reporting requirements with respect to "specified foreign property" be expanded so that more detailed information is available for audit use. These additional measures are needed to ensure that the Canada Revenue Agency has the information and time required to identify and reassess those taxpayers who have not properly reported their income from transactions involving offshore investment fund properties and non-resident trusts.

Non-Resident Trusts

The revised proposals are based on the outstanding proposals with respect to non-resident trusts, but with substantial modifications meant to simplify the outstanding proposals and to better target arrangements that seek to avoid paying the appropriate amount of Canadian tax.

Scope of the Rules

The existing rules in the *Income Tax Act* deem a non-resident discretionary trust to be resident in Canada if it has a Canadian contributor and a related Canadian beneficiary. Such a trust is required to pay tax on its income in the same manner as other residents of Canada. The Canada Revenue Agency, however, has identified complex tax-planning arrangements that attempt to frustrate the fundamental policy objectives of these rules. The outstanding proposals were intended to prevent this type of tax avoidance by broadening the scope of non-resident trusts to which deemed residence would apply.

The outstanding proposals would have applied to non-resident trusts (other than exempt foreign trusts) with a resident contributor regardless of the current existence of a Canadian beneficiary. They would have also applied where the non-resident trust had a Canadian beneficiary and the contributor had been resident in Canada within 60 months of having made the contribution to the trust (referred to as a resident beneficiary under the outstanding proposals). A deemed resident trust would have been taxed on all of its income, regardless of who contributed the property upon which the income was earned or the source of the income. The outstanding proposals would have generally made both resident contributors and resident beneficiaries jointly and severally, or solidarily, liable for tax payable by a trust deemed resident.

The Government has received representations from taxpayers citing the complexity of the outstanding proposals and the difficulty for taxpayers in proceeding with legitimate, non-tax-motivated transactions because of uncertainty as to how those proposals would apply in a variety of particular situations. It is proposed that the scope of the outstanding proposals be simplified and better targeted in several ways.

First, concerns have been expressed that the outstanding proposals would have inadvertently caused a Canadian tax-exempt entity, such as a pension plan, that invested in a non-resident trust to become jointly and severally, or solidarily, liable for the trust's income tax liability despite its tax-exempt status under the *Income Tax Act*. It is proposed that an exemption from resident-contributor and resident-beneficiary status be provided for all persons exempt from tax under section 149 of the *Income Tax Act* (for example, pension funds, Crown corporations and registered charities). However, if a tax-exempt entity were to be used as a conduit to allow a resident of Canada to make an indirect contribution to a non-resident trust, provisions in the outstanding proposals would continue to ensure that the resident of Canada making the indirect contribution is still considered a resident contributor to the trust.

Secondly, concerns have been raised that under the outstanding proposals, an investor would be unable to determine with certainty whether any particular commercial trust would be deemed resident in Canada. Concerns have also been raised about the possibility that a commercial trust might be deemed resident in Canada due to circumstances beyond the investor's control. It has been argued that these uncertainties with respect to the potential application of the outstanding proposals deter genuine commercial investments from being made.

It is not intended that investments in *bona fide* commercial trusts be deterred; nor is it intended that *bona fide* commercial trusts be deemed resident in Canada. Consequently, it is proposed that the provision in the outstanding proposals that would have imposed deemed Canadian residence on a trust by reason only of the trust acquiring or holding restricted property be eliminated. This change will have the effect of expanding the exemption for commercial trusts under paragraph (*h*) of the definition "exempt foreign trust" in the outstanding proposals. Furthermore, a commercial trust will not be deemed resident in Canada if the trust satisfies all the following conditions:

- each beneficiary is entitled to both the income and capital of the trust;

- any transfer of an interest by a beneficiary results in a disposition for the purposes of the *Income Tax Act* and interests in the trust cannot cease to exist otherwise than as a consequence of a redemption or cancellation under which the beneficiary is entitled to receive the fair market value of the interests;

- the amount of income and capital payable to a beneficiary does not depend on the exercise of, or failure to exercise, discretion by any person (discretion only with respect to the timing of distributions will not prevent a trust from being an exempt foreign trust);

- interests in the trust: (i) are listed and regularly traded on a designated stock exchange, (ii) were issued by the trust for fair market value, or (iii) where the trust has at least 150 investors, are available to the public in an open market;

- the terms of the trust cannot be varied without the consent of all the beneficiaries or, in the case of a widely held trust, a majority of the beneficiaries; and

- the trust is not a personal trust.

A commercial trust that is varied in a non-permitted way will lose its status as an exempt foreign trust and, at that time, will be taxable on all the trust's income that has been accumulated (together with an interest amount) since the time it first acquired a resident beneficiary or resident contributor. Taxing the trust on its accumulated income in this manner reflects the fact that the trust would not have qualified as an exempt foreign trust in the first place had the terms of the trust always provided for the trust to be varied in that manner; and consequently, the trust should have been subject to tax in Canada in earlier years. This new anti-avoidance rule is intended to reduce the incentive for Canadians to seek to avoid tax on their personal investments by structuring an arrangement to mimic a genuine commercial trust. However, recognizing that legitimate circumstances may exist in which non-resident beneficiaries may disclaim an interest in a commercial trust for non-tax reasons, a safe harbour will be provided where the interest being disclaimed is under a *de minimus* threshold.

Thirdly, as a result of the proposed changes to the definition "exempt foreign trust", the role of restricted property will be significantly reduced. Restricted property will, however, remain relevant for certain other purposes (for example, in determining whether a particular transfer of property results in an "arm's length transfer" as defined in the outstanding proposals). It is proposed that the definition "restricted property" be narrowed and better targeted. It will be limited to shares or rights (or property that derives its value from such shares or rights) acquired, held, loaned or transferred by a taxpayer as part of a series of transactions or events in which "specified shares" (as defined in the outstanding proposals being, generally, shares with fixed entitlement rights) of a closely-held corporation were issued at a tax cost less than their fair market value.

Finally, it was noted that under the outstanding proposals a conventional loan made by a Canadian financial institution to a non-resident trust in the ordinary course of its business could be viewed as a contribution to that trust, if as part of the terms and conditions of the loan, there was a potential for a transfer of restricted property between the parties (on default of the loan, for example). It is proposed that a new rule be added to ensure that loans made by a Canadian financial institution to a non-resident trust will not result in the financial institution being a resident contributor to the trust as long as the loan is made in the ordinary course of the financial institution's business.

Application of the Rules

Taxation of a Deemed Resident Trust

Where a non-resident trust has a resident beneficiary or a resident contributor, the outstanding proposals would have imposed tax on all of the trust's income and generally made the resident beneficiaries and resident contributors jointly and severally, or solidarily, liable for that tax. It is proposed that a number of refinements to the taxation of a trust deemed resident in Canada be made. For this purpose, it is proposed that the trust's property be divided into a resident portion and a non-resident portion. The resident portion will consist of property acquired by the trust by way of contributions from residents and certain former residents, and any property substituted for such property. The non-resident portion will consist of any property that is not part of the resident portion.

It is proposed that any income arising from property that is part of the non-resident portion, other than income from sources in Canada upon which non-residents are normally required to pay tax, be excluded from the trust's income for Canadian tax purposes. In addition, it is proposed that the trust's income be attributed to its resident contributors in proportion to their relative contributions to the trust (discussed below). The trust will be entitled to a deduction for both the amount of its income that is payable to its beneficiaries in the year and for amounts attributed to resident contributors. As a result, the trust itself will ordinarily pay tax in Canada only on income derived from contributions of certain former resident contributors.

It is proposed that, when income of the trust is not distributed to beneficiaries, the amount of the accumulated income for the relevant taxation year will be deemed to be a contribution by the trust's connected contributors and will form part of the resident portion for the next taxation year. There will be an exception to this deeming rule; accumulated income that arises from property that is part of the non-resident portion will not be subject to the deeming rule if it is kept separate and apart from all the property of the resident portion.

In addition, it is proposed that ordering rules be introduced with respect to distributions to beneficiaries of the trust. Distributions to resident beneficiaries will be deemed to be made first out of the resident portion of the trust's income while distributions to non-resident beneficiaries will be deemed to be made first out of the non-resident portion. Distributions to non-resident beneficiaries out of the non-resident portion of the trust will not be subject to Part XIII tax, but distributions to non-resident beneficiaries out of the resident portion of the trust will be subject to Part XIII tax.

It has been noted that the outstanding proposals do not fully recognize the foreign taxes paid to another country that also treats the trust as a resident for tax purposes. It is proposed to address this concern by permitting a trust that is deemed to be resident in Canada under these rules to claim a foreign tax credit for income taxes paid to another country that treats the trust as a resident of that country for income tax purposes, irrespective of the limits under subsection 20(11) of the *Income Tax Act* but up to the Canadian tax rate (which generally limits the foreign tax credit in respect of property income to 15% of the foreign income).

Attribution

As noted, the outstanding proposals would have generally made both resident contributors and resident beneficiaries jointly and severally, or solidarily, liable for tax payable by a trust deemed resident. This liability has raised concerns on the basis that resident contributors could be held liable for tax on income that has no connection with the property they contributed to the trust.

In response to these concerns, it is proposed that resident contributors to a trust that is deemed to be resident under these rules be attributed, and taxed on, their proportionate share of the trust's income for Canadian tax purposes. They will not be jointly and severally, or solidarily, liable for the trust's own income tax obligations (although resident beneficiaries will be liable with respect to the trust's income tax payable to the same extent as under the outstanding proposals).

Other Tax Measures

Specified Leasing Property Rules

Arrangements to acquire and finance depreciable assets can have varying tax implications depending upon how the arrangement is structured. A taxpayer could borrow money from a financial institution to finance the acquisition, putting the property up as security for the loan, or lease the property from a financial institution that acquired the property for the purpose of leasing it to the taxpayer. Thus, economically, a lease and a loan are highly substitutable. The main difference between the two is the fact that they result in title to the asset being in different hands: in the case of a lease, the financial institution holds the title, whereas in the case of a loan the taxpayer holds this title.

However, unlike accounting rules, the income tax law does not reclassify the legal nature of lease arrangements. Because the income tax law looks at ownership to determine who may claim capital cost allowance, leases have been used to transfer capital cost allowance deductions from the user of an asset to the person financing its acquisition. To seek to neutralize the tax consequences of substituting a lease for a loan, the existing Specified Leasing Property rules in the *Income Tax Regulations* effectively recharacterize such a lease from the lessor's perspective to be a loan, with the lease payments received being treated as blended payments of principal and interest. The rules restrict a lessor's claim for capital cost allowance on the leased property to the lesser of the amount of capital cost allowance that would otherwise be deductible and the amount of lease payments received, less a calculation of notional interest amount for the year. In effect, the Specified Leasing Property rules put lessors in the same position as lenders who receive blended payments of principal (non-taxable) and interest (taxable).

The Specified Leasing Property rules contain certain exceptions. In particular, they do not apply to short-term leases or to leases of property with a value of less than $25,000, since generally such leases provide an immaterial tax benefit or do not, in substance, provide financing to the lessee. The rules also include an exception for certain types of property ("exempt property").

Some taxpayers have exploited these exemptions by leasing exempt property, and claiming capital cost allowance in respect of that property, to a lessee who is not subject to Canadian income tax and therefore cannot make use of the capital cost allowance, either because the lessee is tax-exempt or non-resident.

Budget 2010 proposes to extend the application of the Specified Leasing Property rules to otherwise exempt property that is the subject of a lease to a government or other tax-exempt entity, or to a non-resident. However, such a lease will continue to be exempt if the total value of the property that is the subject of the lease is less than $1 million. In this regard, an anti-avoidance rule will apply if it may reasonably be considered that one of the purposes of dividing property (or a class of property) among separate leases is to meet the $1 million exception.

These measures will apply to leases entered into after 4:00 p.m. Eastern Standard Time March 4, 2010.

Information Reporting of Tax Avoidance Transactions – Public Consultation

Budget 2010 announces a public consultation on proposals to require the reporting of certain tax avoidance transactions. The Government will undertake consultations with stakeholders on these proposals, with a view to improving the fairness of the Canadian tax system. Details of these proposals will be released at the earliest opportunity and the consultation process will be announced at that time.

The fairness of the Canadian income tax system is essential to ensure the integrity of Canada's self-assessment system. Ensuring this fairness requires a balancing between a taxpayer's entitlement to plan their affairs in a manner that legally minimizes their tax liability and the need to ensure that the tax law is not abused. Aggressive tax planning arrangements entered into by some taxpayers can undermine the tax base and the fairness and integrity of the tax system, to the detriment of all Canadians.

The *Income Tax Act* already contains a number of substantive rules intended to counter aggressive tax planning. In some cases, these rules help identify certain transactions and their participants. In other cases, the rules deny the tax benefits sought to be obtained (including, but not limited to, the General Anti-Avoidance Rule).

However, in order to be able to effectively apply these substantive rules, the Canada Revenue Agency must be able to identify aggressive tax planning in a timely manner. In this regard, there are already information reporting requirements for tax shelters, as defined in the *Income Tax Act*. The reporting regime for tax shelters assists the Canada Revenue Agency to ensure that the benefits provided by a tax shelter are not unintended, inappropriate or contrary to a provision of the tax law. However, a significant number of aggressive tax planning arrangements do not meet the definition in the law of a tax shelter. Currently, there is no specific information reporting regime that identifies for the Canada Revenue Agency other types of potentially abusive tax avoidance transactions.

Budget 2010 therefore proposes a regime under which a tax "avoidance transaction" that features at least two of three "hallmarks" would be a "reportable transaction" that must be reported to the Canada Revenue Agency. The proposed hallmarks would reflect certain circumstances that commonly exist when taxpayers enter into tax avoidance transactions. Although the hallmarks are not themselves evidence of abuse, their presence often indicates that underlying transactions are present that carry a higher risk of abuse of the income tax system. In this regard, the proposed regime is similar to, but less strict than, the reporting regimes of other jurisdictions that use hallmarks as a means of identifying aggressive tax planning, such as those of the United States, the United Kingdom and most recently, the Province of Québec. This would minimize the possibility that normal tax planning would be subject to these proposals.

For this purpose, a reportable transaction would be an avoidance transaction, as currently defined in the *Income Tax Act*, that is entered into by or for the benefit of a taxpayer that bears at least two of the following three hallmarks:

1. A promoter or tax advisor in respect of the transaction is entitled to fees that are to any extent

   • attributable to the amount of the tax benefit from the transaction,

   • contingent upon the obtaining of a tax benefit from the transaction, or

   • attributable to the number of taxpayers who participate in the transaction or who have been provided access to advice given by the promoter or advisor regarding the tax consequences from the transaction.

2. A promoter or tax advisor in respect of the transaction requires "confidential protection" about the transaction.

3. The taxpayer or the person who entered into the transaction for the benefit of the taxpayer obtains "contractual protection" in respect of the transaction (otherwise than as a result of a fee described in the first hallmark).

A transaction that is a tax shelter or a flow-through share arrangement will not be impacted by these proposals, but will be subject to the existing requirements for tax shelters and flow-through shares.

Upon discovery of a reportable transaction that has not been reported when required, the Canada Revenue Agency could deny the tax benefit resulting from the transaction. If the taxpayer still wanted to claim the tax benefit, it would be required to file with the Canada Revenue Agency any required information and to pay a penalty. The disclosure of a reportable transaction would have no bearing on whether the benefit is allowed under the law; rather it would simply assist the Canada Revenue Agency in identifying the transaction. In this regard, the disclosure of a reportable transaction would not be considered in any way as an admission that the General Anti-Avoidance Rule applies to the transaction.

These proposals, as modified to take into account the consultations, would apply to avoidance transactions entered into after 2010, as well as those that are part of a series of transactions completed after 2010.

Online Notices

In 2000 the *Personal Information Protection and Electronic Documents Act* introduced a legislative framework by which requirements in federal statutes and regulations, which contemplate the use of paper or do not expressly permit the use of electronic technology, may be administered or complied with in the electronic environment. This gave the Canada Revenue Agency general legislative authority to provide information electronically in most circumstances. However, the provisions of some of the various statutes dealing with notices issued by the Canada Revenue Agency were enacted at a time when electronic alternatives were not contemplated. As a result of the specific language of these provisions, some notices cannot be provided in electronic format even with the general permission accorded by the *Personal Information Protection and Electronic Documents Act*. As such, taxpayers can receive notices, such as notices of assessment under the *Income Tax Act*, from the Canada Revenue Agency only through the mail system or personally.

Budget 2010 proposes that the *Income Tax Act, Excise Tax Act, Excise Act, 2001, Air Travellers Security Charge Act, Canada Pension Plan* and *Employment Insurance Act* be amended to allow for the electronic issuance of those notices that can currently be sent by ordinary mail. However, notices that are specifically required to be served personally or by registered or certified mail will not be eligible to be transmitted electronically.

These measures will provide the Canada Revenue Agency with the legislative authority to issue electronic notices, if authorized by a taxpayer, which will be made available on the Canada Revenue Agency's existing secure online platforms (My Account and My Business Account). The Canada Revenue Agency will inform taxpayers that provide such authorization that a new electronic document is available in their secure online account by sending the taxpayer an email to that effect. The Canada Revenue Agency intends to provide this service in respect of notices of assessment and reassessment of tax under Part I of the *Income Tax Act*, and notices of determination and re-determination in respect of the Goods and Services Tax / Harmonized Sales Tax (GST/HST) credit and the Canada Child Tax Benefit. Legislative authority will also be provided to the Canada Revenue Agency to issue electronic notices for GST/HST, excise tax and duty (other than the duty on beer), and the Air Travellers Security Charge.

The necessary legislative amendments will be effective as of the date of Royal Assent of the implementing legislation. However, the application of these measures will commence at such time as will be announced by the Minister of National Revenue.

Tax Evasion and the Proceeds of Crime and Money Laundering Regime

The *Criminal Code* was amended in December 2001 as part of an internationally coordinated effort by developed countries to counter criminal and terrorist activities. The proceeds of crime and money laundering regime in the *Criminal Code* provides the Crown, in respect of certain criminal and terrorist activities, with enhanced powers to search, to seize and to retain proceeds of crime and to apply minimum terms of imprisonment to convicted criminals and terrorists who do not forfeit their proceeds of crime. In such cases, Canada is also assisted in investigating these serious offences (referred to as "designated offences" in the *Criminal Code*) by foreign governments under mutual legal assistance treaties.

Provisions in the *Criminal Code* can be applied to prosecute tax evasion offenses that constitute fraud, in which case the proceeds of crime and money laundering regime may be applicable. Indictable tax offences prosecuted under the *Income Tax Act,* the *Excise Tax Act*, the *Excise Act* (except for subsections 233(1) and 240(1)) and the *Budget Implementation Act, 2000,* however, were excluded from falling within the ambit of the proceeds of crime and money laundering regime.

Budget 2010 proposes to rationalize the rules concerning the application of the proceeds of crime and money laundering regime, and provide further support for international efforts to counter criminal and terrorist activities, by repealing the exclusion for indictable tax offences under the *Income Tax Act*, the *Excise Tax Act*, the *Excise Act*, and the *Budget Implementation Act, 2000* from the definition of "designated offence" under the *Criminal Code*, such that the Crown will be able to prosecute these tax offences using that regime, regardless of whether prosecuted under the *Criminal Code* fraud provisions or the tax statutes. Budget 2010 also proposes consequential amendments to the *Proceeds of Crime (Money Laundering) and Terrorist Financing Act* consistent with the proposal above with respect to the *Criminal Code.*

Taxation of Corporate Groups

Over the last several years, the Government has taken significant steps to improve the competitiveness of the tax system for Canadian businesses, and followed through on *Advantage Canada* commitments to reduce taxes on business investment. However, there are still specific structural elements of the tax system where it may be possible to make improvements. For example, the Government has heard various concerns from the business community and from the provinces regarding the utilization of tax losses within corporate groups. Going forward, the Government will explore whether new rules for the taxation of corporate groups - such as the introduction of a formal system of loss transfers or consolidated reporting – could improve the functioning of the tax system. Stakeholder views will be sought prior to the introduction of any changes.

Aboriginal Tax Policy

Taxation is an integral part of good governance as it promotes greater accountability and self-sufficiency and provides revenues for important public services and investments. Therefore, the Government of Canada supports initiatives that encourage the exercise of direct taxation powers by Aboriginal governments.

Notices of Ways and Means Motions

Notice of Ways and Means Motion to Amend the *Income Tax Act* and *Income Tax Regulations*

That it is expedient to amend the *Income Tax Act* and *Income Tax Regulations* to provide among other things:

Benefits Entitlement – Shared Custody

(1) That, for amounts in respect of the Goods and Services Tax Credit that are deemed to be paid during months after June 2011,

   (*a*) section 122.5 of the Act be amended to add the following after subsection (3):

   (3.01) Notwithstanding subsection (3), if an eligible individual is a shared custody parent (within the meaning assigned by section 122.6, but with the words "qualified dependant" in that section having the meaning assigned by subsection (1)) in respect of one or more qualified dependants at the beginning of a month, the amount deemed by subsection (3) to have been paid during a specified month is equal to the amount determined by the formula

$$(A + B) / 2$$

   where

   A is the amount determined by the formula in subsection (3), calculated without reference to this subsection, and

   B is the amount determined by the formula in subsection (3), calculated without reference to this subsection and subparagraph (*b*)(ii) of the definition "eligible individual" in section 122.6.

   and

   (*b*) paragraph 122.5(6)(*b*) of the Act be replaced by the following:

   (*b*) in the absence of an agreement referred to in paragraph (*a*), the person is deemed to be, in relation to that month, a qualified dependant of the individuals, if any, who are, at the beginning of that month, eligible individuals (within the meaning assigned by section 122.6, but with the words "qualified dependant" in that section having the meaning assigned by subsection (1)) in respect of that person; and.

(2) That, for overpayments in respect of the Canada Child Tax Benefit that are deemed to arise after June 2011,

   (*a*) paragraph (*b*) of the definition "eligible individual" in section 122.6 of the Act be replaced by the following:

   (*b*) is a parent of the qualified dependant who

   > (i) is the parent who primarily fulfils the responsibility for the care and upbringing of the qualified dependant and who is not a shared custody parent in respect of the qualified dependant, or

   > (ii) is a shared custody parent in respect of the qualified dependant;

   (*b*) section 122.6 of the Act be amended by adding the following definition in alphabetical order:

   "shared custody parent" in respect of a qualified dependant at a particular time means, where the presumption referred to in paragraph (*f*) of the definition "eligible individual" does not apply in respect of the qualified dependant, an individual who is one of the two parents of the qualified dependant who

   > (*a*) are not at that time cohabiting spouses or common-law partners of each other,

   > (*b*) reside with the qualified dependant on an equal or near equal basis, and

   > (c) primarily fulfil the responsibility for the care and upbringing of the qualified dependant when residing with the qualified dependant, as determined in consideration of prescribed factors,

and

   (*c*) section 122.61 of the Act be amended by adding the following after subsection (1):

   (1.1) Notwithstanding subsection (1), if an eligible individual is a shared custody parent in respect of one or more qualified dependants at the beginning of a month, the overpayment deemed by subsection (1) to have arisen during the month is equal to the amount determined by the formula

   $$(A + B) / 2$$

(13) That, in respect of programs that are funded, directly or indirectly, by a province but administered by a third party, paragraph (11) apply for the 2009 and subsequent taxation years.

(14) That, for the 2009 and subsequent taxation years, subparagraphs 241(4)(*d*)(vii.1) and 241(4)(*d*)(vii.5) of the Act be amended to allow taxpayer information to be disclosed for the purpose of administering or enforcing programs described in paragraph (11).

Scholarship Exemption and Education Tax Credit

(15) That, for the 2010 and subsequent taxation years, the portion of the scholarship exemption in paragraph 56(3)(a) of the Act that applies in respect of a scholarship, fellowship or bursary received in connection with the taxpayer's enrolment in an educational program be limited to an amount equal to the sum of the fees paid to a designated educational institution, as defined in subsection 118.6(1) of the Act, in respect of the taxpayer's tuition and costs incurred for program-related materials, if the taxpayer may deduct an amount by reason of paragraph (*b*) of the description of B in subsection 118.6(2) of the Act in respect of that educational program.

(16) That, for the 2010 and subsequent taxation years, a scholarship, fellowship or bursary (in this paragraph referred to as an "award") is not, for the purpose of the scholarship exemption in subsection 56(3) of the Act, considered to be received in connection with a taxpayer's enrolment in an educational program except to the extent that it is reasonable to conclude that the award is intended to support the taxpayer's enrolment in the program, having regard to all the circumstances, including

> (a) any terms or conditions that apply in respect of the award,
>
> (b) the duration of the program, and
>
> (c) the period for which support is intended to be provided by the award.

(17) That, for the 2010 and subsequent taxation years, a program at a post-secondary school level referred to in the definition "qualifying education program" in subsection 118.6(1) of the Act does not include a program that consists primarily of research, unless the program leads to a diploma from a college or a Collège d'enseignement général et professionnel (CEGEP), or a bachelor, masters or doctoral degree (or an equivalent degree).

Charities: Disbursement Quota Reform

(18) That, for taxation years of registered charities that end on or after March 4, 2010,

(a) the definitions "capital gains pool", "enduring property" and "specified gift" in subsection 149.1(1) of the Act be repealed;

(b) the formula in the definition "disbursement quota" in subsection 149.1(1) of the Act be replaced by the following:

$$A \times B \times 0.035 / 365$$

where

A is the number of days in the taxation year, and

B is

(*a*) the prescribed amount for the year, in respect of all or a portion of a property owned by the charity at any time in the 24 months immediately preceding the taxation year that was not used directly in charitable activities or administration, if that amount is greater than

(i) if the registered charity is a charitable organization, $100,000, and

(ii) in any other case, $25,000, and

(*b*) in any other case, nil;

(c) the following definition be added in alphabetical order in subsection 149.1(1) of the Act:

"designated gift" means that portion of a gift, made in a taxation year by a registered charity, that is designated as a designated gift in its information return for the year.

(19) That, for taxation years of registered charities that end on or after March 4, 2010, the word "specified" in subsection 149.1(1.1) of the Act be replaced with the word "designated".

(20) That, for taxation years of registered charities that end on or after March 4, 2010, subsection 149.1(4.1) of the Act be amended

(a) by replacing paragraph 149.1(4.1)(*a*) with the following:

(*a*) of a registered charity, if it has entered into a transaction (including a gift to another registered charity) and it may reasonably be considered that a purpose of the transaction was to avoid or delay unduly the expenditure of amounts on charitable activities;

and

(b) by adding the following after paragraph 149.1(4.1)(*c*):

(*d*) of a registered charity, if it has in a taxation year received a gift (other than a designated gift) from another registered charity with which it does not deal at arm's length, and if it has not expended, before the end of the next taxation year, in addition to its disbursement quotas for those taxation years, an amount at least equal to the total amount of the gift, on charitable activities carried on by it or by way of gifts made to qualified donees with which it deals at arm's length.

(21) That, for taxation years of registered charities that end on or after March 4, 2010, subsection 149.1(8) of the Act be replaced by the following:

(8) A registered charity may, with the approval in writing of the Minister, accumulate property for a particular purpose, on terms and conditions, and over such period of time, as the Minister specifies in the approval, and any property accumulated after receipt of and in accordance with that approval, including any income earned in respect of the accumulated property, is not to be included in the amount described in B in the formula in the definition "disbursement quota" in subsection (1) for any taxation year that the Minister specifies.

(22) That, for taxation years of registered charities that end on or after March 4, 2010, subsection 188.1(11) be replaced by the following:

(11) If, in a taxation year, a registered charity has entered into a transaction (including a gift to another registered charity) and it may reasonably be considered that a purpose of the transaction was to avoid or delay unduly the expenditure of amounts on charitable activities, the registered charity is liable to a penalty under this Act for its taxation year equal to 110% of the amount of expenditure avoided or delayed, and in the case of a gift to another registered charity, both charities are jointly and severally, or solidarily, liable to the penalty.

(12) If a registered charity has in a taxation year received a gift of property (other than a designated gift) from another registered charity with which it does not deal at arm's length, and if it has not expended, before the end of the next taxation year, in addition to its disbursement quotas for those taxation years, an amount at least equal the amount of the gift, on charitable activities carried on by it or by way of gifts made to qualified donees with which it deals at arm's length, the registered charity is liable to a penalty under this Act for that subsequent taxation year equal to 110% of the amount of by which the fair market value of the property exceeds the total of such amounts expended.

Employee Stock Options

Stock Option Cash-Outs

(23) That, for transactions occurring after 4:00 p.m. Eastern Standard Time on March 4, 2010, paragraphs 110(1)(*d*) and (*d*.1) of the Act require, as a condition of eligibility for the deductions provided under those paragraphs (referred to in this paragraph as "the stock option deduction"), that the securities described in an agreement to sell or issue securities referred to in subsection 7(1) of the Act be acquired by the employee, unless

> (*a*) the employer elects in prescribed form in respect of all stock options issued or to be issued after 4:00 p.m. Eastern Standard Time on March 4, 2010 under the agreement, and files such election with the Minister of National Revenue, that neither the employer, nor any person who does not deal at arm's length with the employer, will deduct any amount in respect of a payment, to or for the benefit of the employee, for the employee's disposition of rights under the agreement;

> (*b*) the employer provides the employee with evidence in writing of such election; and

> (*c*) the employee files such evidence with the Minister of National Revenue with his or her return of income for the year in which the stock option deduction is claimed.

(24) That, for dispositions of rights occurring after 4:00 p.m. Eastern Standard Time on March 4, 2010, it be clarified that the rules in subsection 7(1) of the Act apply in circumstances in which an employee (or a person who does not deal at arm's length with the employee) disposes of rights under an agreement to sell or issue securities to a person with whom the employee does not deal at arm's length.

Tax Deferral Election and Remittance Requirement

(25) That, in respect of rights under an agreement to sell or issue securities exercised after 4:00 p.m. Eastern Standard Time on March 4, 2010, subsections 7(8) to (16) of the Act be repealed.

(26) That, in respect of securities acquired by employees after 2010, it be clarified that under section 153 of the Act an amount must be remitted to the Receiver General by the employer in respect of an employment benefit that is taxable under section 7 of the Act (other than an amount to which subsection 7(1.1) of the Act applies), to the same extent as if the amount of the benefit had been paid to the employee in money as a bonus, and, for these purposes, if the requirements of paragraph 110(1)(*d*) of the Act are met in respect of the employment benefit at the time that the securities are acquired, the amount of the benefit be reduced by one-half.

(27) That, in respect of employment benefits realized from acquisitions of securities after 2010, section 153 of the Act provide that the fact that the benefit arose from the acquisition of securities not be considered a basis on which the Minister of National Revenue may reduce the amount required to be remitted under section 153 of the Act.

(28) That paragraphs (26) and (27) not apply in respect of rights under an agreement to sell or issue securities granted before 2011 if the agreement was entered into in writing before 4:00 pm Eastern Standard Time on March 4, 2010 and included, at that time, a written condition that restricts the employee from disposing of the securities acquired under the agreement for a period of time after exercise.

Special Relief for Tax Deferral Elections

(29) That, where a taxpayer disposes of securities before 2015 and the securities gave rise to an employment benefit in respect of which an election under subsection 7(10) of the Act was made, the taxpayer be permitted to elect, in prescribed form, the following tax treatment for the taxation year in which the securities are disposed of:

(*a*) that paragraph 110(1)(*d*) and 110(1)(*d*.1) of the Act be read without reference to the phrase "1/2 of" in calculating the amount deductible by the taxpayer in respect of the employment benefit arising under subsection 7(1);

(*b*) that one-half of the lesser of

   i.   the amount deductible under subparagraph (*a*) and

   ii. the taxpayer's capital loss from the disposition of the securities be included as a taxable capital gain in the taxpayer's income for the taxation year in which the deduction in subparagraph (*a*) is claimed;

(*c*) that a special tax, equal to the taxpayer's proceeds of disposition of the securities (or 2/3 of the taxpayer's proceeds of disposition, if the taxpayer resides in Québec), be payable under the Act for the taxation year in which the deduction under subparagraph (*a*) is claimed; and

(*d*) that the taxable capital gain under subparagraph (*b*) be disregarded for the purposes of the definition "adjusted income" in subsections 122.5(1), 122.51(1) and 180.2(1), section 122.6, and the definition "adjusted net income" in subsection 122.7(1) of the Act.

(30) That, an election described in paragraph (29) in respect of a taxation year that is outside the normal reassessment period (within the meaning of subsection 152(3.1) of the Act) be considered an application for determination by the Minister of National Revenue under subsection 152(4.2).

(31) That, the deadline for a taxpayer to file the election described in paragraph (29) shall be:

(*a*) if the taxpayer disposed of the securities before 2010, the taxpayer's filing-due date for 2010, and

(*b*) if the taxpayer disposes of the securities after 2009, the taxpayer's filing-due date for the year of the disposition.

U.S. Social Security Benefits

(32) That, in computing taxable income for a taxation year that ends after 2009, a taxpayer be allowed to deduct 35 per cent of the total of all benefits received by the taxpayer in the taxation year to which paragraph 5 of Article XVIII of the *Convention between Canada and the United States of America with respect to Taxes on Income and on Capital* as set out in Schedule I to the *Canada-United States Tax Convention Act, 1984,* of the S.C. 1984, c. 20, applies, if

(a) the taxpayer has, continuously during a period that begins before 1996 and that ends in the taxation year, been resident in Canada and received such benefits in each taxation year ending in that period, or

(b) the benefits are payable to the taxpayer in respect of a deceased individual, and

(i) the deceased individual was, immediately before the deceased individual's death, the taxpayer's spouse or common-law partner and was, in the taxation year in which the deceased individual died, a taxpayer described in paragraph (a), and

(ii) the taxpayer has, continuously during a period that begins at the time of the death of the deceased individual and that ends in the taxation year, been resident in Canada and received such benefits in each taxation year ending in that period.

Mineral Exploration Tax Credit

(33) That, for expenses renounced under a flow-through share agreement made after March 2010,

(a) paragraph (*a*) of the definition "flow-through mining expenditure" in subsection 127(9) of the Act be replaced by the following:

(*a*) that is a Canadian exploration expense incurred by a corporation after March 2010 and before 2012 (including, for greater certainty, an expense that is deemed by subsection 66(12.66) to be incurred before 2012) in conducting mining exploration activity from or above the surface of the earth for the purpose of determining the existence, location, extent or quality of a mineral resource described in paragraph (*a*) or (*d*) of the definition "mineral resource" in subsection 248(1),

and

(b) paragraphs (*c*) and (*d*) of the definition "flow-through mining expenditure" in subsection 127(9) of the Act be replaced by the following:

(*c*) an amount in respect of which is renounced in accordance with subsection 66(12.6) by the corporation to the taxpayer (or a partnership of which the taxpayer is a member) under an agreement described in that subsection and made after March 2010 and before April 2011, and

(*d*) that is not an expense that was renounced under subsection 66(12.6) to the corporation (or a partnership of which the corporation is a member), unless that renunciation was under an agreement described in that subsection and made after March 2010 and before April 2011.

Canadian Renewable and Conservation Expenses – Principal-Business Corporations

(34) That, in respect of taxation years ending after 2004, the definition "principal-business corporation" in subsection 66(15) of the Act be amended to include a corporation, the principal business of which is producing fuel or generating or distributing energy, using property described in Class 43.1 or 43.2 of Schedule II to the *Income Tax Regulations.*

SIFT Conversions and Loss Trading

(35) That subsection 256(7) of the Act be modified to add a rule similar to that in existing paragraph 256(7)(*c*) such that where two or more persons dispose of interests in a SIFT trust (as defined in the Act, determined without reference to subsection 122.1(2) of the Act), SIFT partnership (as defined in the Act, determined without reference to subsection 197(8) of the Act) or real estate investment trust in exchange for shares of the capital stock of a corporation, control of that corporation and of each corporation controlled by it immediately before the exchange is deemed to have been acquired at the time of the exchange by a person or group of persons.

(36) That subsection 256(7) of the Act be modified such that where a SIFT wind-up corporation is the only beneficiary of a trust and the trust controls another corporation, on a distribution of the shares of the other corporation that is part of a SIFT trust wind-up event (as defined in the Act), the SIFT wind-up corporation will be deemed not to acquire control of the other corporation because of that distribution.

(37) That the amendments referred to in paragraphs (35) and (36) apply to transactions undertaken after 4:00 p.m. Eastern Standard Time March 4, 2010, other than transactions that the parties are obligated to complete pursuant to the terms of an agreement in writing between the parties entered into before that time. A party shall be considered not to be obligated to complete a transaction if the party may be excused from completing the transaction as a result of amendments to the *Income Tax Act.* If the relevant parties so elect in writing, the amendments referred to in paragraphs (35) and (36) will apply to transactions that were completed or agreed to in writing before 4:00 p.m. Eastern Standard Time March 4, 2010.

Notice of Ways and Means Motion to Amend the *Excise Tax Act*

That it is expedient to amend the *Excise Tax Act* as follows:

GST/HST and Purely Cosmetic Procedures

1. (1) Section 1 of Part II of Schedule V to the *Excise Tax Act* is amended by adding the following in alphabetical order:

"cosmetic service supply"
« *fourniture de services esthétiques* »

"cosmetic service supply" means a supply of property or a service that is made for cosmetic purposes and not for medical or reconstructive purposes;

(2) Subsection (1) applies in respect of

(*a*) a supply made after March 4, 2010; and

(*b*) a supply made on or before that day if

(i) all of the consideration for the supply becomes due after March 4, 2010, or is paid after that day without having become due, or

(ii) any consideration for the supply became due, or was paid, on or before that day, unless the supplier did not, on or before that day, charge, collect or remit any amount as or on account of tax in respect of the supply under Part IX of the Act.

2. (1) Part II of Schedule V to the Act is amended by adding the following after section 1:

1.1 For the purposes of this Part, other than section 9, a cosmetic service supply and a supply, in respect of a cosmetic service supply, that is not made for medical or reconstructive purposes are deemed not to be included in this Part.

(2) Subsection (1) applies in respect of

(*a*) a supply made after March 4, 2010; and

(*b*) a supply made on or before that day if

(i) all of the consideration for the supply becomes due after March 4, 2010, or is paid after that day without having become due, or

(ii) any consideration for the supply became due, or was paid, on or before that day, unless the supplier did not, on or before that day, charge, collect or remit any amount as or on account of tax in respect of the supply under Part IX of the Act.

3. (1) Section 2 of Part II of Schedule V to the Act is replaced by the following:

2. A supply of an institutional health care service made by the operator of a health care facility if the institutional health care service is rendered to a patient or resident of the facility.

(2) Subsection (1) applies in respect of

(*a*) a supply made after March 4, 2010; and

(*b*) a supply made on or before that day if

(i) all of the consideration for the supply becomes due after March 4, 2010, or is paid after that day without having become due, or

(ii) any consideration for the supply became due, or was paid, on or before that day, unless the supplier did not, on or before that day, charge, collect or remit any amount as or on account of tax in respect of the supply under Part IX of the Act.

4. (1) Section 5 of Part II of Schedule V to the Act is replaced by the following:

5. A supply of a consultative, diagnostic, treatment or other health care service that is rendered by a medical practitioner to an individual.

(2) Subsection (1) applies in respect of

(*a*) a supply made after March 4, 2010; and

(*b*) a supply made on or before that day if

(i) all of the consideration for the supply becomes due after March 4, 2010, or is paid after that day without having become due, or

(ii) any consideration for the supply became due, or was paid, on or before that day, unless the supplier did not, on or before that day, charge, collect or remit any amount as or on account of tax in respect of the supply under Part IX of the Act.

5. (1) Section 2 of Part VI of Schedule V to the Act is amended by striking out "or" at the end of paragraph (*n*), by adding "or" at the end of paragraph (*o*) and by adding the following after paragraph (*o*):

(*p*) property or a service

(i) the supply of which

(A) is a cosmetic service supply (as defined in section 1 of Part II of this Schedule), or

(B) is in respect of a cosmetic service supply referred to in clause (A) and is not made for medical or reconstructive purposes, and

(ii) the supply of which would be included in Part II of this Schedule or Part II of Schedule VI if Part II of this Schedule were read without reference to section 1.1 or Part II of Schedule VI were read without reference to section 1.2, as the case may be.

(2) Subsection (1) applies in respect of

(*a*) a supply made after March 4, 2010; and

(*b*) a supply made on or before that day if

(i) all of the consideration for the supply becomes due after March 4, 2010, or is paid after that day without having become due, or

(ii) any consideration for the supply became due, or was paid, on or before that day, unless the supplier did not, on or before that day, charge, collect or remit any amount as or on account of tax in respect of the supply under Part IX of the Act.

6. (1) Part II of Schedule VI to the Act is amended by adding the following after section 1.1:

1.2. For the purposes of this Part, a cosmetic service supply (as defined in section 1 of Part II of Schedule V) and a supply, in respect of a cosmetic service supply, that is not made for medical or reconstructive purposes are deemed not to be included in this Part.

(2) Subsection (1) applies in respect of

(*a*) a supply made after March 4, 2010; and

(*b*) a supply made on or before that day if

(i) all of the consideration for the supply becomes due after March 4, 2010, or is paid after that day without having become due, or

(ii) any consideration for the supply became due, or was paid, on or before that day, unless the supplier did not, on or before that day, charge, collect or remit any amount as or on account of tax in respect of the supply under Part IX of the Act.

7. (1) Section 34 of Part II of Schedule VI to the Act is replaced by the following:

34. A supply of a service (other than a service the supply of which is included in any provision of Part II of Schedule V except section 9 of that Part) of installing, maintaining, restoring, repairing or modifying a property the supply of which is included in any of sections 2 to 32 and 37 to 41 of this Part, or any part for such a property if the part is supplied in conjunction with the service.

(2) Subsection (1) applies in respect of

(*a*) a supply made after March 4, 2010; and

(*b*) a supply made on or before that day if

(i) all of the consideration for the supply becomes due after March 4, 2010, or is paid after that day without having become due, or

(ii) any consideration for the supply became due, or was paid, on or before that day, unless the supplier did not, on or before that day, charge, collect or remit any amount as or on account of tax in respect of the supply under Part IX of the Act.

(i) supplies of select products of the person, made by the person, by way of sales that are arranged for by sales representatives of the person (in this subsection referred to as "select supplies"), or

(ii) where the person is a direct seller (as defined in section 178.1), supplies by way of sale of exclusive products (as defined in that section) of the person made by the person to independent sales contractors (as defined in that section) of the person at any time when an approval of the Minister for the application of section 178.3 to the person is in effect;

(*b*) all or substantially all of the total of all consideration, included in determining the income from a business of the person for the fiscal year, for select supplies is for select supplies made to consumers;

(*c*) all or substantially all of the sales representatives of the person to which network commissions become payable by the person during the fiscal year are sales representatives, each having a total of such network commissions of not more than the amount determined by the formula

$$\$30,000 \times A/365$$

where

A is the number of days in the fiscal year; and

(*d*) the person and each of its sales representatives have made joint elections under subsection (4).

Application

(3) A person may apply to the Minister, in prescribed form containing prescribed information, to have subsection (7) apply to the person and each of its sales representatives, beginning on the first day of a fiscal year of the person, if the person

(*a*) is registered under Subdivision d of Division V and is reasonably expected to be, throughout the fiscal year,

(i) engaged exclusively in commercial activities, and

(ii) a qualifying network seller; and

(*b*) files the application in prescribed manner before

(i) in the case of a person that has never made a supply of a select product of the person, the day in the fiscal year on which the person first makes a supply of a select product of the person, and

(ii) in any other case, the first day of the fiscal year.

Joint election

(4) If subsection (3) applies to a person or a person is a network seller, the person and a sales representative of the person may jointly elect, in prescribed form containing prescribed information, to have subsection (7) apply to them at all times when an approval granted under subsection (5) is in effect.

Approval or refusal

(5) If the Minister receives an application under subsection (3) from a person, the Minister may approve the application of subsection (7) to the person and each of its sales representatives beginning on the first day of a fiscal year of the person or may refuse the application and the Minister shall notify the person in writing of the approval and the day on which it becomes effective or of the refusal.

Evidence of joint elections

(6) Every network seller shall maintain evidence satisfactory to the Minister that the network seller and each of its sales representatives have made joint elections under subsection (4).

Effect of approval

(7) For the purposes of this Part, if, at any time when an approval granted under subsection (5) in respect of a network seller and each of its sales representatives is in effect, a network commission becomes payable by the network seller to a sales representative of the network seller as consideration for a taxable supply (other than a zero-rated supply) of a service made in Canada by the sales representative, the taxable supply is deemed not to be a supply.

Sales aids

(8) For the purposes of this Part, if, at any time when an approval granted under subsection (5) in respect of a network seller and each of its sales representatives is in effect, the network seller or a sales representative of the network seller makes in Canada a taxable supply by way of sale of a sales aid of the network seller or of the sales representative, as the case may be, to a sales representative of the network seller, the taxable supply is deemed not to be a supply.

Host gifts

(9) For the purposes of this Part, if, at any time when an approval granted under subsection (5) in respect of a network seller and each of its sales representatives is in effect, the network seller or a particular sales representative of the network seller makes a supply of property to an individual as consideration for the supply by the individual of a service of acting as a host at an occasion that is organized for the purpose of allowing a sales representative of the network seller or the particular sales representative, as the case may be, to promote, or to arrange for the sale of, select products of the network seller, the individual is deemed not to have made a supply of the service and the service is deemed not to be consideration for a supply.

Notification of refusal

(10) If the Minister notifies a person of a refusal under subsection (5) at any time when the person and a sales representative of the person have made a joint election under subsection (4), the person shall forthwith notify the sales representative of the refusal in a manner satisfactory to the Minister.

Revocation by Minister

(11) The Minister may revoke an approval granted under subsection (5) in respect of a network seller and each of its sales representatives, effective on the first day of a fiscal year of the network seller, if, before that day, the Minister notifies the network seller of the revocation and the day on which it becomes effective and if

(*a*) the network seller fails to comply with any provision of this Part;

(*b*) it can reasonably be expected that the network seller will not be a qualifying network seller throughout the fiscal year;

(*c*) the network seller requests in writing that the Minister revoke the approval;

(*d*) the notice referred to in subsection 242(1) has been given to, or the request referred to in subsection 242(2) has been filed by, the network seller; or

(*e*) it can reasonably be expected that the network seller will not be engaged exclusively in commercial activities throughout the fiscal year.

Deemed revocation

(12) If an approval granted under subsection (5) in respect of a network seller and each of its sales representatives is in effect at any time in a particular fiscal year of the network seller and, at any time during the particular fiscal year, the network seller ceases to be engaged exclusively in commercial activities or the Minister cancels the registration of the network seller, the approval is deemed to be revoked, effective on the first day of the fiscal year of the network seller immediately following the particular fiscal year, unless, on that first day, the network seller is registered under Subdivision d of Division V and it is reasonably expected that the network seller will be engaged exclusively in commercial activities throughout that following fiscal year.

Effect of revocation

(13) If an approval granted under subsection (5) in respect of a network seller and each of its sales representatives is revoked under subsection (11) or (12), the following rules apply:

(*a*) the approval ceases to have effect immediately before the day on which the revocation becomes effective;

(*b*) the network seller shall forthwith notify each of its sales representatives in a manner satisfactory to the Minister of the revocation and the day on which it becomes effective; and

(*c*) a subsequent approval granted under subsection (5) in respect of the network seller and each of its sales representatives shall not become effective before the first day of a fiscal year of the network seller that is at least two years after the day on which the revocation became effective.

Failure to notify on revocation

(14) For the purposes of this Part, a taxable supply (other than a zero-rated supply) of a service made in Canada by a sales representative of a network seller is deemed not to be a supply if

(*a*) the consideration for the taxable supply is a network commission that becomes payable by the network seller to the sales representative at any time after an approval granted under subsection (5) in respect of the network seller and each of its sales representatives ceases to have effect as a consequence of a revocation on the basis of any of paragraphs (11)(*a*) to (*c*);

(*b*) the approval could not have been revoked on the basis of paragraph (11)(*d*) or (*e*) and would not have otherwise been revoked under subsection (12);

(*c*) at the time the network commission becomes payable, the sales representative

(i) has not been notified of the revocation by the network seller, as required under paragraph (13)(*b*), or by the Minister, and

(ii) neither knows, nor ought to know, that the approval ceased to have effect; and

(*d*) an amount has not been charged or collected as, or on account of, tax in respect of the taxable supply.

Failure to notify on revocation

(15) Subsection (16) applies if the following conditions are satisfied:

(*a*) the consideration for a taxable supply (other than a zero-rated supply) of a service made in Canada by a sales representative of a network seller is a network commission that becomes payable by the network seller to the sales representative at any time after an approval granted under subsection (5) in respect of the network seller and each of its sales representatives ceases to have effect as a consequence of a revocation under subsection (11) or (12);

(*b*) the approval was, or could at any time otherwise have been, revoked on the basis of paragraph (11)(*d*) or (*e*) or was, or would at any time otherwise have been, revoked under subsection (12);

(*c*) at the time the network commission becomes payable, the sales representative

(i) has not been notified of the revocation by the network seller, as required under paragraph (13)(*b*), or by the Minister, and

(ii) neither knows, nor ought to know, that the approval ceased to have effect; and

(*d*) an amount has not been charged or collected as, or on account of, tax in respect of the taxable supply.

Failure to notify on revocation

(16) If the conditions described in paragraphs (15)(*a*) to (*d*) are satisfied, the following rules apply for the purposes of this Part:

(*a*) section 166 shall not apply in respect of the taxable supply described in paragraph (15)(*a*);

(*b*) tax that becomes payable or that would, in the absence of section 166, become payable in respect of the taxable supply shall not be included in determining the net tax of the sales representative referred to in paragraph (15)(*a*); and (*c*) the consideration for the taxable supply shall not, in determining whether the sales representative is a small supplier, be included in the total referred to in paragraph 148(1)(*a*) or (2)(*a*).

Sales aids on revocation

(17) For the purposes of this Part, a taxable supply of a sales aid of a particular sales representative of a network seller made in Canada by way of sale to another sales representative of the network seller is deemed not to be a supply if

(*a*) the consideration for the taxable supply becomes payable at any time after an approval granted under subsection (5) in respect of the network seller and each of its sales representatives ceases to have effect as a consequence of a revocation under subsection (11) or (12);

(*b*) at the time the consideration becomes payable, the particular sales representative

(i) has not been notified of the revocation by the network seller, as required under paragraph (13)(*b*), or by the Minister, and

(ii) neither knows, nor ought to know, that the approval ceased to have effect; and

(*c*) an amount has not been charged or collected as, or on account of, tax in respect of the taxable supply.

Restriction on input tax credits

(18) If

(*a*) a registrant that is a network seller in respect of which an approval granted under subsection (5) is in effect acquires or imports property (other than a select product of the network seller) or a service or brings it into a participating province for supply to a sales representative of the network seller or an individual related to the sales representative,

(*b*) tax becomes payable in respect of the acquisition, importation or bringing in, as the case may be,

(*c*) the property or service is so supplied by the registrant for no consideration or for consideration that is less than the fair market value of the property or service, and

(*d*) the sales representative or individual is not acquiring the property or service for consumption, use or supply exclusively in the course of commercial activities of the sales representative or individual, as the case may be, the following rules apply:

(*e*) no tax is payable in respect of the supply, and

(*f*) in determining an input tax credit of the registrant, no amount shall be included in respect of tax that becomes payable, or is paid without having become payable, by the registrant in respect of the property or service.

Appropriations for sales representatives

(19) For the purposes of this Part, if a registrant that is a network seller in respect of which an approval granted under subsection (5) is in effect appropriates, at any time, property (other than a select product of the network seller) that was acquired, manufactured or produced, or any service acquired or performed, in the course of commercial activities of the registrant, to or for the benefit of a sales representative of the network seller, or any individual related to the sales representative, that is not acquiring the property or service for consumption, use or supply exclusively in the course of commercial activities of the sales representative or individual, in any manner (otherwise than by way of supply for consideration equal to the fair market value of the property or service), the registrant shall be deemed

(*a*) to have made a supply of the property or service for consideration paid at that time equal to the fair market value of the property or service at that time; and

(*b*) except where the supply is an exempt supply, to have collected, at that time, tax in respect of the supply calculated on that consideration.

Exception

(20) Subsection (19) does not apply to property or a service appropriated by a registrant if the registrant was not entitled to claim an input tax credit in respect of the property or service because of section 170.

Ceasing to be a registrant

(21) If, at any time when an approval granted under subsection (5) in respect of a network seller and each of its sales representatives is in effect, a sales representative of the network seller ceases to be a registrant, paragraph 171(3)(*a*) does not apply to sales aids of the sales representative that were supplied to the sales representative by the network seller or another sales representative of the network seller at any time when the approval was in effect.

Non-arm's length supply

(22) Section 155 does not apply to the supply described in subsection (9) made to an individual acting as a host.

(2) Subsection (1) applies in respect of any fiscal year of a person that begins on or after January 1, 2010, except that, for the purposes of applying section 178 of the Act, as enacted by subsection (1), in respect of a fiscal year of a person that begins during 2010, the following rules also apply:

(*a*) a person may, despite subparagraphs 178(3)(*b*)(i) and (ii) of the Act, as enacted by subsection (1), apply under subsection 178(3) of the Act, as enacted by subsection (1), to have subsection 178(7) of the Act, as enacted by subsection (1), apply to the person and each of its sales representatives, beginning on a day in 2010 that the person specifies in the application, if the person files the application before that day and that day is the first day of a reporting period of the person that begins during the fiscal year;

(*b*) if the person makes an application in accordance with paragraph (*a*),

(i) each reference in subsections 178(2), (3), (5) and (11) of the Act, as enacted by subsection (1), to "fiscal year" is to be read as a reference to "qualifying period", and

(ii) each reference in subsection 178(12) of the Act, as enacted by subsection (1), to "particular fiscal year" is to be read as a reference to "qualifying period"; and

(*c*) "qualifying period" of a person means the period beginning on the day specified in an application made by the person in accordance with paragraph (*a*) and ending on the last day of the fiscal year.

9. (1) The Act is amended by adding the following after section 236.4:

First and second variant years

236.5 (1) For the purposes of this section, a fiscal year of a network seller in respect of which an approval granted under 178(5) is in effect is

(*a*) the first variant year of the network seller if the network seller

(i) fails to meet the condition referred to in paragraph 178(2)(*c*) in respect of the fiscal year, and

(ii) meets the condition referred to in paragraph 178(2)(*c*) for each fiscal year of the network seller, in respect of which an approval granted under 178(5) is in effect, preceding the fiscal year; and

(*b*) the second variant year of the network seller if

(i) the fiscal year is after the first variant year of the network seller,

(ii) the network seller fails to meet the condition referred to in paragraph 178(2)(*c*) in respect of the fiscal year, and

(iii) the network seller meets the condition referred to in paragraph 178(2)(*c*) for each fiscal year (other than the first variant year) of the network seller, in respect of which an approval granted under 178(5) is in effect, preceding the fiscal year.

Adjustment by network seller if conditions not met

(2) Subject to subsections (3) and (4), if a network seller fails to satisfy any condition referred to in paragraphs 178(2)(*a*) to (*c*) for a fiscal year of the network seller in respect of which an approval granted under subsection 178(5) is in effect and, at any time during the fiscal year, a network commission would, if this Part were read without reference to subsection 178(7), become payable by the network seller to a sales representative of the network seller as consideration for a taxable supply (other than a zero-rated supply) made in Canada by the sales representative, the network seller shall, in determining the net tax for the first reporting period of the network seller following the fiscal year, add an amount equal to interest, at the prescribed rate, on the total amount of tax that would be payable in respect of the taxable supply if tax were payable in respect of the taxable supply, computed for the period beginning on the earliest day on which consideration for the taxable supply is paid or becomes due and ending on the day on or before which the network seller is required to file a return for the reporting period that includes that earliest day.

No adjustment for first variant year

(3) In determining the net tax for the first reporting period of a network seller following the first variant year of the network seller, the network seller is not required to add an amount in accordance with subsection (2) if

(*a*) the network seller satisfies the conditions referred to in paragraphs 178(2)(*a*) and (*b*) for the first variant year and for each fiscal year, in respect of which an approval granted under subsection 178(5) is in effect, preceding the first variant year; and (*b*) the network seller would meet the condition referred to in paragraph 178(2)(*c*) for the first variant year if the reference in that paragraph to "all or substantially all" were read as a reference to "at least 80%".

No adjustment for second variant year

(4) In determining the net tax for the first reporting period of the network seller following the second variant year of the network seller, the network seller is not required to add an amount in accordance with subsection (2) if

(*a*) the network seller satisfies the conditions referred to in paragraphs 178(2)(*a*) and (*b*) for the second variant year and for each fiscal year, in respect of which an approval granted under subsection 178(5) is in effect, preceding the second variant year;

(*b*) the network seller would meet the condition referred to in paragraph 178(2)(*c*) for each of the first variant year and the second variant year if the reference in that paragraph to "all or substantially all" were read as a reference to "at least 80%"; and

(*c*) within 180 days after the beginning of the second variant year, the network seller requests in writing that the Minister revoke the approval.

Adjustment by network seller due to notification failure

(5) If, at any time after an approval granted under subsection 178(5) in respect of a network seller and each of its sales representatives ceases to have effect as a consequence of a revocation under subsection 178(11) or (12), a network commission would, if this Part were read without reference to subsection 178(7), become payable as consideration for a taxable supply (other than a zero-rated supply) made in Canada by a sales representative of the network seller that has not been notified, as required under paragraph 178(13)(*b*), of the revocation and an amount is not charged or collected as, or on account of, tax in respect of the taxable supply, the network seller shall, in determining the net tax for the particular reporting period of the network seller that includes the earliest day on which consideration for the taxable supply is paid or becomes due, add an amount equal to interest, at the prescribed rate, on the total amount of tax that would be payable in respect of the taxable supply if tax were payable in respect of the taxable supply, computed for the period beginning on that earliest day and ending on the day on or before which the network seller is required to file a return for the particular reporting period.

(2) Subsection (1) applies in respect of any fiscal year of a person that begins on or after January 1, 2010, except that, if the person makes an application in accordance with paragraph 8(2)(*a*) in respect of a qualifying period (as defined in paragraph 8(2)(*c*)), for the purposes of applying subsections 236.5(1) to (4) of the Act, as enacted by subsection (1), each reference in those subsections to "fiscal year" is to be read, in respect of a fiscal year of the person that begins in 2010, as a reference to "qualifying period".

10. (1) Section 242 of the Act is amended by adding the following after subsection (2.2):

Request for cancellation

(2.3) If, at any time when an approval granted under subsection 178(5) in respect of a network seller (as defined in subsection 178(1)) and each of its sales representatives (as defined in that subsection) is in effect, a sales representative of the network seller would be a small supplier if the approval had been in effect at all times before that time and the sales representative files with the Minister in prescribed manner a request, in prescribed form containing prescribed information, to have the registration of the sales representative cancelled, the Minister shall cancel the registration of the sales representative.

(2) Subsection (1) is deemed to have come into force on January 1, 2010.

Financial Services

11. (1) Paragraph (*l*) of the definition "financial service" in subsection 123(1) of the Act is replaced by the following:

(*l*) the agreeing to provide, or the arranging for, a service that is

(i) referred to in any of paragraphs (*a*) to (*i*), and

(ii) not referred to in any of paragraphs (*n*) to (*t*), or

(2) The definition "financial service" in subsection 123(1) of the Act is amended by adding the following after paragraph (*q*):

(*q.1*) an asset management service,

(3) The definition "financial service" in subsection 123(1) of the Act is amended by adding the following after paragraph (*r.2*):

(*r.3*) a service (other than a prescribed service) of managing credit that is in respect of credit cards, charge cards, credit accounts, charge accounts, loan accounts or accounts in respect of any advance and is provided to a person granting, or potentially granting, credit in respect of those cards or accounts, including a service provided to the person of

(i) checking, evaluating or authorizing credit,

(ii) making decisions on behalf of the person in relation to a grant, or an application for a grant, of credit,

(iii) creating or maintaining records for the person in relation to a grant, or an application for a grant, of credit or in relation to the cards or accounts, or

(iv) monitoring another person's payment record or dealing with payments made, or to be made, by the other person,

(*r.4*) a service (other than a prescribed service) that is preparatory to the provision or the potential provision of a service referred to in any of paragraphs (*a*) to (*i*) and (*l*), or that is provided in conjunction with a service referred to in any of those paragraphs, and that is

(i) a service of collecting, collating or providing information, or

(ii) a market research, product design, document preparation, document processing, customer assistance, promotional or advertising service or a similar service,

(*r.5*) property (other than a financial instrument or prescribed property) that is delivered or made available to a person in conjunction with the rendering by the person of a service referred to in any of paragraphs (*a*) to (*i*) and (*l*),

(4) Subsection 123(1) of the Act is amended by adding the following in alphabetical order:

"asset management service"
« *service de gestion des actifs* »

"asset management service" means a service (other than a prescribed service) rendered by a particular person in respect of the assets or liabilities of another person that is a service of

(*a*) managing or administering the assets or liabilities, irrespective of the level of discretionary authority the particular person has to manage some or all of the assets or liabilities,

(*b*) providing research, analysis, advice or reports in respect of the assets or liabilities,

(*c*) determining which assets or liabilities are to be acquired or disposed of, or

(*d*) acting to realize performance targets or other objectives in respect of the assets or liabilities;

"management or administrative service"
« *service de gestion ou d'administration* »

"management or administrative service" includes an asset management service;

(5) Subsections (1) to (4) are deemed to have come into force on December 17, 1990, except that, for the purposes of Part IX of the Act, other than Division IV of that Part, subsections (1) to (4) do not apply in respect of a service rendered under an agreement, evidenced in writing, for a supply if

(*a*) all of the consideration for the supply became due or was paid on or before December 14, 2009;

(*b*) the supplier did not, on or before December 14, 2009, charge, collect or remit any amount as or on account of tax under Part IX of the Act in respect of the supply; and (*c*) the supplier did not, on or before December 14, 2009, charge, collect or remit any amount as or on account of tax under Part IX of the Act in respect of any other supply that is made under the agreement and that includes the provision of a service referred to in any of paragraphs (*q*), (*q.1*) and (*r.3*) to (*r.5*) of the definition "financial service" in subsection 123(1) of the Act, as amended by subsections (1) to (4).

(6) Despite section 298 of the Act, the Minister of National Revenue may assess, reassess or make an additional assessment of any amount payable or remittable by a person in respect of a supply of a service referred to in any of paragraphs (*q*), (*q.1*) and (*r.3*) to (*r.5*) of the definition "financial service" in subsection 123(1) of the Act, as amended by subsections (2) to (4), at any time on or before the later of the day that is one year after the day on which this Act is assented to and the last day of the period otherwise allowed under that section for making the assessment, reassessment or additional assessment.

Notice of Ways and Means Motion to Amend the *Customs Tariff*

That it is expedient to amend the *Customs Tariff* to provide among other things:

1. That the List of Tariff Provisions set out in the schedule to the *Customs Tariff* be amended to provide that the Most-Favoured-Nation Tariff rates of customs duty and, where necessary, the applicable preferential tariff rates of customs duty, be "Free", for the following tariff items:

2511.10.00	2804.21.00	2826.19.00	2835.26.90	2843.30.91
2514.00.10	2804.29.90	2826.90.10	2835.29.21	2843.30.99
2515.20.20	2804.30.00	2826.90.90	2835.29.29	2843.90.90
2516.12.10	2804.40.00	2827.10.90	2835.29.90	2846.10.90
2516.20.20	2804.69.00	2827.20.00	2835.31.90	2846.90.00
2516.90.20	2805.12.00	2827.35.00	2835.39.90	2850.00.19
2517.30.00	2805.19.90	2827.39.20	2836.20.90	2852.00.20
2518.20.00	2805.30.00	2827.39.30	2836.91.90	2852.00.30
2530.90.10	2811.19.90	2827.39.90	2836.92.00	2852.00.40
2705.00.00	2811.21.90	2827.41.00	2836.99.90	2852.00.50
2707.40.90	2811.29.10	2827.49.00	2841.50.20	2852.00.60
2707.99.10	2811.29.99	2827.60.10	2841.50.90	2852.00.70
2710.11.19	2812.10.90	2827.60.99	2841.61.00	2852.00.80
2710.19.20	2812.90.90	2829.19.90	2841.69.00	2852.00.90
2710.91.10	2817.00.90	2829.90.20	2841.70.90	2853.00.00
2710.91.91	2819.90.90	2833.24.00	2841.80.00	2903.15.00
2710.99.20	2821.10.00	2833.25.90	2841.90.20	2903.21.00
2710.99.91	2821.20.00	2833.40.90	2841.90.90	2903.39.00
2711.11.00	2823.00.90	2834.10.00	2842.10.10	2903.41.00
2712.90.10	2824.10.00	2834.29.10	2842.90.20	2903.42.00
2713.20.90	2824.90.10	2835.10.00	2842.90.91	2903.43.00
2714.10.00	2824.90.90	2835.22.10	2843.10.00	2903.44.00
2715.00.10	2825.70.00	2835.22.90	2843.21.00	2903.45.00
2804.10.00	2825.90.10	2835.24.00	2843.29.00	2903.46.00

2903.47.00	2907.29.20	2914.23.00	2917.13.99	2921.44.90
2903.49.00	2907.29.90	2914.31.00	2917.14.90	2921.45.91
2903.61.10	2908.11.90	2914.39.00	2917.19.99	2921.45.99
2903.69.90	2908.19.90	2914.40.90	2917.20.00	2921.46.00
2904.10.10	2908.91.00	2914.50.90	2917.32.00	2921.49.00
2904.10.99	2908.99.19	2914.61.00	2917.33.00	2921.51.90
2904.20.00	2908.99.90	2914.69.90	2917.34.10	2921.59.90
2904.90.00	2909.30.00	2914.70.00	2917.34.99	2922.11.00
2905.16.90	2909.41.00	2915.13.90	2917.39.90	2922.12.00
2905.17.00	2909.43.00	2915.24.00	2918.18.90	2922.13.00
2905.19.10	2909.44.90	2915.29.90	2918.19.10	2922.14.00
2905.19.99	2909.49.91	2915.32.00	2918.19.99	2922.19.91
2905.22.00	2909.49.92	2915.33.00	2918.23.00	2922.19.99
2905.32.00	2909.49.99	2915.36.00	2918.29.90	2922.21.00
2905.42.00	2909.50.90	2915.39.90	2918.91.00	2922.29.29
2905.43.00	2909.60.20	2915.50.10	2918.99.90	2922.29.90
2905.49.10	2909.60.99	2915.50.99	2919.90.10	2922.31.00
2905.49.90	2910.10.00	2915.90.92	2919.90.99	2922.39.90
2905.51.00	2910.20.00	2915.90.99	2920.11.00	2922.41.90
2905.59.00	2910.40.90	2916.12.20	2920.19.00	2922.44.00
2906.12.00	2910.90.90	2916.12.90	2920.90.10	2922.49.90
2906.13.00	2911.00.00	2916.19.00	2920.90.99	2922.50.90
2906.19.90	2912.19.10	2916.20.10	2921.11.90	2923.10.90
2906.21.90	2912.19.99	2916.20.99	2921.19.20	2923.20.90
2906.29.00	2912.29.00	2916.31.00	2921.19.91	2923.90.10
2907.12.00	2912.30.00	2916.32.00	2921.19.99	2923.90.99
2907.15.90	2912.50.00	2916.34.00	2921.22.00	2924.11.00
2907.19.10	2913.00.00	2916.35.00	2921.29.90	2924.12.90
2907.19.99	2914.11.00	2917.11.19	2921.30.90	2924.19.10
2907.21.90	2914.19.00	2917.11.90	2921.42.90	2924.19.99
2907.22.90	2914.22.00	2917.12.99	2921.43.90	2924.21.00

2924.23.19	2932.99.00	2937.50.10	3809.93.00	3824.75.00
2924.23.99	2933.19.90	2937.50.29	3810.10.90	3824.76.00
2924.24.00	2933.29.90	2937.50.39	3810.90.00	3824.77.00
2924.29.91	2933.32.90	2937.90.19	3811.11.00	3824.78.00
2924.29.99	2933.33.00	2938.90.00	3811.19.00	3824.79.00
2925.11.00	2933.39.90	2940.00.00	3811.21.90	3824.81.00
2925.12.00	2933.41.00	2942.00.90	3811.29.00	3824.82.00
2925.19.00	2933.49.10	3202.10.10	3811.90.00	3824.83.00
2925.21.90	2933.49.90	3203.00.10	3812.10.00	3824.90.20
2925.29.90	2933.55.00	3205.00.00	3812.20.90	3824.90.30
2926.30.00	2933.59.91	3206.42.90	3812.30.90	3824.90.49
2926.90.90	2933.59.99	3206.49.29	3813.00.00	3824.90.90
2929.90.10	2933.69.10	3206.49.30	3814.00.00	3903.11.00
2929.90.90	2933.69.99	3206.49.90	3815.19.10	3903.19.10
2930.20.10	2933.71.90	3207.10.90	3815.90.10	3903.19.90
2930.20.99	2933.72.00	3207.20.00	3816.00.90	3903.20.10
2930.30.20	2933.79.00	3207.30.90	3817.00.90	3903.20.90
2930.30.99	2933.91.90	3207.40.90	3821.00.90	3903.30.10
2930.50.90	2933.99.22	3212.10.00	3823.11.00	3903.30.90
2930.90.21	2933.99.90	3212.90.90	3823.12.00	3903.90.00
2930.90.29	2934.10.00	3215.11.00	3823.19.00	3904.10.90
2930.90.99	2934.20.90	3215.19.90	3823.70.90	3904.21.00
2931.00.10	2934.30.90	3215.90.90	3824.10.00	3904.22.00
2931.00.99	2934.91.00	3801.30.90	3824.30.00	3904.30.90
2932.19.00	2934.99.10	3801.90.00	3824.40.00	3904.40.00
2932.29.90	2934.99.99	3806.30.90	3824.50.90	3904.50.10
2932.91.00	2935.00.20	3807.00.10	3824.60.00	3904.90.00
2932.92.00	2935.00.99	3809.91.20	3824.71.00	3905.12.00
2932.93.00	2937.19.19	3809.91.90	3824.72.00	3905.19.90
2932.94.00	2937.29.10	3809.92.10	3824.73.00	3905.21.00
2932.95.00	2937.39.19	3809.92.90	3824.74.00	3905.29.90

3905.91.10	3917.22.00	4006.90.90	4104.19.29	4106.31.10
3905.99.10	3917.23.90	4007.00.90	4104.19.31	4106.31.92
3906.10.90	3917.29.90	4008.11.90	4104.19.39	4106.31.99
3906.90.91	3917.31.90	4008.19.10	4104.19.41	4106.32.20
3907.20.90	3917.40.90	4008.19.90	4104.19.49	4106.32.90
3907.30.90	3919.90.99	4008.21.90	4104.19.91	4106.91.20
3907.40.10	3920.10.10	4008.29.10	4104.19.99	4106.91.90
3907.50.00	3920.10.90	4008.29.90	4104.41.12	4106.92.20
3907.60.90	3920.20.20	4009.11.00	4104.41.19	4106.92.90
3907.70.90	3920.20.90	4009.12.00	4104.41.92	4107.11.12
3907.91.00	3920.30.90	4009.21.00	4104.41.99	4107.11.19
3907.99.90	3920.43.90	4009.22.90	4104.49.12	4107.11.92
3909.30.10	3920.49.90	4009.31.90	4104.49.19	4107.11.99
3909.40.91	3920.51.90	4009.32.90	4104.49.22	4107.12.12
3909.50.90	3920.59.10	4009.41.90	4104.49.29	4107.12.19
3910.00.90	3920.61.10	4009.42.90	4104.49.92	4107.12.92
3911.10.10	3920.62.90	4010.11.10	4104.49.93	4107.12.99
3911.90.90	3920.63.00	4010.11.20	4104.49.99	4107.19.12
3912.11.90	3920.71.00	4010.12.19	4105.10.12	4107.19.19
3912.12.00	3920.73.10	4010.12.29	4105.10.19	4107.19.92
3912.20.10	3920.79.10	4010.19.19	4105.10.29	4107.19.93
3912.39.10	3920.79.29	4010.19.29	4105.10.99	4107.19.99
3912.90.90	3920.92.90	4104.11.22	4105.30.12	4107.91.20
3913.10.00	3920.93.00	4104.11.29	4105.30.19	4107.91.90
3913.90.90	3920.94.10	4104.11.31	4105.30.99	4107.92.20
3914.00.10	3920.99.91	4104.11.39	4106.21.29	4107.92.90
3916.10.00	4005.10.90	4104.11.41	4106.21.99	4107.99.20
3916.90.11	4005.20.00	4104.11.49	4106.22.22	4107.99.30
3916.90.99	4005.91.90	4104.11.91	4106.22.29	4107.99.90
3917.10.10	4005.99.00	4104.11.99	4106.22.92	4112.00.90
3917.21.00	4006.10.00	4104.19.22	4106.22.99	4113.10.20

4113.10.90	5111.30.29	5208.32.90	5311.00.90	5603.12.99
4113.20.20	5111.30.91	5208.33.99	5407.52.90	5603.13.30
4113.20.90	5111.30.92	5208.39.90	5407.61.11	5603.13.40
4113.90.20	5111.90.50	5208.41.90	5407.61.93	5603.13.50
4113.90.90	5111.90.91	5208.42.99	5407.61.99	5603.13.99
4114.10.00	5111.90.92	5208.43.90	5407.92.90	5603.14.30
4114.20.90	5112.11.60	5208.49.99	5408.10.90	5603.14.40
4302.11.00	5112.11.90	5208.51.90	5408.21.90	5603.14.50
4302.19.22	5112.19.19	5208.52.90	5408.22.29	5603.14.99
4302.19.29	5112.19.94	5208.59.99	5408.22.99	5603.91.50
4302.19.30	5112.19.95	5209.11.90	5408.23.19	5603.91.90
4302.19.90	5112.20.30	5209.12.90	5408.23.99	5603.92.60
4302.20.00	5112.20.91	5209.19.90	5408.24.19	5603.92.99
4408.31.10	5112.20.92	5209.21.90	5408.24.99	5603.93.60
4408.39.10	5112.30.29	5209.22.90	5408.31.90	5603.93.90
4413.00.00	5112.30.30	5209.29.90	5408.32.90	5603.94.50
4415.20.90	5112.30.91	5209.31.90	5408.33.90	5603.94.90
4416.00.90	5112.30.94	5209.32.90	5408.34.90	5606.00.90
5111.11.50	5112.90.30	5209.39.90	5515.13.99	5801.10.99
5111.19.31	5112.90.91	5209.41.90	5515.22.00	5801.22.29
5111.19.32	5112.90.92	5209.42.90	5516.31.00	5801.22.99
5111.19.39	5113.00.90	5209.43.99	5516.32.00	5801.23.90
5111.19.90	5203.00.90	5209.49.90	5516.33.00	5801.24.90
5111.20.19	5208.12.90	5209.51.00	5516.34.00	5801.25.10
5111.20.29	5208.13.90	5209.59.90	5603.11.30	5801.25.29
5111.20.91	5208.19.90	5211.42.90	5603.11.40	5801.26.90
5111.20.92	5208.21.99	5309.11.90	5603.11.50	5801.31.90
5111.30.12	5208.22.90	5309.19.90	5603.11.99	5801.32.90
5111.30.13	5208.23.99	5309.21.90	5603.12.30	5801.33.90
5111.30.18	5208.29.99	5309.29.90	5603.12.40	5801.34.90
5111.30.19	5208.31.99	5310.90.99	5603.12.50	5801.35.99

5801.36.90	5810.10.90	7019.90.40	7307.29.91	7318.16.00
5801.90.99	5810.91.30	7019.90.90	7307.29.99	7318.19.00
5802.11.90	5810.91.90	7106.92.19	7307.91.19	7318.21.00
5802.19.90	5810.92.90	7106.92.21	7307.91.20	7318.22.90
5802.20.90	5810.99.90	7106.92.22	7307.91.90	7318.23.00
5802.30.90	6804.10.00	7107.00.00	7307.92.90	7318.24.00
5803.00.19	6804.23.00	7108.13.20	7307.93.10	7318.29.90
5803.00.22	6805.10.20	7109.00.00	7307.99.20	7320.10.00
5803.00.29	6805.10.90	7111.00.00	7307.99.91	7320.20.90
5803.00.99	6805.20.20	7115.10.00	7307.99.99	7320.90.90
5804.10.30	6805.20.90	7115.90.90	7309.00.90	7324.29.10
5804.10.90	6805.30.20	7202.60.00	7310.10.11	7325.91.10
5804.21.90	6805.30.90	7202.70.00	7310.10.19	7325.91.90
5804.29.90	6806.10.10	7202.91.00	7310.10.90	7407.10.11
5804.30.30	6806.10.90	7202.92.10	7310.21.00	7407.10.12
5804.30.90	6806.20.00	7202.92.90	7310.29.00	7407.10.21
5806.10.19	6806.90.90	7202.93.00	7311.00.90	7407.10.29
5806.10.99	6814.10.90	7202.99.00	7315.12.91	7407.21.21
5806.20.90	6814.90.00	7205.10.10	7315.12.99	7407.21.22
5806.31.40	6815.10.20	7206.90.00	7315.81.90	7407.21.90
5806.31.50	7019.31.90	7303.00.00	7315.82.91	7407.29.21
5806.31.90	7019.32.20	7307.11.10	7315.82.92	7407.29.29
5806.32.99	7019.32.90	7307.11.90	7315.89.91	7407.29.90
5806.39.99	7019.39.99	7307.19.91	7315.89.92	7408.11.31
5806.40.90	7019.40.20	7307.19.99	7315.90.91	7408.11.32
5807.10.19	7019.51.20	7307.21.10	7315.90.99	7408.19.00
5807.10.29	7019.51.99	7307.21.91	7318.11.00	7408.21.20
5807.90.90	7019.52.20	7307.21.99	7318.12.00	7408.21.90
5808.10.90	7019.52.99	7307.22.90	7318.13.90	7408.22.10
5808.90.90	7019.59.20	7307.23.10	7318.14.00	7408.22.90
5809.00.90	7019.59.99	7307.23.90	7318.15.90	7408.29.10

7408.29.90	7614.10.00	8111.00.12	8311.10.00	8438.20.10
7411.10.00	7614.90.00	8111.00.22	8311.20.00	8438.40.10
7411.21.00	7616.10.90	8111.00.40	8311.30.00	8438.60.10
7411.22.00	7801.10.90	8112.51.00	8311.90.90	8443.13.20
7411.29.00	7801.99.00	8112.52.00	8401.10.00	8451.80.10
7412.10.00	7804.11.90	8112.59.00	8401.40.00	8457.30.00
7412.20.00	7804.19.00	8112.92.90	8403.10.00	8458.11.10
7413.00.00	7804.20.00	8112.99.20	8407.33.90	8458.19.10
7415.10.00	7806.00.10	8112.99.90	8407.34.10	8458.91.90
7415.21.00	7806.00.90	8113.00.00	8407.34.21	8459.21.10
7415.29.00	8003.00.20	8205.70.20	8407.34.29	8459.29.10
7415.33.90	8007.00.20	8207.19.20	8409.91.20	8459.31.10
7415.39.00	8007.00.30	8207.19.90	8409.91.90	8459.39.90
7603.10.00	8101.99.90	8207.20.10	8410.11.20	8459.40.10
7603.20.00	8102.95.10	8207.30.10	8410.12.20	8459.61.10
7604.10.12	8102.95.20	8207.40.10	8410.13.20	8460.29.10
7604.10.20	8102.99.00	8207.50.90	8410.90.30	8460.90.91
7604.21.00	8103.90.00	8207.60.10	8411.81.20	8461.50.11
7604.29.12	8104.11.00	8207.80.10	8411.81.90	8461.50.91
7604.29.20	8104.19.90	8209.00.10	8411.82.20	8462.21.91
7605.19.00	8104.30.00	8209.00.92	8411.99.20	8462.29.91
7605.29.00	8104.90.00	8301.20.90	8415.20.90	8462.31.10
7606.11.20	8105.20.90	8301.30.00	8415.83.10	8462.39.10
7606.12.90	8105.90.00	8301.40.10	8415.90.22	8462.49.21
7606.91.90	8107.90.00	8301.60.00	8415.90.29	8462.91.99
7606.92.90	8108.20.90	8307.10.90	8421.23.20	8463.10.10
7607.11.19	8108.30.00	8307.90.00	8421.23.90	8463.30.10
7607.19.90	8108.90.90	8308.10.90	8421.31.90	8463.90.10
7608.10.00	8109.20.90	8308.90.90	8436.80.91	8467.11.10
7611.00.90	8109.30.00	8309.10.00	8437.10.91	8467.19.10
7613.00.00	8109.90.90	8309.90.90	8437.80.10	8467.21.10

8467.22.10	8501.40.39	8528.49.11	9028.10.00
8467.29.10	8501.51.90	8528.49.19	9028.20.90
8468.90.10	8501.52.20	8528.59.11	9028.30.00
8477.10.10	8501.53.91	8528.59.19	9029.20.90
8477.20.10	8501.53.99	8528.71.40	9029.90.20
8477.51.11	8501.61.90	8528.72.34	9030.10.90
8477.51.21	8501.62.90	8528.72.97	9030.31.10
8477.59.11	8501.63.90	8536.70.10	9030.33.10
8477.59.21	8501.64.91	8536.70.20	9030.84.10
8480.20.00	8501.64.99	8536.70.30	9030.89.10
8480.30.00	8502.11.90	8542.31.90	9031.20.90
8480.71.10	8502.12.00	8542.32.90	9031.49.90
8480.79.00	8502.13.00	8542.33.90	9031.80.90
8482.10.10	8502.20.90	8542.39.90	9032.89.90
8482.80.10	8502.40.00	8545.19.28	9033.00.90
8483.20.00	8506.90.90	8545.19.29	
8483.30.00	8507.10.00	8548.90.90	
8483.40.91	8507.20.10	9001.10.90	
8501.10.12	8507.30.20	9001.20.00	
8501.10.99	8507.40.10	9013.10.00	
8501.20.90	8507.80.20	9013.20.00	
8501.31.20	8507.90.90	9013.80.90	
8501.31.30	8511.10.00	9013.90.30	
8501.32.20	8511.20.00	9015.90.10	
8501.32.90	8511.30.00	9016.00.10	
8501.33.20	8511.40.90	9016.00.90	
8501.33.30	8511.50.00	9017.90.10	
8501.34.20	8511.80.90	9017.90.90	
8501.34.30	8511.90.90	9024.10.90	
8501.40.22	8516.10.20	9024.80.90	
8501.40.29	8516.80.90	9025.90.90	

2. That the List of Tariff Provisions set out in the schedule to the *Customs Tariff* be amended to provide that the Most-Favoured-Nation Tariff rates of customs duty for the tariff items set out in column 1 below be the rates of customs duty set out in column 2 below and that the Most-Favoured-Nation Tariff rates of customs duty, and where necessary the applicable preferential tariff rates of customs duty, in respect of those items set out in column 1, be gradually reduced to "Free" by no later than January 1, 2015.

Column 1	Column 2	Column 1	Column 2
2830.10.00	3%	3908.90.00	6%
2833.21.90	3%	3909.10.10	4%
2839.19.00	5%	3909.20.90	6%
2839.90.10	2.5%	3916.20.00	6%
2847.00.00	5%	3919.10.10	5%
2905.11.00	3%	3919.90.10	5%
2905.12.00	5%	3921.11.90	3%
2905.31.00	5%	3921.12.91	5%
2905.39.00	5%	3921.12.99	5%
2905.45.00	6%	3921.13.91	5%
2907.13.00	5%	3921.13.99	3%
2915.70.10	4%	3921.14.90	3%
2915.70.99	4%	3921.19.90	3%
2915.90.10	3%	3921.90.12	5%
2916.15.00	4%	3921.90.19	5%
2917.12.10	5%	3921.90.94	5%
2917.13.10	4%	3921.90.99	3%
2917.19.10	6%	4408.10.10	5.5%
3204.17.91	4%	4408.90.10	5.5%
3204.17.99	5%	4410.11.10	2%
3206.19.90	4%	4410.12.00	2%
3206.20.00	5%	4410.19.10	2%
3206.49.89	4%	4412.10.10	4.5%
3901.10.90	6%	4412.10.90	5.5%
3901.20.90	6%	4412.31.90	4.5%
3901.30.00	4%	4412.32.90	4.5%
3901.90.00	4%	4412.39.10	5.5%
3902.10.00	4%	4412.39.90	8.5%
3902.30.00	6%	4412.94.90	5.5%
3902.90.10	6%	4412.99.90	5.5%
3908.10.00	3%	5106.10.90	6%

Column 1	Column 2	Column 1	Column 2
5106.20.00	6%	5210.49.19	10%
5107.10.90	6%	5210.49.90	7%
5107.20.90	6%	5210.51.90	7%
5111.11.90	7%	5210.59.00	7%
5204.11.10	4%	5211.11.00	7%
5204.11.90	6%	5211.12.90	10%
5205.11.90	6%	5211.19.00	10%
5205.12.90	6%	5211.20.19	10%
5205.13.90	6%	5211.20.90	10%
5205.14.90	6%	5211.31.00	10%
5205.21.90	6%	5211.32.90	10%
5205.22.90	6%	5211.39.00	7%
5205.23.90	6%	5211.41.90	10%
5205.24.90	6%	5211.43.90	10%
5205.31.90	6%	5211.51.00	10%
5205.32.90	6%	5211.52.90	10%
5205.41.90	6%	5211.59.00	7%
5205.42.90	6%	5212.11.30	6%
5206.11.00	6%	5212.11.90	10%
5206.12.00	6%	5212.12.30	6%
5206.13.00	6%	5212.12.90	10%
5206.22.00	6%	5212.13.40	6%
5206.31.00	6%	5212.13.90	10%
5206.32.00	6%	5212.14.40	6%
5206.34.00	6%	5212.14.90	10%
5206.35.00	6%	5212.15.30	6%
5206.41.00	6%	5212.15.90	7%
5206.42.00	6%	5212.21.30	6%
5206.43.00	6%	5212.21.90	10%
5206.44.00	6%	5212.22.30	6%
5209.52.90	7%	5212.22.90	10%
5210.11.00	7%	5212.23.30	6%
5210.19.00	7%	5212.23.90	10%
5210.21.00	7%	5212.24.30	6%
5210.29.00	7%	5212.24.90	7%
5210.31.00	7%	5212.25.30	6%
5210.32.00	7%	5212.25.90	10%
5210.39.00	7%	5308.90.90	6%
5210.41.00	7%	5401.10.00	6%

Column 1	Column 2	Column 1	Column 2
5402.11.90	6%	5508.10.10	6%
5402.19.90	6%	5509.11.00	6%
5402.20.90	6%	5509.12.90	6%
5402.31.90	6%	5509.21.90	6%
5402.32.90	6%	5509.22.30	6%
5402.33.90	6%	5509.22.90	6%
5402.34.90	6%	5509.31.00	6%
5402.39.00	6%	5509.32.90	6%
5402.51.90	6%	5509.41.90	6%
5402.52.99	6%	5509.42.00	6%
5402.59.90	6%	5509.52.90	6%
5402.61.00	6%	5509.53.90	6%
5402.62.90	6%	5509.61.00	6%
5402.69.90	6%	5509.62.00	6%
5407.10.20	8%	5509.91.00	6%
5407.10.90	7%	5509.92.00	6%
5407.20.99	7%	5509.99.00	6%
5407.30.90	10%	5510.11.90	6%
5407.41.90	7%	5510.12.90	6%
5407.42.90	7%	5510.20.90	6%
5407.43.00	10%	5510.30.90	6%
5407.44.00	10%	5510.90.00	6%
5407.51.90	7%	5512.11.99	10%
5407.52.19	8%	5512.19.99	7%
5407.53.00	7%	5512.21.90	10%
5407.54.90	7%	5512.29.99	10%
5407.61.19	10%	5512.91.90	10%
5407.69.90	7%	5512.99.99	10%
5407.71.00	7%	5513.11.99	10%
5407.72.00	7%	5513.12.99	10%
5407.73.90	7%	5513.13.99	10%
5407.74.00	7%	5513.19.00	7%
5407.81.90	7%	5513.21.00	7%
5407.82.99	7%	5513.23.19	7%
5407.83.99	7%	5513.23.99	10%
5407.84.90	7%	5513.29.90	7%
5407.91.90	10%	5513.31.90	10%
5407.93.90	7%	5513.39.19	10%
5407.94.90	7%	5513.39.99	10%

Column 1	Column 2	Column 1	Column 2
5513.41.90	7%	5602.90.90	10%
5513.49.90	7%	5604.90.10	6%
5514.11.99	7%	5811.00.10	10%
5514.12.90	7%	5811.00.29	10%
5514.19.90	7%	5811.00.90	10%
5514.21.00	7%	5901.10.90	10%
5514.22.90	7%	5901.90.90	10%
5514.23.90	10%	5902.10.00	6%
5514.29.90	7%	5902.20.00	6%
5514.30.99	7%	5902.90.00	6%
5514.41.00	7%	5903.10.19	10%
5514.42.00	10%	5903.10.29	10%
5514.43.90	10%	5903.20.19	10%
5514.49.90	10%	5903.20.23	8%
5515.11.90	7%	5903.20.29	10%
5515.12.90	7%	5903.90.10	10%
5515.19.90	10%	5903.90.29	10%
5515.21.90	10%	5906.10.90	10%
5515.29.90	10%	5906.91.99	10%
5515.91.90	10%	5906.99.19	10%
5515.99.19	10%	5906.99.22	8%
5515.99.99	10%	5906.99.29	10%
5516.13.90	10%	5907.00.13	6%
5516.14.90	7%	5907.00.18	10%
5516.21.99	7%	5907.00.19	10%
5516.22.90	7%	5910.00.19	7%
5516.23.99	10%	5910.00.90	7%
5516.24.90	7%	5911.10.90	10%
5516.41.00	7%	5911.20.90	10%
5516.42.00	7%	5911.31.10	5%
5516.43.00	7%	5911.32.10	5%
5516.44.00	7%	5911.40.90	10%
5516.91.99	7%	5911.90.20	7%
5516.92.90	7%	5911.90.90	8%
5516.94.90	10%	6001.10.90	10%
5601.21.29	3%	6001.21.00	10%
5601.29.90	3%	6001.29.90	10%
5602.10.90	10%	6001.91.00	10%
5602.21.99	10%	6001.92.90	7%
5602.29.00	10%	6001.99.90	10%

Column 1	Column 2	Column 1	Column 2
6002.40.40	8%	6006.24.90	10%
6002.40.90	10%	6006.31.90	10%
6002.90.19	8%	6006.32.90	7%
6002.90.90	10%	6006.33.90	10%
6003.10.99	10%	6006.34.90	7%
6003.20.40	8%	6006.41.90	10%
6003.20.90	10%	6006.42.90	7%
6003.30.99	10%	6006.43.90	10%
6003.40.99	10%	6006.44.90	7%
6003.90.40	8%	6006.90.90	10%
6003.90.90	10%	6815.10.90	3%
6004.10.19	8%	7019.40.99	13%
6004.10.90	7%	7607.20.90	5.5%
6004.90.30	8%	7609.00.00	3%
6004.90.90	10%	8402.11.00	6%
6005.21.30	8%	8402.12.00	3%
6005.21.90	10%	8402.19.00	6%
6005.22.30	8%	8402.20.00	2.5%
6005.22.90	10%	8402.90.00	2.5%
6005.23.30	8%	8404.10.10	4%
6005.23.90	10%	8410.11.10	8%
6005.24.30	8%	8410.12.10	8%
6005.24.90	10%	8410.13.10	8%
6005.31.90	10%	8410.90.20	8%
6005.32.90	7%	8411.82.90	8%
6005.33.99	10%	8413.70.99	5%
6005.34.90	7%	8477.80.91	8%
6005.41.90	10%	8502.39.10	5%
6005.42.90	10%	8536.20.90	2%
6005.43.99	10%	8536.90.91	4%
6005.44.90	10%	8536.90.92	2%
6005.90.29	10%	8537.10.21	2%
6005.90.99	8%	8537.10.31	2%
6006.21.10	10%	8537.10.93	2%
6006.21.90	10%	8544.11.90	3%
6006.22.10	10%	8544.19.90	3%
6006.22.90	7%	8544.49.90	3%
6006.23.29	10%	8544.60.91	4%
6006.23.90	10%	8544.60.99	5%
6006.24.10	10%		

3. That the List of Tariff Provisions set out in the schedule to the *Customs Tariff* be amended to add tariff item No. 1513.19.10 for goods "For use in the manufacture of animal feeds" currently classified under tariff item No. 1513.19.00 which is being revoked. The Most-Favoured-Nation Tariff rate of customs duty, and where necessary the applicable preferential tariff rates of customs duty, will be "Free" for the new tariff item.

4. That the List of Tariff Provisions set out in the schedule to the *Customs Tariff* be amended to add tariff item No. 1513.19.90 to maintain the current rates of customs duty on goods currently classified under tariff item No. 1513.19.00 except for those goods "For use in the manufacture of animal feeds".

5. That the List of Tariff Provisions set out in the schedule to the *Customs Tariff* be amended to add tariff item No. 5402.34.20 for "Multifilament single yarn, solely of polypropylene, textured, measuring 715 decitex or more but not exceeding 2,290 decitex, for use in the manufacture of woven fabrics" currently classified under tariff item No. 5402.34.90. The Most-Favoured-Nation Tariff rate of customs duty, and where necessary the applicable preferential tariff rates of customs duty, will be "Free" for the new tariff item.

6. That the List of Tariff Provisions set out in the schedule to the *Customs Tariff* be amended to add tariff item No. 5407.93.50 for "3-thread twill weave fabrics, of polyester filaments in the warp and viscose rayon filaments in the weft, of a weight not exceeding 100 g/m^2, for use in the manufacture of apparel" currently classified under tariff item No. 5407.93.90. The Most-Favoured-Nation Tariff rate of customs duty, and where necessary the applicable preferential tariff rates of customs duty, will be "Free" for the new tariff item.

7. That the List of Tariff Provisions set out in the schedule to the *Customs Tariff* be amended to add tariff item No. 5515.12.40 for "Plain woven fabric, from yarns of different colours, containing 70% or more by weight of polyester staple fibres in the weft, and 20% or more by weight of polyester filament yarns in the warp, of a weight not exceeding 140 g/m^2, for use in the manufacture of men's and boys' suit jackets, blazers or sports jackets" currently classified under tariff item No. 5515.12.90. The Most-Favoured-Nation Tariff rate of customs duty, and where necessary the applicable preferential tariff rates of customs duty, will be "Free" for the new tariff item.

8. That the List of Tariff Provisions set out in the schedule to the *Customs Tariff* be amended to add tariff item No. 5516.11.10 for "Solely of rayon, bleached, of a width exceeding 280 cm, having a sum of yarns per 10 cm in the warp and the weft of 1,060 or more, for use in the manufacture of bed linen, duvet covers, pillow shams, cushions and cushion covers" currently classified under tariff item No. 5516.11.00 which is being revoked. The Most-Favoured-Nation Tariff rate of customs duty, and where necessary the applicable preferential tariff rates of customs duty, will be "Free" for the new tariff item.

9. That the List of Tariff Provisions set out in the schedule to the *Customs Tariff* be amended to add tariff item No. 5516.11.90 to cover goods currently classified in tariff item No. 5516.11.00 except for "Solely of rayon, bleached, of a width exceeding 280 cm, having a sum of yarns per 10 cm in the warp and the weft of 1,060 or more, for use in the manufacture of bed linen, duvet covers, pillow shams, cushions and cushion covers". The Most-Favoured-Nation rate of customs duty will be "7%" for the new tariff item and this rate of customs duty, and where necessary the applicable preferential tariff rates of customs duty, will be gradually reduced to "Free" by January 1, 2013.

10. That the List of Tariff Provisions set out in the schedule to the *Customs Tariff* be amended to add tariff item No. 5516.12.91 for "Solely of rayon, of a width exceeding 280 cm, having a sum of yarns per 10 cm in the warp and the weft of 1,085 or more, for use in the manufacture of bed linen, duvet covers, pillow shams, cushions and cushion covers" currently classified under tariff item No. 5516.12.90 which is being revoked. The Most-Favoured-Nation Tariff rate of customs duty, and where necessary the applicable preferential tariff rates of customs duty, will be "Free" for the new tariff item.

11. That the List of Tariff Provisions set out in the schedule to the *Customs Tariff* be amended to add tariff item No. 5516.12.99 to cover goods currently classified under tariff item No. 5516.12.90 except for "Solely of rayon, of a width exceeding 280 cm, having a sum of yarns per 10 cm in the warp and the weft of 1,085 or more, for use in the manufacture of bed linen, duvet covers, pillow shams, cushions and cushion covers". The Most-Favoured-Nation rate of customs duty will be "10%" for the new tariff item and this rate of customs duty, and where necessary the applicable preferential tariff rates of customs duty, will be gradually reduced to "Free" by January 1, 2015.

12. That the List of Tariff Provisions set out in the schedule to the *Customs Tariff* be amended to add tariff item No. 5516.91.92 for "Plain weave fabric, of unbleached yarns, composed predominately of viscose rayon staple fibres, mixed mainly with horsehair, cotton and polyester staple fibres, of a weight not exceeding 225 g/m², for use in the manufacture of apparel" currently classified under tariff item No. 5516.91.99. The Most-Favoured-Nation Tariff rate of customs duty, and where necessary the applicable preferential tariff rates of customs duty, will be "Free" for the new tariff item.

13. That the List of Tariff Provisions set out in the schedule to the *Customs Tariff* be amended to add tariff item No. 5909.00.10 to maintain the current rates of customs duty on "Fire hoses" currently classified under tariff item No. 5909.00.00 which is being revoked.

14. That the List of Tariff Provisions set out in the schedule to the *Customs Tariff* be amended to add tariff item No. 5909.00.90 to cover the goods currently classified in tariff item No. 5909.00.00 except for "Fire hoses". The Most-Favoured-Nation rate of customs duty will be "10%" for the new tariff item and this rate of customs duty, and where necessary the applicable preferential tariff rates of customs duty, will be gradually reduced to "Free" by January 1, 2015.

15. That the List of Tariff Provisions set out in the schedule to the *Customs Tariff* be amended to add tariff item No. 6001.22.10 for "Weft knit fabrics, solely of brushed polyester fibres, of a width exceeding 175 cm, not impregnated, coated, covered or laminated, of a weight exceeding 260 g/m² but not exceeding 290 g/m², for use in the manufacture of yarn" currently classified in tariff item No. 6001.22.00 which is being revoked. The Most-Favoured-Nation Tariff rate of customs duty, and where necessary the applicable preferential tariff rates of customs duty, will be "Free" for the new tariff item.

16. That the List of Tariff Provisions set out in the schedule to the *Customs Tariff* be amended to add tariff item No. 6001.22.90 to cover goods currently classified in tariff item No. 6001.22.00 except for "Weft knit fabrics, solely of brushed polyester fibres, of a width exceeding 175 cm, not impregnated, coated, covered or laminated, of a weight exceeding 260 g/m² but not exceeding 290 g/m², for use in the manufacture of yarn". The a Most-Favoured-Nation rate of customs duty of will "7%" for the new tariff item and this rate of customs duty, and where necessary the applicable preferential tariff rates of customs duty, will be gradually reduced to "Free" by January 1, 2013.

17. That the List of Tariff Provisions set out in the schedule to the *Customs Tariff* be amended to add tariff item No. 6001.92.40 for "Warp pile fabric, cut, solely of polyester, including the ground fabric, brushed, for use in the manufacture of coffin interiors" currently classified under tariff item No. 6001.92.90. The Most-Favoured-Nation Tariff rate of customs duty, and where necessary the applicable preferential rates of customs duty, will be "Free" for the new tariff item.

18. That the Description of Goods of Tariff item No. 8477.80.91 in the List of Tariff Provisions set out in the schedule to the *Customs Tariff* be replaced by the following:

----For blending plastics

19. That the Description of Goods of tariff item No. 8716.90.10 in the List of Tariff Provisions set out in the schedule to the *Customs Tariff* be amended by replacing the reference to "Brake drums, hubs and rotors for use in the manufacture of brakes and brake assemblies mounted on axles for semi-trailers;" with a reference to "Brake drums, hubs and rotors for use in the manufacture or repair of brakes and brake assemblies mounted on axles for semi-trailers;".

20. That any enactment founded on sections 1 to 19 be deemed to have come into force on March 5, 2010.

Notice of Ways and Means Motion to Amend the *Universal Child Care Benefit Act*

That it is expedient to amend the *Universal Child Care Benefit Act* to provide among other things that, for payments in respect of months after June 2011:

> (*a*) section 2 of the Act be amended by adding the following definition in alphabetical order:
>
> > "shared custody parent" has the meaning assigned for the purpose of Subdivision a.1 of Division E of Part I of the *Income Tax Act*;
>
> (*b*) subsection 4(1) of the Act be replaced by the following:
>
> > 4. (1) The Minister shall pay to an eligible individual, for each month at the beginning of which he or she is an eligible individual, for each child who is a qualified dependant of the eligible individual at the beginning of that month,
> >
> > > (*a*) a benefit of $50, if the eligible individual is a shared custody parent of the qualified dependant; and
> > >
> > > (*b*) a benefit of $100 in any other case.

Notice of Ways and Means Motion to amend the *Income Tax Act*, the *Excise Tax Act*, the *Excise Act, 2001*, the *Air Travellers Security Charge Act*, the *Canada Pension Plan*, and the *Employment Insurance Act* relating to Online Notices

That it is expedient to amend the *Income Tax Act*, the *Excise Tax Act*, the *Excise Act, 2001*, the *Air Travellers Security Charge Act*, the *Canada Pension Plan* and the *Employment Insurance Act* to provide among other things that the provisions of these acts relating to the issuance of online notices be modified in accordance with the proposals described in the budget documents tabled by the Minister of Finance in the House of Commons on March 4, 2010.

Notice of Ways and Means Motion to Amend the *Air Travellers Security Charge Act*

That it is expedient to amend the *Air Travellers Security Charge Act* as follows:

1. (1) The portion of paragraph 12(1)(*a*) of the *Air Travellers Security Charge Act* before subparagraph (i) is replaced by the following:

(*a*) $7.12 for each chargeable emplanement included in the service, to a maximum of $14.25, if

(2) The portion of paragraph 12(1)(*b*) of the Act before subparagraph (i) is replaced by the following:

(*b*) $7.48 for each chargeable emplanement included in the service, to a maximum of $14.96, if

(3) The portion of paragraph 12(1)(*c*) of the Act before subparagraph (i) is replaced by the following:

(*c*) $12.10 for each chargeable emplanement included in the service, to a maximum of $24.21, if

(4) The portion of paragraph 12(1)(*d*) of the Act before subparagraph (i) is replaced by the following:

(*d*) $12.71 for each chargeable emplanement included in the service, to a maximum of $25.42, if

(5) Paragraph 12(1)(*e*) of the Act is replaced by the following:

(*e*) $25.91, if the service includes transportation to a destination outside the continental zone.

(6) The portion of paragraph 12(2)(*a*) of the Act before subparagraph (i) is replaced by the following:

(*a*) $12.10 for each chargeable emplanement by an individual on an aircraft used to transport the individual to a destination outside Canada but within the continental zone, to a maximum of $24.21, if

(7) The portion of paragraph 12(2)(*b*) of the Act before subparagraph (i) is replaced by the following:

(*b*) $12.71 for each chargeable emplanement by an individual on an aircraft used to transport the individual to a destination outside Canada but within the continental zone, to a maximum of $25.42, if

(8) Paragraph 12(2)(*c*) of the Act is replaced by the following:

(*c*) $25.91, if the service includes transportation to a destination outside the continental zone.

(9) Subsections (1) to (8) apply in respect of an air transportation service that includes a chargeable emplanement on or after April 1, 2010 unless,

(*a*) **if any consideration is paid or payable in respect of the service, all of the consideration is paid before April 1, 2010; or**

(*b*) **if no consideration is paid or payable in respect of the service, a ticket is issued before April 1, 2010.**